The Mormons...the Catholics

A Tale of Two Cities

By

Rev. William Taylor

A Tale of Two Cities

Copyright © 2022 by Rev. William Taylor.

All rights reserved.

Content

Preface

Almost forty-five years ago, I was Campus Minister at Idaho State University, in Pocatello, Idaho. While I was there, a I wrote a little book called *A Tale of Two Cities, the Mormons, the Catholics.* I wrote it for students who were encountering Mormonism in a place where Mormons were in the vast majority. It was a pre-emptive effort. I wanted my students to understand the LDS religion. But even more, I wanted to give them an explanation about the depth and beauty of their Catholic faith. The book sold 40,000 copies.

A priest friend read the book and said, "It is beautiful, but nobody lives their Catholic faith at the level you are describing." True enough. Most of us are in the middle of busy, distracted lives. Many of us are getting along on a grade school grasp of our faith, stirred together with whatever we remember from a spotty religious education in high school, and the sermons we hear at Mass. But I wanted to share what I had come to know and love over a lifetime. It was like showing you a picture of a high mountain lake. There is something beautiful up there, I said. Do you want to make the difficult climb with me, and see it for yourself?

Many years have passed, but the need for this book remains. And so I am writing *The Mormons…The Catholics.* My basic purpose has not changed. I want to give an honest, respectful explanation of Mormonism. But even more, I want to offer Catholics a vision of the Catholic Church at its best. I try to give Catholic and Mormon readers an understanding of a Church populated by its share of sinners, including me, many great saints, and legions of humble saints. This is the Church I know and love.

In a way, this is a kind of reference book. If you look at the Table of Contents, you will see a point by point comparison between the Catholic faith and the Mormon faith. When I explain Catholic beliefs, I base what I say on my own experience over a long life as a priest, and on the wisdom of the Church found in the Catholic Catechism and the writing of some theologians. I have compared Catholic life and faith to blue lakes in a mountain cirque surrounded by sheer cliffs. My favorite places on earth. Some have climbed that high. Give it a shot.

Introduction

Who are the Mormons, anyway? Their sixteen million member church now outnumbers several major Protestant denominations, and they are making their way into the American mainstream. Right now they are in a small slump, but Mormons are organizers. It will not be long before they are pushing hard again. Their traditional name has been the Church of Jesus Christ of Latter-day Saints, or the Latter-day Saints, or the Saints, or the LDS, or the Mormons. And most recently they have decided to call themselves the Church of Jesus Christ. For simplicity sake, I will call them LDS, Latter-day Saints, the Saints, or Mormons.

Mormons have admirable conservative values and a strong commitment to family. They don't smoke. They don't drink. They take care of their own. Many non-Mormons wish their own churches could copy the LDS commitment to youth and to fallen-away members. Even though some dismiss the Mormons as members of a cult, more and more non-Mormons now count the Latter-Day Saints among the Christian churches.

My credentials as I write this book

I grew up in Pocatello, Idaho, a town with a huge LDS majority. Some of my best memories are loving contact with my many Mormon relatives. Family reunions were a special delight. Looking back, I realize that our family gatherings were a snapshot of the Mormon religious world. Grandpa was the family patriarch, whose words and blessing came from the power and authority of his Mormon priesthood, accepted by a grateful family that hoped to accompany him into eternity. It was a while before I understood that I was not expected to join them on that journey.

My ancestors were Danish converts who made the long journey from Europe to the high harsh area known as the Bear Lake Country, where Utah, Idaho, and Wyoming come together. There, they lived lives marked by hard work and a fervent loyalty to their church. My tight-knit expanded family continues the spiritual legacy. Family members have occupied offices at the lower levels of Latter-day Saint authority structure, and some of my uncles and aunts—well past the age of sixty—bravely served as missionaries in Missouri, Illinois, and Ireland.

As I tell this story, I remember once again that I am the product of a most unlikely circumstance. Somehow, a sturdy Catholic branch managed to sprout from a rugged Mormon juniper tree. It all goes back to my mother, the rebel who abandoned the traditional ways of her family and went on a spiritual journey of her own. The Union Pacific Railroad brought my family to Kemmerer, Wyoming. My mother began to explore the small town and found herself in front of a Catholic Church. She entered on a whim, and found herself in a place of quiet and the smell of incense. This was her first experience of sacred silence. For a long hour, she basked in the awareness of God come close. She returned to that church often and gradually discovered a new way to God. It was in her heart that the city of Salt Lake met the city of Rome. She was pregnant with me when she discovered that little Catholic church. It was almost inevitable that I would try to bring the two legacies together.

Four points before we proceed

First, Mormons use familiar Catholic terms, but every word has a completely different meaning

Please pay close attention. When Catholics and Mormons talk about their faith, they share words like God, Jesus, the Holy Spirit, salvation, and the Gospel of Jesus Christ. Surely, the Mormons are Christians, like the Baptists or the Presbyterians. Some might feel that the jump from Catholicism to Mormonism is a short one.

This book will help you discover that Catholics and Mormons do not share a common religious DNA. The Latter-day Saints worship someone they call God, but he is a god Catholics never heard of. The Mormons love a person they call Jesus, but he is not the Jesus known to Catholics and other Christians.

Second, we go forward in the spirit of ecumenism

God's reach knows no limits. The Vatican Council made this clear. In *Lumen Gentium*, a key document that explores the mystery of the Church, the bishops taught us that many elements of sanctification and of truth are found outside the visible confines of the Church of Rome. To begin with, all Christians belong to the Body of Christ.

But that is not where the vision stops. The Church's respect for other religions extends beyond Christianity to include Jews, Moslems who adore one God, and those who in shadows and images seek the unknown God. Whatever of good or truth is found amongst them is considered by the Church to be a preparation for the Gospel and given by him who enlightens all men and women that they may at length have life. In the light of the

Council, Catholics believe that the Holy Spirit is present wherever people are, whatever
their faith or lack of faith. The law of love is written in every heart, even when the owner of that heart does not recognize the God who wrote it there. Catholics will not be surprised to discover a heaven crowded with other Christians, Jews, Moslems, Buddhists, etc., and even a large gathering of astonished atheists. I will try to be guided by the respectful attitude of the Vatican Council as I discuss Mormon church structure and beliefs.

Third, Our discussion will focus on comparisons, but we will have areas of disagreement

I do not want to attack a church where so many members of my family find a spiritual home. But I also know that the LDS Church is very aggressive in its missionary efforts, putting special pressure on non-Mormon youth who live in heavily LDS areas. For instance, a few years ago, I spoke about Mormonism in several towns in an agricultural area of eastern Washington that has witnessed a strong influx of Mormons. Incredibly, more than a thousand youth and their parents attended the talks. Their very numbers announced a desperate need for answers and understanding. For this reason, along with pointing out differences in an objective manner, I also feel obliged to debate some issues Mormons use to attack the Catholic Church. This will occur in the second and seventh sections of the book.

Fourth, a red-button issue: how much can I say about Joseph Smith?

Latter-day Saints refuse to sit still for any critical evaluation of their prophet, Joseph Smith. I suppose I would feel the same way if someone wanted me to sit still for a criticism of the pope. And yet, Joseph Smith claimed visions and revelations that made him the prophet, seer, and revelator of an entirely new religion. And so, for better or for worse, the truthfulness of Joseph Smith is more important than any of his doctrines. This question has to be asked: Was he a truthful man? If I think he was I need to leave the Catholic Church. I will ask this question in the second section of this book. I promise to address the problems presented by Joseph Smith with great care.

PART ONE

Foundations

Our two churches stand on completely different foundations, and a Catholic who does not see this will never understand the Mormon Church. He will imagine that the LDS Church is another Christian church, like the Lutherans or the Methodists. But if he leaves his Catholic Church for the Mormon Church, he will be leaving Christianity behind

1

A Look at A Mormon Family

As a child, I spent a lot of time with the hard working and deeply religious Mormon members of my family, and so, basing my story on a few uncles, aunts, and cousins, I would like to tell you about Glen and Thelma Hansen. I don't have any relatives by that name, of course. What I want to do is paint a respectful picture of a good family living the strict commands of its LDS faith. I apologize for any distortions.

Living a righteous life: a family on its way to godhood

Galen Hansen grew up on Idaho Falls, Idaho, deep in the heart of Mormon country. He studied and practiced his faith, with a little prodding from his parents. A key moment came in his life when he was only 12, and became a "deacon" with a small role in his faith community. After he graduated from high school, he fulfilled a family dream by volunteering to go on a mission. At age nineteen, he was an "elder" sent to work in the mission fields of Argentina. Although he didn't make a lot of converts, the experience gave him poise and self-confidence. When he returned after two years, he attended Ricks College, a church-run institution in Rexburg, Idaho that is now called BYU Idaho. There he met Thelma Rich, a quiet, deeply religious girl from the tiny mostly LDS town of Paris, Idaho. They were attracted to each other from the start and, at the end of the second semester, he asked her to be his wife. They decided to marry in the Idaho Falls temple. It was a crucial step, because it allowed them to dream of a time when Galen would actually become a god, with Thelma his eternal companion.

A key step on this spiritual journey was marriage in the Idaho Falls Temple. In order for this to happen, Galen and Thelma had to go to their respective bishops for a worthiness interview. Each bishop questioned his subject in considerable detail about the state of his or her moral life, including the possibility of any pre-marital sexual involvement.[1] Satisfied that they were morally pure and devoted to their church, their bishops signed their temple recommends, which permitted them to enter the temple. The relatives and friends who accompanied them also possessed temple recommends, a witness to their good stature in the church.

With joyful hearts, Galen and Thelma entered the sacred precincts of the Idaho Falls Temple. There, they received something called the Temple Endowments. Finally, they knelt facing each other at a white altar while a General Authority sealed their marriage for time and for eternity.

Fast forward a few years. The Hansens now occupy a comfortable home in Idaho Falls and try to live as faithful Saints. Both wear special undergarments as a sign of their temple marriage, and give their church full tithing and fast offerings, which exceeds eleven percent of their gross income. Ordained to the Melchizedek Priesthood when he became a missionary, Galen is careful to remain sexually pure and is conscientious about the Word of Wisdom, a Mormon teaching which forbids smoking, alcohol, or caffeine. He works in a firm employing mostly LDS people, socializes within a Mormon circle, and is a good neighbor in his mostly LDS neighborhood. Thelma also works, but

---

[1] In *The Miracle of Forgiveness*, by deceased president Spencer W. Kimball

makes a great effort to be a busy housewife and mother who is obedient to her husband and also careful about the Word of Wisdom.

As the father of his family, Brother Hansen feels a heavy spiritual responsibility. He tries to give sound spiritual leadership to his wife and children. He makes sure they pray twice a day, leads the family council meeting held on Sundays to discuss family rules and other business, and conducts the Family Home Evening gatherings on Monday evenings. Galen has risen to the level of high priest leading a priesthood quorum, and serves as a Boy Scout leader. Sister Hansen sings in the choir and has served as counselor to the president of the Relief Society in her ward. Both give about six hours a week in volunteer time to their church.

The Hansen children have been raised to follow strict Mormon rules. There is no dating until the age of sixteen, no caffeine, no drugs, tobacco, or alcohol at any age, and no pre-marital sex. Like their parents, the children are expected to give their church many hours of their time. For the teenagers, this means about fourteen hours a week spent in church-related events. Also like their parents, they are expected to pay a tithe on the money they get from allowances, baby-sitting, or student level jobs.

Galen Jr. has applied to become a missionary and has already had an interview with his bishop. A missionary savings account, begun when Galen was only six, will pay all of his missionary expenses. When he returns from his mission in two years, he will have full stature as a Mormon. In the meantime, he watches his email for an official announcement of his call.

LaVerna is a senior in high-school this year. She writes emails to her fiancé, who serves a mission in Denmark. When he returns, he will enroll as a sophomore at BYU Idaho, and they will be married in the Idaho Falls Temple.[2]

Devon is sixteen years old, and moderately active in his Aaronic priesthood quorum. Ordained a teacher by his father, he occasionally goes to the homes of fellow ward members to deliver a small lesson on some religious topic. Sister Hansen wakes him up early on school days so that he can attend 7:00 A.M. seminary classes, held five days a week in the LDS Institute Building across the street from the local high school.

Norma is fourteen and very active in her young women's group, called the MIA Maids. She meets weekly with other Mormon girls of the same age to plan service and social activities. When she was ten, she asked her father to help her start her own missionary savings account, and plans to go on her own mission.

Jared, age eleven, is preparing for his role in the Aaronic Priesthood. During the coming year, he will begin preparation for his ordination to the rank of deacon, the lowest level in the Aaronic Priesthood.

Lynn, age seven, is looking forward to the day when he can join the priestly rank and follow the path of his father. He is a happy, friendly boy who has just begun to discover that Mormons are different. He is a bit puzzled why he cannot play with the children of a gentile family down the block.

Thou shalt keep holy the Sabbath Day

The Hansens are very serious about honoring the Sabbath. It is the first Sunday of the month, a day the Mormons call Fast Sunday. The whole family will abstain

---

[2] Missionaries are encouraged to marry soon after returning from the mission.

from meals until evening. The money they saved on food will be given to the church. As they get ready for church, the males in the family don conservative suits and ties, while the females wear long dresses.

The Hansens arrive early, each member prepared to attend at least three different meetings. Galen and his oldest sons begin their day with a priesthood meeting. Both the Melchizedek and the Aaronic Priesthood members gather together for a few minutes at the beginning of the hour to receive general instructions from the bishop and his two counselors concerning their duties and opportunities for ward service. Brother Hansen's involvement with his Melchizedek Priesthood tasks takes up to seven additional hours each week. The members of the two priesthoods split quickly into quorums for quorum business and instruction. Meanwhile, Thelma attends Relief Society, the two girls join their young women's groups, and the younger boys go to programs of their own.

At ten o'clock, all the Hansens attend Sunday School. The two youngest go to Primary, where they learn the basics of their faith. Those twelve and older attend classes identified by age groups for the youth and by interest for the adults. Thelma has been appointed teacher in one of the primary classes, and Galen Sr. is teaching a class on the Book of Mormon.

At eleven-thirty, the young people and adults attend the Sacrament Meeting. Since it is Fast Sunday, the members of the congregation are invited to give testimonies as soon as the announcements are over. Those who feel moved by the holy spirit bear testimony to their belief in church authority, church doctrine, and church practice. Then it is time for Sacrament Meeting. As a deacon, Devon takes his turn preparing the bread and the water that will be used as the sacrament, and watches while a male member chosen from the congregation offers the opening prayer. The sacrament is administered by those who hold Aaronic priestly authority. A youth breaks bread into pieces, kneels, and blesses it with the proper formula given by revelation to Joseph Smith. Devon and other young deacons then distribute the bread to the congregation. The youth then blesses the water, which is also distributed.

The Hansen family hurries home, but they will continue their fast and will do their best to honor the Sabbath. There will be no gardening, or sports, or shopping at the mall. The rest of the day will be spent in prayerful reading, visiting family, writing letters to loved ones, doing genealogy work, or perhaps some special work assigned for that day. When the children try to ignore that agenda, Galen lays down the law. In the evening after a well-cooked meal that ends the fast, Galen and Thelma discuss a special trip to the Idaho Falls Temple on the coming weekend.

In Summary

The ideal picture I have just painted surely contains inaccuracies and I apologize for that. Its lofty tone doesn't mean that all is peace and light in the Hansen family. The children have their difficulties with each other, and Galen and Thelma face the tense moments other couples face. Their church teaches them to follow a very patriarchal family structure, and so Galen plays a dominating leadership role, and his wife and children are taught by their church to yield to his authority. But sometimes the kids are confused by the larger culture they meet at school, or on television and in movies. The Hansen teenagers sometimes question Mormon beliefs and chafe under the strong authority of their parents. But in the end, the creed and practice of the LDS Church plays a deciding role in their lives.

Catholic growth points

This description of an ideal Mormon family should cause any Catholic to thoughtfully consider his own life and the Catholic life lived in his family. The first question anyone should ask is this, *Do I take personal responsibility for my religious life as a Catholic?* Have I concluded that my religion is important enough to merit a slice of my time, the gift of my talents, a portion of my treasure? Do I assist at Mass? Attend classes in my parish? Find a way to do ministry? Do I consciously try to discover God's love and think about God's plan for me? Have I made spiritual growth a priority, setting aside time to pray, to reflect on the blessings I have received, to give thanks? Do I read the Bible, Catholic magazines, and spiritual books?

If I am a parent, do I accept my personal responsibility to share faith with my spouse? Do we both understand what it means when we say our marriage is a sacrament? Can I call myself a committed Catholic and consider the example I need to give to my children? Have we found a way to pray together? Do we make attendance at Mass together as a family a high priority? Have we shared faith with our children from the time they were very small?

Do we make sure they attend religious formation classes? Do we give them a strong moral example and try to teach them how to live with the heart of Christ? If our children are teens, do we give the parish youth program our energy and support, or do we leave it up to others? Have our children ever heard us give witness to our love of God and the importance of faith in our lives?

2

Two Different Gospels, Two

Different

Stories of Salvation

One of the most important words we need to discuss is the simple but profound word, "God." Imagine the Hansens standing beside the Finnegans. Each couple is good and solid, a gift to their family and community. Both couples try to honor the First Commandment, which says "I am the Lord your God, you shall not have strange gods before me." Now, imagine the Finnegans reading the gospel and faith narrative of the LDS Church, presented in this chapter. Imagine the Hansens reading the gospel and faith narrative of the Catholic Church, also presented in this chapter. When they are done, each couple will decide, without disrespect or derision, that the other couple worships a strange god. Now, it is your turn. Read below two different accounts of two different gospels and two different faith narratives. Can you see that the God of the one cannot be the God of the other? Which God is your God?

Two different gospels

As I said in my introduction, Mormons and Catholics use the same words, but they live within two completely different spiritual realities. The word "Gospel" is a good example. Both churches say that they are founded on the "Gospel of Our Lord Jesus Christ." The reader will quickly learn that they are not talking about the same thing.

21

The gospel according to the Church of Jesus Christ of Latter-day Saints

With all due respect, the LDS gospel jars the ears of the average Christian. In the first pages of *The Miracle of Forgiveness*, president and prophet Spencer W. Kimball described the Mormon gospel in this way:

> ...God created man to live in mortality and *endowed him with the potential to perpetuate the race, to subdue the earth, to perfect himself and to become as God, omniscient and omnipotent. Because God is* literally *our father, we are "god(s) in embryo."*[3](My emphasis)

You gasp. God is *literally* our father? We are *gods in embryo? Yes* and *yes.* To put it briefly: The god of Mormons was once a male member of the human race who lived on an unknown world during a time long, long ago. Mormons say he is an "exalted" *human being* named Elohim, who is surrounded by an unknown number of exalted human women who are his wives in every sense. These "eternal companions" or "heavenly queens," have no names. Thy have born Elohim billions of "spirit children." He rules over the planet Earth as its "Heavenly Father."

Mormons teach that every human being who has ever lived is a son or daughter of that god, in the most literal sense. Every male has come to earth to gain a body of "crude matter" and prove himself worthy to become a god in his own right. To sum it up in a single sentence,

---

[3] Kimball, p. 3

Heavenly Father invites all worthy males to become gods like him and one day live an "exalted" life forever with their own heavenly queens and spirit children. This is the Mormon gospel.

The Catholic gospel

Something done by God

The word "gospel" means good news or good tidings. It comes from the German: *got spiel,* or *good speech.* According to my biblical dictionary, the Hebrew word that is translated "gospel" means *the news of a victory or a deliverance.*

The Catholic Gospel is not a list of beliefs as much as the good news that the God who created the universe has come close to us in our world dominated by sin. The Second Person of the Trinity, the Father's Word of Love, united himself to the human nature of a child conceived in the womb of a virgin named Mary. We call him the Word made human flesh. Mary named him Jesus, "God saves." All this was done by the power of the Holy Spirit. When the Word became Jesus, God became part of human history. The One God has revealed himself as a trinity of persons. In Jesus, the infinite God has become our brother. Through his suffering, death, and resurrection, Jesus Christ has destroyed the power of sin and established the Kingdom of God as the culmination of human history. This Good News becomes our story and our victory when we embrace it in faith, repentance, and baptism. The Church follows the teaching of Jesus Christ as she labors for the sake of Kingdom, and awaits His return in glory. He will bring about the Kingdom of God in its fullness and, when He does, human history will arrive at its destiny. This is the Catholic gospel.

Catholic growth points

We learn from the Latin roots of the word *Credo*, which is translated as "I believe." *Credo* is formed from two other Latin words: *Cor*, which means "heart," and *Da-re*, which means to "give" or to "place." Our faith is an invitation *to give our hearts* to Jesus who has revealed the compassion of the Father for us by the power of the Holy Spirit. Our faith is an invitation to live within the life of the Trinity. As people called into life by the Father, we are one with Christ our brother, and live by the light and wisdom of the Spirit. Our faith is an invitation to give ourselves to each other in love, mercy, and compassion. Our faith is an invitation to help establish a world of love and peace.

Two different narratives

Every religion, nation, or successful movement needs to remember and tell stories about its beginnings and the great heroes who made it happen. When we tell the stories upon which a religion stands, we talk about God, our place in the universe, God's purposes, and the men and women who were there at the beginning. Involved in these stories is a strong element of faith, because those great figures are sometimes so far in the past that we know little or nothing about them, except what is contained in the story.

The LDS story, a drama in four acts

Act One: Pre-existence, Heavenly Father, spirit-children, and a great Plan

Life in a pre-existent world

A long time ago, a pair of missionaries gave me the book *God, Man, and the Universe,* a scholarly description of Mormon belief. Today's LDS are a bit more circumspect with their answers, but I don't know if this reflects a change in their doctrine or a change in their strategy as they try to make converts. Here is what Hyrum L. Andrus had to say in 1968.

Joseph Smith, the founder of the Mormon Church, received revelations which force Mormons to reject the Big Bang theory about the beginning of the universe. Mormons believe that the universe has no beginning and no end. The Cosmos is filled to every corner with particles of "eternal matter" and governed in all things by "eternal Law." There are two kinds of eternal matter: Gross matter and spirit matter. Every particle of gross or spiritual matter contains some measure of life, or intelligence. Joseph Smith taught that these particles are "self-existent," a term Christians would only apply to God.

These self-existent primary particles can be organized, acquiring more life or intelligence. This is especially true of particles of spirit matter. Who does the organizing? Mormons believe in a universe occupied by gods beyond counting. Each god possesses his own sphere of influence. As I said in our brief presentation of the Mormon gospel, these gods belong to the human species and inhabit the Cosmos in uncountable numbers, going back into infinity. Each god is the literal son of another god, who is the literal son of another god.

Each god is a family man with eternal wives. Through some kind of divine sexual activity, they have "organized" spirit matter filled with life into billions upon billions of spirit children. We have no personal relationship with the countless other gods in this cascading stream of divine beings. The only god we serve is Elohim[4], also known as "Heavenly Father." He lives near a star called Kolob, which is the center of the stellar system under his control.

As Joseph Smith put it in his "King Follett Discourse," Heavenly Father is "like yourselves in all the person, image, and very form of a man." When he was a youth, he aspired to the rank of divinity and, by observing certain eternal laws and covenants, *rose by his own effort to the level of godhood.* But even though he is now a god, he remains a being of the human species, with "body, parts, and passions." Heavenly Father lives today in his heavenly realm, an unimaginably potent exalted man surrounded by an unknown number of incredibly fertile wives who are his "queens and high priestesses." Their spirit children live around the mansion of their heavenly father in numbers beyond counting.

The Great Council in Heaven, a chance to be gods or married to a god

We have no idea how many eons have passed since Elohim "reached exaltation" and became Heavenly Father. At some unknown moment, he summoned his children to a great council. Attending the council were four of Heavenly Father's most important spirit sons: *Jehovah,* his First-born, the *Holy Ghost, Michael,* and...*Lucifer.*

Mormons believe that you and I were also present in that multitude. As the missionaries once told me, we looked with wonder at our Heavenly Father with his exalted body, and longed for exalted bodies of our own. We then gasped

---

[4] Elohim is the generic name for God used by many people in the ancient Middle East besides the Jews. El is the singular form, and Elohim is plural.

in amazement as Heavenly Father proclaimed a great Plan which would allow all the males present to reach exaltation and eventually become gods in their own right. Our sisters would never be gods, but they, too, could achieve exaltation and live with a husband-god as eternal companions and heavenly mothers.[5]

The Plan unfolds in three steps

Our Heavenly Father's Plan would unfold in three steps: *creation*, the *fall*, and *atonement*. But the Plan also involved great danger. It would require living within a material body with a darkened mind and will, subject to sin and death. This could become a trap without an exit. Heavenly Father told his children there was only one way to solve the dilemma. One of his sons *would have to volunteer to come as a savior and die an atoning death on a cross*, thus allowing the Plan to continue.

"Whom shall I send?" Heavenly Father asked. There were two volunteers among the spirit children. *Jehovah* offered to fulfill his Father's plan to the letter, thus giving the Father the glory, but *Lucifer* boldly offered an alternative plan which would bring glory only to himself. When Heavenly Father chose Jehovah to be the redeemer, Lucifer rebelled and became *Satan*. One third of the spirit children joined Satan in this rebellion, and a great war broke out in heaven. Satan and his followers were cast out of the Father's kingdom and fell down to earth. Doomed to live forever without material bodies, they vowed to thwart the Father's plan. Their efforts continue to this day.

[5] Mormons themselves disagree on this. I talked to some young female missionaries, who were sure they would be goddesses.

Step One: Creation

The organization of the earth

I have used the word "creation," but for Mormons, the better word is "organization." As I have explained, Mormons believe in the eternal existence of gross and spirit matter. Because matter is eternal, there is no such thing as creation from nothing. There is only organization. *Jehovah* and *Michael* organized eternal material elements into the planet called Earth.

Michael then went down to inhabit a body fashioned by Jehovah from the dust of the earth. Now named *Adam*, he lived in the Garden of Eden. He was joined by a spirit-sister who received a body fashioned from his rib, and became his wife, named *Eve*. Andrus adds confusion to this story when he says that the god of the Old Testament was Jehovah, the first-born son of Heavenly Father.

Step Two: The Fall

Even though they were now living in the Garden of Eden, Adam and Eve were still beings with immortal bodies. Jehovah gave them two baffling and contradictory commands. First, he warned them, *Do not eat of the fruit of the Tree of Life, for if you do, you will die.* Second, he ordered them to be *fruitful, multiply, and fill the earth.* The two straddled the uncomfortable space between a rock and a hard place. If they honored the first commandment and avoided death, they would break the second commandment, because immortal bodies cannot conceive and bear children.

As I was writing this book, I wrote this: "At this point in their narrative, the Saints must have a good chuckle. Satan slithered into the scene and tempted Eve to eat the forbidden fruit." In my later reading, I realized that Satan was playing an *essential* role in the Plan of Salvation. Mormons teach something they call the "law of opposition." If Satan had not arrived as tempter, there would have been no salvation. This pattern continues. There is no growth unless we pick between good and evil. Adam and Eve *had* to make this choice, or the story of LDS salvation would not have continued. As soon as Eve ate the fruit, she fell into the mortal state. Adam–who was still immortal–saw what his wife had done and what she had become. For her sake, he nobly chose to share the fruit and so he joined her in the mortal state. To paraphrase one Mormon writer, the Fall was not some catastrophe that came out of nowhere. It was part of the Plan. Adam and Eve now had mortal bodies. They could be fruitful, multiply, and fill the earth.

The role of Adam in Mormon theology

Because of his key role in this complicated drama, Latter-day Saints consider "Father Adam" one of the "most noble and intelligent characters who has ever lived."[6] In their theology, he occupies the highest place. He is head of all gospel dispensations and presiding high priest (under the authority of Jehovah) over all the spirit-children who will ever come to this earth. He is the one who holds the keys of salvation, "Michael, who will reign forever." Even though his mind was now darkened, thanks to revelation, he knew all the details of

---

[6] Mormon Doctrine, Op. Cit. p. 17 [8] Ibid.

the plan, including the coming of a messiah who would die on a cross in atonement for sin.[8] The true church dates back to him.

As a corollary to this teaching about the Fall, Mormons teach that there is no such thing as original sin. Adam's sin, if it was a sin, was forgiven retroactively when Jesus died on the cross. Mormons reject the Protestant teaching that we are a fallen race, with hell as our natural destiny. God does not hold us responsible for Adam's sin, only for the sins that we ourselves commit.

The inevitable collapse of the first dispensation

Adam and Eve had no memory of their life in pre-existence. Somehow the gospel was revealed to them, and they lived by faith. Thanks to their fall into the mortal state, they began to have children. With the conception of each mortal body in the Eve's womb, a spirit child would come down from heaven to enter that body "like a hand in a glove," according to one pair of missionaries. And so began his or her "probationary estate" with all its struggle and pain.[7] Mormons call this time the "dispensation of Adam."

The children of Adam and Eve had to prove themselves worthy of godhood. But their minds were darkened and their weakened wills were prone to sin. Satan lurked, ready to strike. Inevitably, the dispensation of Adam vanished in apostasy.

Four more times, men were chosen by revelation to become prophets of a new dispensation. Again and again, sin and darkness played their devastating role. Each dispensation lost its way.

---

[7] Bruce McConkie, *A New Witness to the Articles of Faith*, Deseret Book, Salt Lake City, Utah, 1985, p. 85

Evil and death became the central experience of the human race. Humanity waited uneasily for its redeemer.

Step Three: The Atonement

Finally, at the "Meridian of Time," Heavenly Father, with his "body, parts, and passions," came down to earth and had a child by Mary, who had been one of his spiritual daughters in pre-existence. Mormons have trouble explaining it in physically sexual terms, and have to explain away the implication of incest. Jehovah, the God of the Old Testament and Heavenly Father's first-born son, had waited for this moment. He entered into the mortal body conceived by that union, and became Jesus of Nazareth, the Heavenly Father's "first-born son in the flesh."

Jehovah-become-Jesus did not start a new church. He restored the Church of Adam. He picked his twelve apostles, ordained them to the Melchizedek Priesthood, and taught them the fullness of the gospel. Then it was time for him to die on the cross. His death atoned for the sins of humankind and his resurrection restored the gift of immortality. It was again possible for Heavenly Father's children to continue their progress toward exaltation and godhood.

Jesus founded his church in America

After his resurrection, Jesus also appeared to the two groups of people who populate the *Book of Mormon*. Called the Nephites and Lamanites, they lived in South or Central America from around 587 BC to 400 AD. Jesus organized his church in their midst and proclaimed the true gospel. He appointed apostles, bestowed the Priesthood, and established the covenants and ordinances that would lead to exaltation.

The Great Apostasy and restoration through Joseph Smith

But even the church founded by Jesus Christ lost its way. Mormons teach that, sometime after the apostles died, Christ's church fell into a "Great Apostasy." A just and righteous God took the Melchizedek Priesthood back to heaven and, when that happened, the true church disappeared once more. What survived was an apostate church. Although other good men and women might appear in the hundreds and hundreds of years that followed, the true church no longer existed on earth.

Joseph Smith, Jr. was born in Vermont, in 1805. His poverty-ridden family migrated to Palmyra, in upstate New York, where they settled down as marginal farmers. As a youth, Joseph experienced two amazing visions. When he was only fifteen, Heavenly Father and his Son Jesus appeared and warned him that all churches were false. Mormons believe that this vision marked Joseph Smith as a prophet. When he was seventeen, an angel named Moroni appeared and revealed the location of mysterious gold plates, which he had hidden on Hill Cumorah hundreds of years before. According to the angel, the plates explained the origin of the American Indians, and contained the "fullness of the gospel." Smith was able to locate and translate the plates, which were published as the *Book of Mormon*, in 1830.

During that same year, Smith founded his church. At some unknown time during the next two years, Smith was ordained by Peter, James and John to the Melchizedek

Priesthood, and given the Power of the Keys. With these priestly powers, he fully restored the lost Church of Christ. He was only twenty-five years old.

The surrounding churches raised the alarm about Smith's new scripture and his new church. Beset by persecution, Smith moved from New York to Ohio, then to Missouri. Driven from Missouri, Smith and his followers moved to the banks of the Mississippi River in Illinois and founded a city called Nauvoo. Converts arrived by the thousands. Nauvoo grew and Smith reached the peak of his power, In the midst of these public accomplishments, Smith was also secretly teaching the doctrine of Celestial Marriage, or polygamy. He married thirty-three or perhaps even fifty-five women[8] and implanted the practice among his most trusted disciples. But other disciples opposed the doctrine and raised the alarm.

Heedless of the danger, Smith boldly plunged into Illinois politics. By voting as a group, the Mormons decided the results of several local elections and two state elections. But Smith's ambitions did not stop there. His disciples proclaimed him King of the World, and he began to secretly plan a theocratic kingdom uniting church and state. At the same time, he proclaimed himself a presidential candidate, a decision that threatened to upset the national election of 1844.

Many assume that Smith's downfall was caused by his practice of polygamy. But some historians say that while this triggered scorn and derision, it did not stir up the kind of rage that would lead to murder. It was politics. After Smith betrayed a promise he made to the Whigs, which caused them to lose the state election in Illinois, his enemies began to plot his downfall. He gave them a perfect excuse

---

[8] LDS authorities have finally admitted the extent of Smith's polygamy, raising the number of wives to 55.

when he ordered the destruction of the *Nauvoo Expositor,* a newspaper founded by a few dissident Saints. As the news spread, men in the surrounding communities followed a grim American tradition and began to gather into mobs. Judges issued writs for Smith's arrest and he found himself in Carthage jail. On the twenty-fourth of June, 1844, he was murdered by a crowd of men with blackened faces. He was only thirty-eight years old.

We look at the life of Joseph Smith with amazement. In a few short years, he had, by the "power of revelation and prophecy," translated the *Book of Mormon,* established a church which had more than twenty thousand members, created an authority structure which would lead the church into the future, and authored three books of "modern scripture." His murder turned Smith into a martyr, and his legacy would endure. In the eyes of Mormons, he is the prophet of the seventh dispensation, a dispensation will endure until the end of the world.

The Catholic story of salvation

In the beginning, there was nothing. Nobody could say, "Look! Over there! The Big Bang! *Nothing* means there was no space to stand, no time to keep, and no way to watch it happen. But at God's word, creation stepped forth, blazing, growing, and building, reaching toward infinity. Thirteen and a half billion years later, we live on a rocky planet that revolves around a yellow star located on one of the spiral arms on a medium sized galaxy, which is one of possibly two hundred billion galaxies in the universe. Catholics believe that God holds this universe in the palm of his hand.

Two stories in the Book of Genesis

The Catholic faith narrative unfolds in two creation stories that appear at the beginning of the Book of Genesis. The first story teaches us that we are made in the image and likeness of God. Because of this, we are beings with worth beyond measure. This does not imply the Mormon belief that we are the literal children of a deity So what does "image and likeness mean?" In the ancient world, a governor who ruled a province in the name of a king was called the image and likeness of the king. When the Genesis story applies this expression to Adam and Eve, itis telling us that human beings are the stewards who rule God's creation in his name.

The second creation story, the story of Adam and Eve, is about God's dream for us, and our reply. The man made from the red earth was put in the garden to till it and keep it. Labor was part of his destiny. God then gave him and his wife a command to obey. This story teaches us that our lives of freedom and contentment are meant to be lived within limits. If we abuse our freedom and exceed those limits, the result is sin, shame, separation from God, separation from each other, and chaos and death.

Going deeper

The Mormons teach that you and I and every particle of eternal matter is self-subsistent. That means we stand by ourselves, rooted only in ourselves, forever. But the two stories from Genesis teach us that we are beings held in the hands of God. We are like words written in chalk dust, clinging to a blackboard. We can never boast that we are stand-alone beings who depend on nothing and no one but ourselves.

A lesson from quantum physics

Cosmologists, those scientists who study deepest reality, tell us about "quantum particles." In their research, they have watched these tiniest of all particles vanish into *nothing*. You and I are made of these particles, and this means that, somewhere within us and at this very second, we are vanishing into nothing. Gone. But then the cosmologists tell us something else. Think of an enclosed space completely emptied of every smallest trace of energy and matter. Think of an emptiness less than any vacuum we can ever create. And then, these scientist tell us, something emerges there. It simply "foams forth." We, who disappear into nothing, constantly emerge from the void. In my amazement, I call this a glimpse of the hand of God the Creator at work.

I believe that God has never stopped creating us from nothing. Creation is not a one-time event that happened thirteen and a half billion years ago. God says "let there be" in the midst of every emerging nano-second ticked off from the beginning of time to its end. We are not just talking about you or me waking up in the morning. We are talking about the Cosmos and every galaxy, star, planet, and every cell, molecule, atom, and sub-atomic particle in the world around us and within us. All that is, all that lives, and all that knows bursts forth *now* as a good and bountiful gift from the One whose very name is the outpouring of love past understanding.

A tragic step in our story: The Fall

God seems to have made the human race for his glory and sorrow. We are creatures of history and consciousness, blessed and cursed with freedom, able to give love, and hold it back. We are unpredictable. Our ability to act and our ability to remember give us the capacity to make a history that will lead us toward God or away from God. A poet explained the Fall in a handful of tragic words: *God called us to love's meeting place, and we refused to go.* The Bible chooses a striking metaphor to tell the tale of this tragedy. Adam and Eve ate the forbidden fruit. The man fashioned from the earth by God's own hand, who alone received God's own breath, turned away from his maker. The woman born from beside man's fickle heart joined her husband in disobedience. The community of God-man-woman shattered into pieces, replaced by shame, oppressive fears, harmful desires, and isolated self-destruction.

Original sin

Catholics reject Protestant pessimism, which views human beings as totally fallen. Catholics say that, even after the Fall, God looked at Adam and all his descendants and recognized children created in his image. This means that, even after the fall, we can look at each other and the world around us and catch a glimpse of the face of God. Even after the Fall, God calls us to build community because the Triune God is a community of persons.

But although the world always gives us a glimpse of the God who created it, and even though we remain in God's image, imperfect nature endlessly falls into destructive chaos. Unwilling to trust completely in the goodness of God, we choose to go our own way. Our freedom to live in the Spirit is weakened by our desire to live in the Flesh. Men and women can no longer flourish in peace and trust, choosing instead the way of lust and domination. Death, which should be a door opening into God's arms, opens instead to fear and dread.

In the words of a modern theologian, our world

> ...has lost its center and has begun to disintegrate into confusion, suspicions, injustice and oppression, general fear, and warfare. An individual who is self-centered is an individual whose focus is so badly off-center that all aspects and dimensions of life are distorted and inauthentic to some degree....[9]

Traditionally, we use the word "original sin" to describe this desperate situation. We are not talking about personal sin with its burden of guilt. We are talking about a *condition* with mysterious roots into which we are all born. As soon as we emerge from the warmth of our mother's womb, we are thrust into this imperfect universe, where our sin-afflicted parents teach us to be their sin-afflicted children.

The Catholic story of salvation begins with the Jewish people

We know this part of the story by heart. It is the experience of real men and women, and we can still walk on the same dusty roads that felt their footsteps. Moses led slaves out of Egypt and across the Red Sea to Mount Sinai. There, they made a Covenant with God and became the Israelite people.

In the centuries that followed, a gathering of tribes became the Kingdom of David, whose covenant with God

---

[9][12] Monika K. Hellwig, *Understanding Catholicism,* Paulist Press, N.Y. 1981, p. 172

was celebrated by solemn sacrifices offered in a magnificent temple built by Solomon, his son. But with pomp and power came greed and division. The golden kingdom of Solomon split into Judah and Israel, two squabbling brothers. In 727, Israel fell to Assyria. In 587 BC, it was Judah's turn, as a Babylonian army crushed Jerusalem and obliterated the Temple.

After a dark night of captivity in Babylon, the people of Judah returned to their ruined city. Humbled by suffering and finally aware that they were only a fragment in a world of contending empires, they saw that they were never going to be a rival power. They realized that their true destiny was to be a remnant people who obeyed the Law and studied the Word of God in Scripture, awaiting the Day of the Lord. On that day, God would intervene through a man anointed as David was anointed. Until that day came, they were called to be faithful. If they were faithful, the Messiah would surely come and restore the kingdom.

Jesus and the coming of the Kingdom

As the Catholic story continues, dreams of human glory are turned upside down. The next part of the story unfolds in a humble village on the outskirts of the Jewish world. There, an angel put salvation into the hands of Mary, perhaps only fifteen years old. She said yes to God's messenger and, by the power of the Holy Spirit, she conceived in her womb. During the split second of that conception, the Second Person of the Trinity united himself with that emerging reality, became one with the whole human race, and took its pains and sorrows to himself.

Nine months later, Jesus was born in Bethlehem, the city of David. The upside-down story of salvation continued. Mary was forced to birth her son in a stable. He lived most of his life in the humble village of Nazareth, in the province of Galilee, far from the places of power. His stepfather Joseph was an artisan, and he followed the same trade. But when he was about thirty years-old, he made a sudden separation from his family. Baptized by John in the Jordan, he traveled to the Sea of Galilee, and began to gather disciples whose hands were scarred by hard labor. He called God his Father and announced the coming of the long-awaited Kingdom of God. Attracted by his words and miracles, his disciples dared believe that Jesus was the promised Messiah. They followed him to Jerusalem, expecting to become part of the restored kingdom of David. But their dream of worldly glory came to nothing. Jesus was arrested by the religious authorities, who turned him over to their Roman conquerors, who murdered him in the most painful way possible, nailing him to a cross.

But the usual triumph of the powerful over the weak took a sudden and totally unexpected turn. Again, the story of salvation turned human reality upside down. Jesus rose from the dead and appeared to his stunned disciples. After asking them to wait in Jerusalem for the gift of the Holy Spirit, he ascended into heaven. On Pentecost, the Holy Spirit came in wind and fire. This scene, paralleling the story at the beginning of the Book of Genesis, marks a New Creation. Filled with new life in the Spirit, the disciples recognized the crucified and risen Jesus as the Christ, the promised Messiah. But, infinitely more, they realized that he was the Son of God whose death brought the forgiveness of sins and the discovery of a new hope for the human race.

On Pentecost day, the Church, which had existed in embryo during the life of Jesus, burst into life. She recognized that, by the power of the Holy Spirit, Jesus Christ, Messiah and Son of God, still lived in her midst. She came to understand that she was his Body. His mission was now her mission. It was her task to proclaim his Gospel of redemption and salvation, to minister to the poor and afflicted in His name, and to call the world into a community of love and mutual forgiveness.

Almost two thousand years have gone by and the Church is still busy at her task, chipping away at the stubborn heart of a world filled with sin. Sadly, she herself has not been able to avoid this contagion. A bride whose dress has been tattered by her own sinful foolishness, she has been forced to learn, again and again, the true meaning of salvation. Repentant, trusting in God's faithfulness, she awaits the return of her Savior, who will come again in glory to gather His faithful ones into the Kingdom of His Father.

Catholic growth points

We have looked at two different gospels and two different stories of salvation. We have discovered the abyss that lies between the two churches. We do not worship the same God. We do not share the same dream of salvation.

In the meantime, my LDS relatives are very serious about their faith. People who aspire to be gods or married to gods have to set the bar very high. My honest, hard-working expanded family live lives marked by self-sacrifice and moral purity. They contribute up to twelve percent of their gross income to their church. They are also very generous with their time, performing their church duties as well as they can. Church attendance is a priority. They have great loyalty to their leaders. This does not mean that they manage to be perfect. But it does mean that they make great efforts to live their faith and meet its requirements.

The very goodness of so many Mormons presents a challenge to Catholics. Thousands of people attend the English and Spanish Masses at my parish every Sunday. Once in a while, I sit in the congregation in the middle of the folks. It has been a discovery. I cannot describe the people around me as lost in pious thoughts, although some clearly enter deeply into prayer. But there are kids to tend to, pages to turn, and—from my own experience—the struggle to pay attention to the sermon and focus on the mystery of the Mass. Even though the pews can be a restless, even noisy place, I think Jesus is very comfortable in our midst.

As I sit in the pew, I hope that the people around me have truly accepted their life in Christ. I pray that they allow their hearts to be his holy place. I trust that they share their Catholic life with their spouses, children, and friends. I pray that they will welcome the stranger. I know we are sitting there together, saints and sinners.Let me speak directly to the Catholics who are reading this book. Are you willing to let the large story of our faith be your story? We are called to walk with Christ, die with Christ, live with Christ. Do you see yourself on a journey with Jesus and his band of disciples? Do you share your faith with your children? Do you let Christ form you values? Have you tried to give yourself in love to Jesus? Do you pray? Do you meet God in the Mass and in the sacraments? Are you aware of your common inheritance with Mary and the Saints? Are you generous with your Church? Is your home a place where visitors can recognize a love for God and the desire to live within God's New Creation? Do you dream with the Church a larger vision for the world, and do you do your bit to make it happen?

3

Are Mormons Christian? Where do Mormons fit in the religious spectrum?

By now, you understand that Mormons and Catholics live within two completely different religious realities. This causes people to ask the question: Are Mormons even Christian? For years, Catholics in the United States asked Church authorities in Rome to give an authoritative answer, but Rome took its time.

An answer in the form of a question

Are Mormons Christian? On June 5, 2001, the Congregation for the Doctrine of the Faith finally replied, but in a complicated way. The Congregation framed its answer in the form of a question. *Is the baptism conferred by the Church of Jesus Christ of Latter-day Saints a valid Baptism?* Baptism is like a key that fits into a lock. As far as we know, it is our only way to open the door into the Christian church. If LDS baptism is a valid Christian baptism, then the LDS faithful are to be considered Christians. But, if their baptism is not valid, then they cannot be numbered among the Christian faithful.

The Latter-day Saints use water baptism by immersion, which is one of the ways of celebrating Baptism honored by the Catholic Church. The LDS baptismal formula resembles the Trinitarian formula used by Catholics: "*Being commissioned by Jesus Christ, I baptize you in the name of the Father, and of the Son, and of the Holy Spirit.*"[10] But as we have begun to see, the Saints do not believe in God as a Trinity, but in a godhead made up of three separate and unequal totally material gods. Their Heavenly Father is an exalted member of the human race, with multiple human wives and billions of spirit children. Jesus is his literal firstborn son born in a previous existence, who achieved exaltation by passing through his own time of probation to become a lesser god.

Pondering LDS belief, the Congregation writes:

> *The differences are so great that one cannot even consider that this doctrine is a heresy which emerged out of a false understanding of Christian doctrine.*[11]

If Mormon baptism is valid, the Congregation could accept the Mormons as Christian even if they were heretics. But we read instead:

> *The Catholic Church has to consider invalid, that is to say cannot consider true Baptism, the rite given that name by the Church of Jesus Christ of Latter-day Saints.*[12]

In simpler words, without a true Christian Baptism, the LDS Church cannot be considered a true Christian church.

---

[10] *Doctrine and Covenants, 20:73*

[11] Navarette, Ibid. II,2

[12] Ibid, IV, 2

The Congregation stressed that the Church is not judging those who are members of the LDS Church. Catholics are not saying that Latter-day Saints are excluded from the Kingdom of God. It was simply saying that the Church of Jesus Christ of Latter-day Saints is not a Christian church.

Even though the Mormons greeted the Congregation's decision with a sneer and a shrug, we trust that Catholics and Mormons will enjoy heaven together. As the Vatican Council stated in its Constitution on the Church,

> "Those who...do not know the Gospel of Christ or his Church, but who nevertheless seek God with a sincere heart, and, moved by grace, try in their actions to do his will as they know it...these too may attain eternal salvation."[13]

Hopefully, there can be further study, dialogue, and good will between the two churches, leading to greater understanding and greater respect.

Locating the Mormons in the religious world

One: the LDS Church is a *"restoration church"*

Some churches, like the Lutherans or Presbyterians, are *reformation* churches. We call them this because they are rooted in the Protestant Reformation, a sixteenth century movement which tried to "reform" the grave abuses afflicting the Catholic Church during that time. But even though the Reformers broke away from the Catholic Church, they did not try to start Christianity over again from scratch.

About two hundred years ago, *Restoration* churches began to appear. They were the first to claim that a *great apostasy* had completely destroyed the church Jesus

---

[13] *Lumen Gentium*, 16

founded. They said that the thread linking this age to the age of the apostles has snapped. When they told the story of the Christian Church, they ended with the Church of the martyrs, or even with the apostles themselves. Reformation was fruitless; the only hope was restoration. The Restoration churches claim that they have restored the church of the first century through a fervent faith based on a correct reading of the Bible.

Representatives of these highly energetic churches control most of the religious programs appearing on radio or television today. They are fundamentalist in their interpretation of the Bible and believe that the end of the world and the Final Judgment are very close at hand. Often claiming exclusive possession of the name "Christian," they can be very critical of both the Catholic and Reformation churches. But like other Protestants, they base their religion on the Bible alone, confer a valid Baptism, and form a growing part of Christianity.

The Mormons adopted the idea of a restored church. But then they deliver a body blow to the Reformation and Restoration churches alike. They say that any attempt based on the Bible alone is a useless effort, because the Bible has been badly damaged and does not tell the whole truth. Only the Church of Jesus Christ of Latter-day Saints can achieve a true restoration, because it alone has a living prophet, it alone possesses a restored apostolic authority, and it alone is blessed with the gift of ongoing revelation.

Two: the LDS Church is a *millennial church*

What is a millennial church? Millennial churches believe that these are the last days. History is about to end and Christ will soon reign with the just for a thousand years. The millennial churches are the most energetic of all churches today. Some of them are Christian, such as the

Assembly of God or the Foursquare Gospel and many others. They are the ones who believe in the "Rapture." At some time just around the corner, God will snatch the just from earth, and everyone else will be left behind.

An urgent conviction that these are the latter-days also drives the LDS Church. The strongest symbol of this belief is the figure of the Angel Moroni standing at the top of every LDS temple, a trumpet to his lips, ready to announce the end of history and the return of Christ.

The LDS want the world to accept them as Christian

Jesus worshiped in Jewish synagogues and led his followers into the Temple in Jerusalem. But the Church he established broke free from Judaism and began to call itself by a different name. Catholics describe a difficult but Spirit-led journey. Bible scholars tell us that the ancient Church had difficulty seeing that their church was separate from the Jewish faith. This is obvious in the Acts of the Apostles. The Apostles continued to go to the Temple and continued to attend synagogue services. Things changed when Paul began to baptize non-Jewish converts without following the Mosaic Law. Jewish leaders made it easier when they began to expel Christians from their synagogues after the destruction of Jerusalem and its temple in 67 AD.

If the disciples of Jesus were no longer Jews, what were they? Some called their newborn church "The Way." But others adopted a name that was first given them by the scornful pagan inhabitants of the great city of Antioch. From then on, they were "Christians."

An historian in the 1800's might have assumed that the LDS Church was going to follow a roughly parallel path. Leaving the Christian world behind, the first LDS converts had chosen to walk behind a new prophet with new revelations about different gods. It would have seemed logical for Mormons to leave the word Christian behind. For a time, this seemed to be the journey Mormons were taking. When I was a youth, the LDS did not identify themselves as a Christian group. I remember a 1960's radio advertising campaign promoting the church, which boasted, "We are not Christians –we're Mormons!"

But today, the Saints are trying very hard to assume the name Christian. At this moment, their leaders are redefining themselves in this way. They seem to hope that nobody will notice the difference between the Jesus of the Christian Trinity, and the Jesus who is the firstborn son of an exalted male of the human species. Mormon author Stephen E. Robinson presents the Mormon position in *Are Mormons Christians?*[14]He defiantly asks, "Is not the name of our church, The Church of *Jesus Christ* of Latter-day Saints? Do we not worship Christ? Is not the book of Mormon another testament of Jesus Christ?"

Robinson quotes *Webster's Third New International Dictionary*, where the term "Christian" is defined. According to Webster, a Christian is:

> *One who believes or professes or is assumed to believe in Jesus Christ and the truth as taught by him; an adherent of Christianity: one who has accepted the Christian religious and moral principles of life: one who has faith in and has pledged allegiance to God thought of as revealed in Christ; one whose life is conformed to the doctrines of Christ."*

But this definition actually supports the charges leveled by the other churches. It says a Christian is "an adherent of

---

14 Stephen E. Robinson, *Are Mormons Christian?* Bookcraft, Salt Lake City, Utah, 1984

Christianity." The churches that are part of Christianity believe in the Triune God who created the universe from nothing. They believe that the Second Person of the Trinity united himself to the human reality conceived in the womb of Mary. But the LDS Church scorns all of these churches as part of a great apostasy, and the Mormon belief in many gods with wives and spirit children is a universe away from the Christian belief in One God who is a Trinity of persons. It is difficult to understand how Mormons can call themselves Christian.

Three: the LDS Church is entangled in *Gnosticism*

The Mormon restoration sounds familiar to someone who has studied the history of the ancient Christian church. As soon as the Apostles left the safe confines of Israel, they collided with a loosely organized religious-philosophical movement called Gnosticism. As they moved from place to place, the Gnostics, like the Borg of Star Trek fame, tried to assimilate other groups into their own social and spiritual reality. Like spiritual parasites, they would enter the bloodstream of the host religion by adopting its words and beliefs, but the end result was something the orthodox members of the host religion could not recognize.

When the Gnostics met Christianity they recognized its power and beauty and tried to twist it to their own purposes. Following their usual strategy, they adopted Christian words and Christian concepts. The first Christian heresies resulted from this brush with Gnosticism. For the first centuries of her existence, the Church was involved in a life and death battle with this invasive force that tried to devour her from within.

A description of Gnosticism

The word *"Gnostic"* means "the possession of secret knowledge." *The Interpreters Dictionary of the Bible* gives us a description of Gnosticism, and some of its ancient beliefs offer amazing parallels to the Mormon story we have just discussed. This includes: 1) A fall or journey from a pre-existent world and the call to return again to that world. 2) A claim that the original Christian message has been lost through some kind of apostasy. 3) And/or, a claim that the original Christian message is incomplete and needs correction. 4) The lost or incomplete message has been restored through secret knowledge. Often, this secret knowledge begins with the knowledge of an unknown god. 5) This secret knowledge is revealed by a redeemer who descends to earth and brings about redemption by providing this lost or secret knowledge. 6) Frequently, the secret knowledge is restored through the discovery of lost books, or through new revelations given to a prophet. 7) This knowledge is revealed to those who "by origin" are related to the redeemer. 8) Secret rites appear, which prepare the living for their return to the realms above.

Anyone familiar with Joseph Smith and the origins of Mormonism can recognize the gnostic pattern. What was lost through repeated apostasy has been restored again through a new prophet and the discovery of lost books Gnosticism appears most vividly in the First and Second books of Nephi in the *Book of Mormon*, and in the *Book of Moses* and *The Book of Abraham*, which are found in the fourth book of Mormon scripture called the *Pearl of Great Price*.

Mormons teach that we have left a pre-existent world behind and, after a time of probation, will return to that world. We have mentioned Smith's claim to restore the fullness of the gospel through the power of prophecy. We begin to understand that the god of Mormons is completely strange to Jews and Christians.

Mimicking the tactics used by the ancient Gnostics, Mormons use the same precious words cherished by two thousand years of Christianity. They talk about God, Jesus, grace and salvation. But they are citizens of an entirely different religious universe We will talk about angelic visions and a mysterious language on golden plates that became the *Book of Mormon*. In a later chapter, we will also discuss the LDS temples and the role they play in the Mormon story of salvation.

But in the end, Mormons truly love Jesus as they understand him. Are they *some* kind of Christian?

Rome has spoken. The Latter-day Saints are not a Christian church. But a person like myself has to consider the loving witness that he has seen in his many LDS relatives. There are pictures of a masculine, red-robed Jesus in their living rooms, and a profound love for Jesus in their sturdy religious hearts. In one of my earliest memories, my mother is holding me in front of a picture of the Child Jesus in the Temple. "This is Jesus," she tells me. "He died for you and he loves you." The intensity of her words and the sight of the figure of the young Jesus lodged forever in my soul. When my mother told me that, she was still a Mormon, and her words reflected her Mormon faith.

So what about the Mormon claim to the name Christian? In the most generic description anyone can think of, a Christian is "someone who tries to be a lover and follower of Christ." I think of a young Mormon who just sent me an email. He told me, "I have tried to get closer and closer to the Savior all of my life." How can we disrespect his search? This is the social definition of Christian suggested by the Congregation of the Doctrine of Faith. I will follow that suggestion and conclude that, even though their church is not a Christian church, and even though their Christ is not the Christ of the Christian churches, Mormon's love for Jesus as they know him gives them the right to be called social Christians.

Catholic growth points

The four gospels were written, in part, to defend the infant Church against Gnosticism and its claims to lost books and new revelations. Have you read one of the gospels, from beginning to end? Maybe you could begin with the Gospel of St. Mark, whose description of a very down-to-earth Jesus was written to oppose Gnostics.

The Catholic Catechism is a long explanation of our faith. Do you own a Catechism? Have you read any of its sections? Do you try to understand the key elements of your faith from an adult point of view? Do you explain to your children why you are a Catholic? Do you help your children clarify their Catholic faith and try to answer their questions?

PART TWO

The Challenge of the Missionaries

You probably bought this book because you or someone you love has had an experience with the Mormon missionaries. Alarmed and feeling defensive, you want answers NOW. Who are these guys who are visiting my son or daughter? What are they trying to teach my sister or brother? I decided we needed some insight into a faith so different from ours before discussing the missionaries. I won't make you wait any longer.

As we discuss the missionaries, I change my tone a bit. What has preceded this chapter has been a calm conversation comparing basic religious truths. But the Mormon missionaries do not want to have a win/win conversation with you. They want your soul. Even though they present themselves well and can be very charming, you are their religious hunting ground. They want to change your understanding of God and turn your religious world upside down. What follows is my kind but dead-serious reaction

4

Who are the Missionaries?

Since I wrote this chapter, the Mormons have revised their missionary program to some extent, but basically, this is what happens.

The missionary structure

If I were God, I would tell the American bishops they can learn a thing or two from the LDS missionary program. It is a proven way to make converts that would not break the back of a busy pastor and his staff. Second, and perhaps even more important, it offers a way for ordinary Catholic youth to share their faith, returning home as mature men and woman ready to participate in their church with energy and dedication. Imagine the Jesuit Volunteers on a national or international scale.

The entire Mormon missionary program is a separate organization that reaches past town, state, and country. Under the authority of the LDS President and directed from Salt Lake, the program exists within the larger church, but with its own parallel authority structure. It accepts missionaries from every Mormon community and prepares them for their task. They might toil in a missionary district anywhere in the world, under the authority and direction a mission president.

A proving ground for mature men and women

Every year, more than seventy thousand young people go off to do difficult work in the name of God and Mormon

Church. They are admired and revered. Most LDS families look forward to the time when a son or a daughter will go off on their own mission. Mormon children at every education level hear dramatic stories about the exploits of the missionaries and imagine themselves knocking on doors in a far-away place As soon as they can, they start a "missionary savings-account" so they can pay all of their own expenses.

A Mormon youth who hopes to have a high standing with family and church will think seriously about becoming a missionary. Many girls dream about the day when they will marry a returned missionary, and more and more young women want to take their own place in the mission field. Understanding that only the pure and the faithful can be missionaries, Mormon high school students guard their moral lives, avoiding extramarital sex and the drugs and drinking that lead so many youth to their downfall.

Who can apply?

Young men at least 18 and young women at least 19 can send applications to their bishop. But the church will demand an interview with the bishop, who will ask some very specific questions. His list of questions might look like this: What about church attendance? Give me evidence about personal prayer. Do you study the scriptures? What about sexual purity? Do you smoke? Drink caffeinated beverages? Drink alcohol? Use drugs? Do you hang out with non-Mormon friends? Give me proof that you tithe. Do you have a testimony about the truth of your faith?

After successful interview, the whole family will be waiting for their son or daughter to receive a call to mission, which will come via email from the LDS president himself. When it does, the whole family will celebrate. The call will specify the place where our missionary will serve. In

Mormon eyes, the president's decision is a matter of divine revelation. If the young man or woman begins to waver, an authority will ask, Do you believe in revelation?

After receiving his/her call, the missionary goes to one of ten Missionary Training Schools scattered throughout the world. The training period lasts for only three weeks. If the missionary has to learn a language, the training program will last for nine weeks. When I first met the missionaries, they based their work on the lesson plans contained in six short pamphlets. But now they follow a book called *Preach my Gospel*, which gives them more freedom and more creativity. As soon as they enter the training program, the missionaries begin to follow the demands of a strict dress code. They are assigned a companion and will always work as a pair. This gives them mutual support and makes them responsible to and for each other.

Off to their mission

With that very short three to nine week preparation under their belts, it is off to their mission. Travelers who land in the Salt Lake City airport are familiar with happy families either waving goodbye to missionaries on their way, or opening their arms to those just returned. A missionary assignment could be any place in the world. For instance, one of my cousins served in Thailand. Another served in North Carolina. Wherever they go, they will be supervised by a mission president who will apply generations of missionary experience to his task.

Our newly arrived missionary is a mere beginner, so his first companion will be someone who has had more experience. The location of his work within the missionary district and the names of his companion will change as time goes on. Thanks to their conservative, American style dress, the two will always stand out. On bicycles or on foot, people will know, even from a distance, that they are Mormon missionaries. Those in doubt only need to wait until they come closer and look for the name-tag announcing that the young persons are either "elders" or "sisters."

Six days a week, they will rise at 6:30 and go to bed at 10:00. Almost every minute of every waking day will be focused on their mission, which will include study, prayer, fasting, and "proselyting." (uniquely Mormon word). They won't watch TV, listen to the radio, go to movies, or use the internet (except for study and to email family). They will read only books, magazines, and other material authorized by church authority. They will study their religion, the religion of others, practice their new language, and learn how to use *Preach my Gospel* in a more and more expert fashion.

Cooperation from local Mormons

Wherever they go, the local ward (parish) will have a committee ready to cooperate with the missionaries, giving them an occasional meal and emotional support. The committee will point out prospects, create a welcome for possible converts who attend services in their church, and help settle new converts in new spiritual homes. That leaves the Mormon bishop free to do his many other tasks, confident that the search for converts is in other capable hands.

Where do missionaries find their converts?

Missionaries have become more and more creative in their presence at public gatherings and in their use of the Internet. But a recent article assured me that they that continue to fish in what they call a "conversion pool." When they arrive in town, the leaders of the local ward will give them a list of inactive Mormons, non-Mormon spouses, friends and relatives of Mormons, friends, and relatives of people of who have just become Mormons, people who have just moved into town, and the location of high possibility neighborhoods, especially Hispanic neighborhoods.

Missionaries will have to go door to door. Introverts like me probably find it an excruciating effort, especially after they receive their first brutal rejection. Knocking at a strange door requires bravado and a thick skin. They will have to knock on hundreds of doors and will have to be satisfied with scant results. Based on a CNN report in 2016, the average missionary makes only 4.7 converts in a year.

In this era dominated by social media, the Mormon missionary effort is trying hard to adapt. I have not had time to research this, but I imagine that missionaries do skillful smart-phone work, and are busy on social media. I know that there are Mormon sites on the Internet which appeal to people on a religious quest. I know that they are more successful with this self-selected group of curious people who are already on the search.

How long will the mission last? Two years for men, eighteen months for women. The lack of large success won't be a waste. They will have passed through a grueling rite of passage, returning home as strong young people ready to be leaders in their church and community.

5

Missionaries at Work

Why people choose to become Mormons

Friends follow friends

Good friends will often lead other friends into their church. Many a non-Catholic is attracted to the Catholic Church by a Catholic friend, often the person who will become a spouse. But the door goes both ways. On the high school level, most kids are part of a group. If a young person is welcomed into a group containing Mormons, he might follow his friends to the LDS Seminary across the street from his high school. The same is true in college, with LDS institutes vacuuming in Catholic kids who are led there by a wonderful new friend. Strategists as always, Mormons have developed a "friendshiping" program which teaches members how to make comfortable contact with non-Mormons, hoping to lead them to an encounter with the missionaries. This is usually an adult/adult effort conducted by LDS members trained in the tactic, but it does operate at the high school level, and some LDS students are very good at it.

Someone seeking to prove their independence might change religion

Ours is a country built by people who crossed the ocean, leaving everyone else behind. We are a nation of individualists where family ties sometimes hang by a thread. If connection to family is thin, connection to church might even be thinner. People change jobs and move from one part of the country to the other. Added to this, our American culture tells its youth that they have to separate from their parents and be their own person. As a result, our young people feel the strong need to assert their independence, and look for a way to symbolize that process. A change in religion can be a dramatic way to say to Mom or Dad, I am in charge of my own life!

A more emphatic and more painful change caused by alienation from parents or family

Young people learn how to pull their parents' string. Often enough, they pull that string in times of anger or bitterness. And no string goes closer to the heart than religion. Some young people change their religion out of rebellion, and it is a wonderful way to get revenge.

I think of "D," a high school student I knew a long time ago. I prayed for her every time I gave her Communion. Her body language said it all: Rigid posture, angry eyes, pouting lips, and scarcely suppressed fury. As soon as "D" turned eighteen, she moved to Salt Lake. Within a month, she was listening to the missionaries. One day, she returned home accompanied by two missionaries. She demanded that her parents put up the missionaries at their house. Her mother heard one of the missionaries urging her daughter to do what she was supposed to do. And so she announced that she was joining the Mormon Church. I told her tearful parents to always treat her with respect and love. Many years later, I met her parents again, who told me she was now married with a family of her own, deeply involved in the Mormon Church, still the rebel, still a self-proclaimed exile from her family.

Boyfriend and girlfriend, and marriage

Friendship has blossomed into love. This is a time when young people often abandon their faith to join a boyfriend or girlfriend in theirs. But they don't just flip a coin when they make this choice. I have noticed this in my own nieces and nephews. One person has a stronger personality than the other. The stronger is the one who will lead the way into his/her church. Related to this: One person is often more in love than the other. With less to lose, the one who is least in love will control the relationship and lead the other into his/her church.

When it comes to marriage, I witness a repeated story. A Catholic marries a Mormon, telling her parents not to worry, because her new husband is not active in his faith. But remember, the Mormon spouse still has Mormon parents and siblings, who do not want to lose a loved one for eternity.

Some, like my own Mormon grandparents, let my mother have her way, deeply hurt and angry until they day they died. But other parents don't give up so easily. Sooner or later, they help their son have a sudden spiritual conversion. Now he wants to live his LDS faith to the full. But his non-Mormon wife blocks his path to life as a god with wives and spirit-children. She will have to become a Mormon so they can marry in the temple and reach this ideal. He feels great power because he has the example of his father, the priesthood holder who might have ruled his family like a patriarch. He has the example of his mother, who played the role of faithful Mormon wife. The pressure is on and the missionaries are at the door. The pressure will get worse as the children arrive. One young wife told me that the missionaries showed up again and again. These young strangers argued that she had to convert for the sake of her family. After a couple of years, her marriage came to an end.

Catholics can drive other Catholics out of the Church

I define faithful Catholics as very forgiving people They have to be, because when Catholics are honest, they admit that theirs is a sinful church. Right now we are living with the consequences of the sex abuse scandal. In the recent past, priests abused children and young people, while their bishops covered it up. Those men, so jealous of their authority and the prestige of the Church, threw their moral authority away and brought a lot of faithful priests and bishops down with them. Because of this, only God knows how many Catholics are leaving the church and turning to other churches like the Mormons, or to no church at all.

But it is not just that. People often leave the Church when they encounter unkind or greedy, or worldly, or uncaring priests. Or maybe the priest is a rigid man who pays no attention to the struggles and pain of his people. Or maybe he preaches endless bad sermons and presides over uninspiring liturgies. When people left the church from my parish, I used to blame myself, but now I realize how often cold and indifferent parishioners don't reach out to strangers or even to each other. I had a parish like that, full of people who managed to be wonderful but very closed within themselves. A Catholic couple that had been attending a Mormon Church showed up with three little children. I introduced them to the parish. The parish ignored them. I begged. I pleaded. In the end, that wonderful couple with their kids went back to the Mormon Church.

Watching the missionaries at work

I want to describe two tactics the missionaries use with considerable effect.

First key tactic, *develop an adult-child relationship*

Even though they are only in their late teens or very early twenties, the missionaries know how to take control of the discussion with a possible convert, turning their lessons on Mormon faith into a parent-child relationship where they hold spiritual authority over the person they call their "investigator." The missionaries might not really understand that this is what they are doing. But if a person refuses to yield to their authority, they will often pull their line out of this part of the conversion pool, and go fishing somewhere else.

It is a matter of strategic manipulation. It *begins* with the badges the well-dressed pair of young missionaries are wearing, which identify them as "elders," or "sisters." These labels demand the respect that is actually deserved only through time and experience. In the Bible, the title "elder" is given to a man who is forty years old or older, a sturdy patriarch surrounded by his extended family. The title "sister" gives a soberly dressed very young pair of female missionaries instant status among Catholics, for whom "sister" means a vowed person given to God after preparation in a religious order. But, just like your own son or daughter at the same age, the missionaries are bare beginners in the spiritual journey. They can point to no special wisdom giving them a big step up the ladder leading to God. What they have instead is a high school background, that very short stay at the Missionary Training School, their memorized instructions for a six week course in their faith, the strength of their own personalities, and what they learn as their short mission unfolds.

The manipulation continues as the missionaries walk up your sidewalk, with the most experienced companion leading the way. They will size up your yard and your house, looking for some kind of hook to introduce themselves and get across your threshold. Along with an energetic door knock and a beaming smile, they will use a few tricks familiar to any door-to-door salesman.

Instructed by a small booklet about missionary tactics, the lead missionary might use a tactic salesmen call "act like yes." He has already opened your screen door and his foot is on your threshold. He will say, "Can we please come in?" As he says this, *he takes a step forward.* As he steps forward, you will probably take an automatic step back, leaving an open space at your door. Admit it; he just got you. In a blink, he and his companion are safely inside. Once inside, he will make pleasant small talk based what he saw in your yard, what sees in your house, and what he senses in your demeanor. After knocking on countless doors, he knows how to give you his best side and how to make you feel comfortable.

When he senses the time is right, *he will try to talk you into listening to just one lesson about Jesus Christ.* When Catholics hear this, they usually assume that this is going to be a discussion among Christians. They do not realize that they are being invited to a journey outside of the Christian world.

If you quickly agree to the lesson, the missionaries' quest is over and it is time to make an appointment. But if you disagree, he is ready with another salesman tactic found in another short pamphlet written to help missionaries on the hunt. Simply put, *a no is not really a no.* After you say no, the pamphlets tell the missionary to rephrase his question or

64

ask another question. If you say no again, but in a different way, or if you try to offer an excuse, the pamphlets urge the missionaries to stay at it, because you have still not really said no.

The first lesson

Whether you gladly accepted the offer of just one lesson, or if you gave in and finally said yes, the missionaries have made an appointment and now they are in your home. After some small talk to break the ice, it is time to get to work. It is time to use another "act like yes tactic." A how-to-do-it pamphlets tells the missionary to say, "Let us pray," *even as he and his partner are already going down to their knees.* The pamphlet boasts, "This will bring everybody down to their knees, as well." While you are there, I hope you contemplate this fact: You have just helped this very young person establish his spiritual authority over you and your family.

Once everyone is down on their knees, *the missionary will ask you, as the father, to say the prayer*. This will give you a case of instant stage fright, if, like many a Catholic father, you do not lead your family in prayer. There you are, on the spot in front of your wife and kids. After your possibly clumsy effort, the impeccably dressed and utterly self-confident young men *will praise you for a wonderful job*. In student/teacher terms, *you just got a star*, and the authority of the missionaries has advanced another step. The missionaries will continue to focus on you, as the father of your family. If they gain control over you, your conversion will probably mean the conversion of your wife and kids. They will especially focus on, and flatter, the father of a Hispanic family. In expanded Hispanic families, the conversion of one family can lead to the conversion of several others.

As the lesson begins, the lead missionary will probably *ask you to read a selected passage from your own Bible*. Oh, oh. If you are like too many normal Catholics, a Bible might not be in sight, or doesn't exist. The missionaries have you again. But the problem gets worse. If you finally find your Bible, or if he gives you his own Bible, you might not know how to turn to the right place in the text. Another score for the spiritual authority of the missionary. With a flourish, he will show you where to read.

Now, he *will do all the talking*. When he does have to stop for a breath, he will be careful to *end with a question*, which leaves him in control of the conversation, and you. And so it will go. It will always be respectful, but he will lead you where he wants you to go. Little by little, you will lose ground and yield to this person only a year or two out of high school.

Somewhere along the way, and maybe more than once, you will get a glimpse of another key tactic, which I will discuss in a moment. The missionaries will bear solemn witness to the truth and beauty of what they are teaching. This is called "testimony," and it is one of the most effective tools in the missionary bag of tricks. You will hear the missionaries bear their testimony many times as the lessons continue.

Finally the first lesson draws to an end. The missionary's next task is to *try to get you to* agree to another appointment, as soon as possible. He will also offer you a free Book of Mormon with important passages outlined in yellow, with the request, "I have underlined some important verses. Will you read and pray about them before we return?" He will persist until he extracts your sincere promise, and will not be content with a half-hearted "I will give it a try." Don't take a breath in relief after he leaves. The next day, he is almost certain to call or text to see how you are doing.

The second lesson

When it comes time for the second appointment, the missionary who has taken the lead will ask whether you did your homework. If you did, another star. If you didn't, he will express deep disappointment, and will assure you that God is disappointed, too. If you feel sheepish, he is already the parent and you are already the child.

The missionaries will lead you and your family through the second lesson. You will still imagine you are listening to missionaries from a Christian church, because the missionaries are very strategic about what they say. They will probably omit a discussion of some topics, such as eternal progression, saving it for a time when you are safely inside their church. Again, the missionaries will bear well-rehearsed testimonies at some points in the lesson. Then it will be time to talk you into the third lesson.

The third lesson: An invitation to a service in a Mormon ward

Now the missionaries press for a third lesson and, if you accept, important things will begin to happen. The missionaries will invite you to join them at a service in a local ward. This does not mean you will sit quietly in the back as an anonymous guest and observe what is going on. Each Mormon Ward has a committee primed and ready to give you a royal welcome.

Prayers to a strange god

While you are sitting there surrounded by sudden new friends, ponder this: The god they are praying to is that exalted male of the human species with numerous wives and billions of spirit children. They believe that he is literally their father. In a Catholic Church, you believe that the God of the universe is there in your midst and in your heart. But the Mormon Heavenly Father is far away in his mansion near the great star Kolob. He is contacting you through that impersonal force or power they call the holy spirit. You will not hear them pray to Jesus, because for Mormons, he is a lesser god. They will only pray in his name. They will not pray to the Holy Ghost, because he is an even lesser god.

Crunch time

At this time, the missionaries will probably urge you to name a date for your baptism. They have asked you to pray about what you have learned in their lessons. They have given you small pamphlets to read to back up their lessons, and they have underlined a few passages in the Book of Mormon. Your decision will be based on good feelings, a minimum of information, and a minimum of time. Based on this flimsy foundation, they are asking you to make one of the most important religious decisions you can make. If you have allowed them to be the parents in an adult-child relationship, you might quickly say yes. If you are suggestible or a people pleaser, it might be especially difficult to say no.

Second key tactic: *Pray for a testimony*

By now, you have heard the missionaries bear their testimony a number of times. Using strong words and maybe with some emotion, they have proclaimed their belief in some aspect of their lesson. Their testimonies have been impressive. You do not know that they have been rehearsing those testimonies again and again, polishing them to perfection. To convince you to ask for baptism, the missionaries will challenge you to pray for your own testimony about the truth of what they are saying. They know this can be a key to your conversion, and they are prepared to explain the steps that will help you find that testimony.

How effective is the use of testimony?

A few years ago, a three hundred pound swindler who had been raised within the LDS tradition named himself Immanuel David and announced that he was God. His disciples gave him their time, their freedom, their money, and followed his "revelations" no matter how strange they seemed to outsiders. Even after Immanuel David committed suicide to avoid jail, his disciples continued to believe. Said one follower, "I can tell you this much: I had spiritual experiences in that group....They were experiences to keep you hooked, to keep you thinking that 'If I had this experience, then this must be right.'"[15] In other words, the man had experienced frequent "testimony," and surely the holy spirit was telling him to follow Immanuel David. This extreme story provides a kind of cautionary tale.

Let me make this crucial point again. *Testimony* is a key tool in the missionary toolbox, as I will explain in the next chapter. Over and over again, the LDS pray to amplify their testimony, which they describe as the warm and pleasant feelings about the truths of their faith. They consider these feelings a revelation from God himself.

Now the missionaries challenge you to have a testimony of your own. They have prepared for that moment by asking you, again and again, *to share your feelings about what you have just heard*. They might ask, for instance, "How did you *feel* when we were teaching you about Jesus' death for

---

[15] From an article by Bill Morlinin the *Idaho Spokesman Review*, April 10, 2000, p. A10

us on the cross?" When you, as a Catholic steeped in a love for Christ on the cross, express good feelings, the missionaries will praise you and tell you that those feelings are *a witness of the holy spirit testifying to the truth of their teaching*. I think of the daughter of a good friend who confessed such good feelings. The female missionaries who were visiting her told her this was a sign from God and began to press her for baptism.

The experience of testimony can be a thunderbolt. I know of a young man who told his parents that God himself had commanded him to become a Mormon. If the missionaries are doing their job, you will be invited to have the same thought. The missionaries will happily help you "feel the spirit." They will stay close, hoping you will not take the time to talk to your priest or any other important figure in your life, people the how-to-do-it missionary pamphlets include among the *forces of evil*. If the emotional feelings and strong convictions finally overwhelm you, they will assure you that, by divine revelation, the holy spirit is calling you to become a Mormon.

This is no RCIA program

In contrast to the six lesions given by the missionaries, the Catholic program for converts, called the RCIA, leads people interested in the Church through a months' long process that involves instruction, witness, a lot of prayer, and constant discernment. The missionaries may not realize that they give their converts a minimum of information, a minimum of time, and a maximum of subtle psychological pressure. They want you baptized within their church within as little as three weeks.

It is this kind of behavior that causes other churches to call the LDS Church a cult. Apart from the lesson plan and a small pamphlet from the missionaries, what does a potential convert really know about Joseph Smith and the Mormon Church? Before caving in to feelings, a person listening to the missionaries should follow advice from Joseph Smith himself and *study it out in his mind, first.* This means you need to continue with this little book, and find one of the three books I will recommend for a long look at the life and character of Joseph Smith. The whole Mormon message comes from his claim to be a prophet and the mouthpiece of God. Read his story carefully. Is he a person you can trust with the fate of your soul?

6

A Catholic Survival Kit

I will always remember the woman who came to me with tears in her eyes. Every Sunday she sat in her pew, accompanied by her husband and several tall sons. One of her sons had met a Mormon girl, and he was about to become a Mormon. She and her husband actually sat down with their son and the missionaries, and tried to convince him not to become a Mormon. But he was deeply in love and in no mood to displease the beautiful young woman who was about to become his bride. It was my encounter with his mother that gave me the energy to write this book again.

Confronting the missionaries

I am not writing this book so that you can rush out, find some missionaries, and go at it mano a mano. This is about a dignified discussion with missionaries who are talking to a Catholic and have a distinct advantage. They hope you do not know that they are really not Christians. Or maybe they actually think they are Christians, but do not understand the difference. They do know how to develop a parent-child relationship. And they know how to use testimony as a clincher. I am going to show you how to make the discussion a discussion between equals.

A young man with a badge saying "elder."

The sight of the well-dressed missionaries on the street or at your door can be intimidating, perhaps because there are two of them, and many of them are tall, handsome young men who might be lifting weights in their spare time. But I remind you, even though male missionaries wear a tag labeling them "elder," the young man might be only eighteen, while the young woman wearing the tag "sister" could be nineteen. So, we are talking about young people just out of high school, and usually no older than any college freshman or sophomore.

This does not fit the biblical definition of an elder. In the Bible, an elder was a grey bearded man over forty in a world where the average life span was around thirty-five. He was a battle-scarred veteran among his people. He had life or death power over his children. His family looked upon him with awe, and he had burly sons to back him up when he argued with other elders in front of the village gate. With all due respect, the missionaries who come to your door are just conservatively dressed kids who have not met the deep life challenges faced by their own mothers and fathers. They have very little to say from personal religious experience; mostly, they are giving lessons from a book.

I am destined to be a god, or married to a god!

A friend who had attended public high school in a city with a majority LDS population told me how she watched her Mormon classmates change. She had known them since grade school, and began to see the changes when they entered junior high. They were learning something about their destiny that would make anyone gasp and strut with pride. A Mormon boy was called to the Melchizedek Priesthood, which meant he could one day act in God's own name and was destined to become a god himself! A Mormon girl was also amazed, and began to look at the boys around her in a new way. She was destined to be married to a god! She would live as a queen in her husband's mansion and bear him children beyond counting. She would watch with joy as they became gods in their own right, or married to gods. She might even imagine, as many Mormon women do today, that she would become a goddess.

Mormon missionaries often possess a certain mystique. Their sense of a divine destiny surely adds a swagger to their steps. They are members of the only true church on earth. They belong to the Elect. With a certain sense of superiority, they will boldly preach the gospel to people three times their age.

I don't want to attack missionaries. I have invited more than one pair into my house to teach me the six lessons and I have encountered other missionaries in other situations. They were respectful young men and women. When I handed them milk and cookies, I have to say I was impressed. It takes a lot of moxie to school a Catholic priest about religion. What I mean to do here is help Catholics turn their meeting with the missionaries into a conversation between adults.

The missionaries come to your door

The time to bring the conversation down to earth is when the missionaries ring your doorbell. You are not obliged to open the door. Many families, especially Hispanic families, have a little sign by their door that identifies them as a Catholic family and politely tells Mormons and Jehovah's Witnesses to stay away. If you don't have such a sign, keep your screen door locked. If your screen door is not locked, you might find it open and a missionary standing there, right at your threshold, inside your space. Do not step back if he steps forward and asks if he can come in. Stand your ground. Unless you want him to come in, tell him no, smile, and shut the door.

If you let the missionaries into your house you are now at a disadvantage as you try to find a polite way to get them to leave. The missionary taking the lead will immediately try to break the ice with compliments about your yard and some of the things he sees in your house. When he feels you are kindly disposed, he will make his pitch for a discussion about Jesus. Remember, you are not talking to a Christian who comes in a different flavor. The Jesus of Mormons is the literal son of an exalted male human being who has become a god in a vast universe filled with other exalted male human beings, who became gods before him or after him. He is the son of a god, who is the son of a god, who is the son of a god. If you are male, the missionaries want to invite you to climb to the level of exaltation and become a god in your own right, with eternal wives and billions of spirit children. If you are female, the missionaries will invite you to become the wife of a god. And so you have to remind yourself again and again that a conversation with the missionaries is no discussion between Christians. It is a discussion between a Christian and two young men who do not worship the God of the Christian tradition.

If you say yes, it could open the door to six lessons and a major effort to turn you and your family into Mormons. This is probably the time to say no and point to the door. But remember, for the missionaries, a no is not really a no. So, you might have to be a broken record, saying no in the same way, over and over, politely but firmly. Or…you could do what my dad used to do, invite the missionaries in for a beer and a smoke. They always had other places to go.

But I want to listen to the missionaries

If you are intrigued and really want to listen to the missionaries, make an appointment. But think about it before they come around the second time. *They are prepared, you are not*, and this giv0es them a serious advantage. Use the time before your appointment to read parts of this book again. You will also have time for second thoughts. When they return, you can always hunker down out of sight and tell the kids to keep quiet. Or you could go to a movie. Or you could open your door a crack and tell them you changed your mind and you have other things to do.

Warning! Warning! A note to Hispanics, the suggestible, people pleasers, and me

In their missionary lore, Mormons boast that converting Hispanics is a piece of cake. I think that the main reason is the famous Latin hospitality. "You are in your own house," the Spanish phrase goes. But they also offer Hispanics, who are often poor, financial incentives. In one part of my state, some Mormon farmers threaten to fire their Hispanic workers if they do not attend the local LDS ward. Whatever the situation, the missionaries will always have an advantage because they are so well dressed and so dignified, and they look official with their books with pages rimmed with gold. One of them might even speak Spanish.

Attention! "Suggestible" people have a special problem. For some reason, I am among that number. I have to take a breath when faced by a strong person's request. Such is the plight of someone who was the middle child. Mom was a toughie who would keep at it until I finally gave way. And then there were my big sister and my next to big sister and my big brother. Whoo! As a result, my first instinct is to automatically say yes. I struggle with the problem to this day. It damaged my ability as a pastor.

On top of that, I am a people pleaser. Again, operating with the habits that sometimes afflict a middle child, I try to keep everybody happy, and I hate even indirect confrontations. My blood pressure rises, my heartrate kicks up. I once found a book called *Don't Say Yes When you Want to Say No* and read it about half a dozen times. But as soon as I met that hard-nosed "Concerned Parishioner," the urge to please kicked in and I forgot everything the book said.

So, if you are a Hispanic, a suggestible person, or a people pleaser like me, don't open the screen door which, hopefully, you keep locked. Say no thank you, no thank you through the screen. Smile. Shut the door.

Help! The missionaries are on my couch!

However, they wrangled an invitation, the missionaries have come to keep their appointment for the first lesson. Welcome them in and offer them cookies and milk. They are wholesome youth and are trained to be really nice guys. But the polished and confident missionaries do not want to be your friends. They want you to be their convert. They are gods in embryo, members of the Elect, and they are there to turn your spiritual world upside down. As I have explained, they will try to control the discussion and they know how to take charge.

How do I avoid the parent-child trap?

Remember. The missionaries know how to turn their visit into an encounter between a child (you) and two parents (them). If you made an appointment and really want a discussion, you have time to rehearse tactics. I think you will have to understand this section of my book thoroughly. It will involve some rehearsal and you will have to set up your home for the encounter. It is important not to be aggressive. Practice speaking in a measured, respectful manner. The missionaries might want your soul, but they are polite about it. Give them a good example and be civil as well.

The first visit

In preparation for your appointment, do not go into the lion's den alone. *This is your first encounter, but they have done it many times before.* They have the psychological advantage. They have worked hard to prepare themselves spiritually for what they are doing. Every day, they fast, pray, study, practice their testimonies and consider how to make you their convert. So invite a friend who is a strong, well-informed Catholic to take the lessons with you. Look for a friend who is an extravert, someone who can think on his feet and is not afraid to speak out. If one of those friends is a former Mormon, be sure and let the missionaries know. Before the missionaries arrive, say a prayer together. After they leave, discuss what happened and say a prayer again.

Have signs and symbols around that show that yours is a Catholic home. Have a cross in a prominent place, along with a picture of Jesus and a picture of Mary. When one of the missionaries goes to your bathroom, he should be face to face with some kind of Catholic picture or symbol. Just for the heck of it, buy or borrow a copy of *No Man Knows My History*, by Fawn Brodie. I will suggest this as a way to get to know Joseph Smith. It is a good read. Have it on prominent display on your coffee table where the missionaries can see it. This famous biography of Joseph Smith will show the missionaries that they are going to have to offer you more than the usual small pamphlet about their prophet, because you already know a lot about Smith's controversial life.

Start with a few questions and maintain your status as an adult

Begin by giving the missionaries what they might really need: a reality check. During the get-acquainted time preceding the lessons, hand over another cookie and ask the missionaries how old they are. Ask them where they got their education. You will learn that they are as young as eighteen or nineteen, with nothing but high school or maybe two years of college under their belt. Point to their "elder" tag. Ask them again how old they are. If they are under the age of twenty-one, point out with smile that they are not old enough to buy a cigar.

Let me repeat myself yet one more time about the men called elders in the Bible. They were forty years old or older, in a country where the average lifespan was thirty-five. They had very few teeth, grey hair, and matching long grey beards. They were the revered heads of large families with many sons and daughters and grandchildren, over whom they exercised the life or death authority of a patriarch. They had experience debating other elders in front of the city gate. This must have been pretty lively sometimes, because one psalm talks about the elder's need for sturdy sons like polished arrows by their side. Explain this to the missionaries. Ask them what they have done to earn the title "elder." Any authority role within their church? Any special wisdom about life learned from the school of hard knocks? Any major responsibilities in their community? For how long? Any grey hairs? Do they have all their teeth? (Smile if you ask that). But be humble about this if you are not very well grounded in your own faith.

How missionaries get the upper hand from the get-go

Remember what I said somewhere above. When the missionaries are ready, the one leading the discussion will say, "let us pray." Even as he is speaking, he and his companion will be going down to their knees. This will force you and anyone with you to kneel, as well. There you are, awkward, clumsy, and manipulated. The missionary will nod and, with a smile, ask you to lead the prayer. Alert! Alert! Here, at the very beginning, the missionaries are trying to turn you into a child while they become the controlling adults.

Before you even start to kneel down, think about who you are and what you are doing. Do you lead your family in prayer on a regular basis? Do the words of prayer come easily to your lips? When you start to pray, faith is your support. So what do you mean by faith? You are a Catholic steeped in the ancient good news about Christ which has come down from the apostles. The Triune God is the God you have known all your life. He is the God of the infinite Cosmos who lives at the same time within your deepest heart. You have met Jesus Christ in prayer and in the Mass, especially when you receive Communion. You have spoken out to God in times of difficulty.

Remind yourself again that the missionaries are asking you to pray to a god you never heard of before, a god who was an ordinary human being in some previous life, somebody with "body, parts, and passions" still bound by the laws of space and time. If you want to meet Heavenly Father face to face, you will have to travel to his mansion near the star Kolob, which you will not find on any astronomical chart. As you make that long journey, you will see that the Mormon god does not rule the Cosmos. He inhabits a mere fragment somewhere among those two hundred billion galaxies and their trillions of stars. His only subjects are the women who have chosen to be his eternal wives, and their spirit-children, who call him Heavenly Father. There are limits to his kingdom. Travel very far, forward or backward, left or right, and you will be trespassing on the turf of another god.

Preparation before "let us pray"

To prepare for this first formal moment with the missionaries, you need to practice. "Let us pray," the missionary says, as he and his companion go down to their knees. It seems so simple, but if you and your family blindly follow the missionaries to your knees, you will be surrendering to their authority. Bad plan. And so you don't go to your knees. Instead, you sit down or stay seated. Take a sip of your 7up. Smile a friendly smile and tell them you have some questions to ask before you are ready to kneel down and pray with them. If you are an introvert who has to take time to think things out and then say what is safe, let the extravert you have invited do the talking.

Remember what I have already carefully explained: the missionaries are not praying to your God, but their god. Tell them something like, "*I want to join in your prayer, but I have some questions. Is it true that Mormons pray to a god who is an exalted male human being who is literally your father in a previous life? Does he actually have wives and billions of children, including Satan? Do you believe that you will become a god?* Now they are the ones who feel awkward, especially if they are still on their knees. Don't let them try to avoid the question by saying they will talk about it later. Demand a direct answer.

The Mormon way of prayer

Let me explain Mormon prayer. When they pray, Mormons always kneel and fold their arms across their chests. They pray only to that human being-become-god they call Heavenly Father. They will finish their prayer by saying something like, "in the name of Jesus Christ, our Lord." But note, they will never pray to Jesus. They do not pray to Jesus because they see him as a lesser god. They do not pray to the holy spirit, because the holy spirit is not a person, but a mysterious power that pervades the universe, like the Force in Star Trek or an algorithm guiding a computer. Instead of Holy Spirit, Mormons use the old fashion term "Holy Ghost." But they do not pray to the Holy Ghost, an even lesser god.

And so, after the missionaries have admitted the real nature of their god, make your response in a practiced, reasonable voice. Say something like this: "*I'm sorry, but I will not join in your prayer to a god who is only an exalted human being. As Catholics, we believe there is one God, who is a Trinity of persons holding the whole universe in his hand. My family and I will pray to the God of the Catholic Church. He is the God who lives in our hearts.*" Start and end with a Sign of the Cross. Say a prayer you have already written and rehearsed. It could be in three parts, addressed to the Father, Jesus, and the Holy Ghost. *Be sure say Holy Ghost.*

> *Father, I thank you for creating heaven and earth and for making us your sons and daughters. Jesus, I thank you for dying for us and for your presence in our hearts. I pray that you will continue to hold our family in your hand. Holy Ghost, I ask you for wisdom as we begin this discussion. Give us your light and love as the discussion continues.*

When your prayer is done, the missionary lesson plan tells them to praise you for your effort, no matter how clumsy. This is one more way to give you a star and turn you into the child in a parent/child relationship. But because you knew it was coming and you had time to write, prepare and practice, your prayer will be confident and impressive. You won't be some person who stammered with stage fright in front of his wife and kids and barely managed a few words. The missionaries will not be able to demean and manipulate you by telling you what a good job you just did and put that sticker on your forehead.

I would suggest that you pray to the Father, Jesus, and the Holy Ghost *every* time they ask you to pray. Always start and end with a Sign of the cross. Be sure to thank the Holy Ghost for his presence in your heart. I suggest this because the missionaries will be stunned to hear you speak to the Holy Ghost in this way. They would never name him in in their prayers. They believe that he is a companion only to faithful Mormons, but he does not live in their hearts because he is a material being limited by space and time. Will they able to congratulate you for saying a prayer in a way they can't believe in?

Avoid a car wreck with the Bible

A failure in this area will leave you deflated and the missionaries offering each other a high five. The missionaries will try to get yet another step above you by asking you if you have a Bible, and will ask you to look up a certain verse. Well, do you have a Bible? In sight? In a place of honor? And will you be able to briskly turn, say, to Mark 12/6? Make sure you have your Bible in a special place of honor, and be sure you know how to find your place when the missionaries mention chapter and verse. If you just tried to turn to Mark 12, you know that each book of the Bible is divided into chapters and verses. In order to get around in your Bible, you have to read it often and know how to find your way from place to place.

The missionaries will show up clutching a King James version of the Bible and a thick book containing the *Book of Mormon*, the *Doctrine and Covenants*, and the *Pearl of Great Price*. Mormons consider *all* of these books sacred scripture and so they are leather bound, with gold pages. But Catholics and all other Christians accept only the Bible as scripture, the Word of God.

As your first lesson proceeds, the missionaries will continue to refer to the Bible. Maybe they might ask you to read a passage aloud, or maybe the missionaries will read a passage. But somewhere along the way, you might experience a salesman's trick called the "bait and switch" maneuver, which once happened to me. Without telling you, the missionary might say, "the Word of God tells us…." And then he reads a passage from a book with gold edges and written in the style of the King James Bible. You assume it is from the Bible and so you think he has made his point.

But be alert! He might be reading from that impressive volume that contains the three books of Mormon scripture. Maybe he has just given you the old switcheroo, and is asking you to submit to the word of Mormon scripture. In my case, it was a passage from the *Doctrine and Covenants.* To defend yourself, you could always ask the missionary to let you find the passages he quotes in your own Bible. If they aren't there, tell him you can only honor words from the Bible. If the passage is from the Bible, mark it, and bring it to your pastor or youth minister for further comments.

The role of questions

If you are reading this book, you are doing some important research on LDS beliefs. Remember, questions help salesmen, and missionaries, control the discussion. Questions will freeze you in place. And so you should be prepared to answer a question with a question. Extraverts will be good at this. Maybe take notes. This takes away control, especially if you ask the missionary to repeat himself so you can get things on paper. The missionaries will doggedly try to bring you back to their lesson plan, but don't be afraid to upset the rhythm once in a while and ask something like "I heard about eternal progression. What does that mean?" Or, "if it is true that god has more than one wife, what is the name of your heavenly mother?" You just changed the subject big time and the flow is broken. Pesky "What about?" questions are ways to break into the chain of thought. Kelley Conway, who was a spokesperson for President Trump, was an expert at this tactic, which left questioning reporters in the dust.

I was always sparing with my questions when I listened to the missionaries because I wanted them to get on with their lesson and I was not surrendering to their authority. I learned to be especially careful if I was in the presence of female missionaries. I pushed one young missionary a bit hard, she broke into tears, and the Catholic woman they were trying to convert looked at me with daggers in her eyes.

But if you have made a pest of yourself, and the missionaries threaten to end the discussion and go home, they are trying to get their authority back. Is that what you want them to do? Once upon a time, accompanied by a couple of Protestant ministers, I was listening to the missionaries. I had to admire their gumption. One of the ministers was giving the lead missionary a tough time. Finally, the young man threatened to bring the discussion to an end. Maybe it was time for us to show the young god-in-embryo to the door and say goodbye. But we really did want to hear what he had to say, and so we toned things down a bit. As a people pleaser, it was easy for me to do. But we still tossed in a question once in a while. The missionary learned he wasn't king of the mountain. It was important to continue our conversation, adult to adult.

A second visit

If they ask for a second visit, you have the right to say no. They will offer you a free *Book of Mormon* and a small pamphlet, and ask you to read them. If you decide to say yes, don't let them force you into any kind of solemn promise that you will read and pray about short passages they have underlined. You are not a kid obeying his teacher. Maybe you will, and maybe you won't. If you do the homework, take the short pamphlet and the *Book of Mormon* with its underlined verses to your priest or your youth minister and ask him to help you develop a list of questions about what you read. In a later chapter, you might find some what about questions you can raise about the *Book of Mormon*.

When they return for the second lesson, the missionaries will ask how you felt about the first lesson. Remember, the first lesson includes Jesus, his love for us, and his death on the cross. As Catholics, you are naturally going to have good feelings when they teach this. Tell them that you were touched, but remember that your Jesus is not the Mormon Jesus. This is not a discussion between Christians.

Then he will ask you if you read and prayed over the underlined passages in the book he gave you. If you didn't do the homework and they tell you they are disappointed, don't apologize. If they tell you God is disappointed, remember they are talking about *their* god, who is not your

God. You have escaped their control. All this will turn your time together into a discussion between equals.

The second lesson will begin to ease you into the Mormon world. Remind yourself again and again that these missionaries have nothing to do with Christianity. Ask questions. Ask for answers. Maybe even take notes.

Attention, teenagers and young adults

You walk into the home of an admired LDS friend or the home of an LDS boyfriend or girlfriend. When you enter the living room, the missionaries are sitting there, well-dressed as usual and loaded for bear. If you are taken by surprise, you are being set up and it is time to head out the door. But maybe you are too embarrassed to do something like that. Understand that the missionaries are hoping you will be too flustered to resist whatever plans they have for you. Alert! You are being manipulated.

But perhaps you already agreed to listen to the missionaries, not really imagining what you were getting into. The missionaries are not there for the fun of it. It's time for a reality check. You might be on the Dean's list or a 200 pound right tackle, but when you take your place on the couch next to the person who has won your heart, you are outmatched. Look around and count the odds. You are outnumbered *five to one*. Your boyfriend or girlfriend is there and the parents are there, but not just to serve cookies and milk.

This is serious business for those parents. They fear you because you might get married to their son, and if you do, you will threaten his eternal salvation. If he marries you, a non-Mormon, he will lose celestial glory and the chance to be a god. Mormon teaching says he will be separated from her family forever. He will be damned. Your continuing relationship with their son might depend on whether or not you agree to become a Mormon. Your boyfriend stares at you with hope and expectation and you feel the pressure.

And then, of course, there are the missionaries, manly, polished, confident. This meeting will be a first experience for you, but they have done it many times before. They have practiced what they are going to say and how they are going to say it. The psychological and spiritual mismatch could not be worse. Pamphlets written for the missionaries boast that *someone lured into this situation will almost certainly become a Mormon.*

If your friend or the missionaries encourage you to keep all this secret from your parents, this is manipulation on steroids. They are trying to increase the odds in their favor. They are trying to separate you from your family. *This is one of the strategies used by the cults*, who try to keep a person isolated from influential figures in his or her life, and then put on the pressure. Your freedom has been reduced to a minimum.

The same will be true if you go with your friend to the LDS seminary next to your high school or to the LDS Institute at some university. There, you will quickly be drawn into another religious world, away from your family and non-LDS friends. Unless you give in, you will not fit in, and it is natural as rain to try to fit in.

Remember, the missionaries will push you for baptism in as little as three weeks. Since this will be one of the most important decisions of your life, wisdom demands that you take as much thought about a new religion as you would about a new car or a new cell phone. You have the right to say no under pressure, no matter how much it disappoints your girlfriend or boyfriend. Could you? Can you?

If you are a parent

If you are a parent and your son or daughter is listening to the missionaries, keep calm. Don't bad mouth the Mormons. Tell your kid you are proud to see him asking the questions an adult would want to ask, and you are glad to see his curiosity about religion. Share some of your own religious struggles when you were young. Ask him to consider how much he really knows about his own faith, but don't turn this into an accusation. Maybe tell him that such discussions helped you discover how much you needed to really know about your Catholic faith. Cautiously tell him how young the missionaries really are. Ask him what Christians believe about God, and explain that Mormons are not Christians because they believe in a god who is only a human being. The missionaries believe they will become gods one day. Tell him he is going to hear testimony from the Mormons. Read my next chapter on testimony and explain what a testimony is. Share moments when you have felt a testimony about your own faith. Ask him how he feels when he receives Communion. If he has had some recent experience with a high school religious group, ask him how he felt and explain that he was experiencing a testimony. Encourage him to bring his questions to you, or his priest, or the youth minister in his parish. Give him this book to read, and point out this chapter.

If your son or daughter is under the influence of a Mormon girlfriend or boyfriend, this is a delicate time and they might refuse to listen. That is when you discover how God feels when we stubbornly take our lives in our own hands. He does not blast us with lightning bolts. Just pray, give good example, and never stop loving. I have had to do this as I watched a nephew and several nieces go off on their own, away from the Church. Did it hurt? Yes. But we don't disown people we love.

Turning the visit with the missionaries into a time of spiritual growth

The missionaries have turned out to be more than you bargained for. You invited the them in, you argued with them, and they have you on the ropes. As I pointed out, an experienced missionary gets pretty good at what he does, and at least one of the missionaries in your house will be quite experienced. This series of meetings could be a step over a spiritual cliff. But it *could also be a step forward in your spiritual life*. If you do some of the things I now suggest.

Remember, the missionaries are very young and they have no spiritual authority beyond a claim to something called the Melchizedec Priesthood. Unlike your pastor, who spent years in study, a missionaries have almost no preparation. Despite their sober clothing and the tag that says "elder," or "sister," the missionaries are youths with no advanced religious education or spiritual formation. They spent only three weeks in training. They are operating out of a book. If you are near their age and have been living your own Catholic life, they have no spiritual advantage over you. If you are a mom or dad with a job and three kids, you learned more about the ups and downs and struggles of life in one year than the two of them together..

Deal with your doubts The missionaries might force you to realize that your knowledge and experience of your faith is more sketchy than you imagined. They can name the sins of the Church, and know how to ask you questions you might not be able to answer. Now you have that shaky feeling we call a doubt. If you are like me, you have probably wondered why you are a Catholic. Maybe, also like me, you even wondered if there really is a God.

This is not a catastrophe. A doubt can be a blessing because it can bring you to a growth point. If you are sincerely looking for answers, respond to the challenge. You can do this by talking to your priest, to an RCIA director, or to a youth minister. It is a time to go through your *Catechism of the Catholic Church,* read a good book on the Catholic faith, or follow an Internet site that explains the faith, such as *Catholic Answers.* Get interested in the study-field called apologetics, which gives you good answers as you defend your faith. Keep a diary of your thoughts and questions.

Live a deeper faith life. The missionaries are busy fasting and praying, and they are in close contact with higher missionary authorities. They don't make much headway with people who are active members of the parish community, or a familiar part of their youth group and not ashamed to turn to their priest or youth minister with serious questions. Learn how to pray. Go to Mass. Receive the sacraments. Learn about the Bible. Pray to the Holy Spirit. While the missionaries are trying to get you to focus on your feelings, remember you have to use your mind as well as your heart.

Dig into your resources I have tried to make this book a good source for you to use. Another excellent source is the Internet. I found a good site called *exmormon.org*, in which former LDS members discuss in a respectful manner the difficulties they have had with their own faith. As I just said, a good Catholic source is "Catholic Answers" on EWTN and the Internet.

To counter their testimony, find your own testimony during moments in your Catholic life. Catholics are not trained to constantly keep track of their feelings about their faith experiences the way Mormons are. Each first Sunday of the month is "Fast Sunday," and Mormons are invited to stand up and bear their testimony about any number of things. Speakers in church give their testimony again and again.

If you are a Catholic, you have almost certainly experienced what Mormons call a testimony, but you were not paying attention. I watch Catholics receive Communion and then kneel, lost in prayer. They are experiencing the deep feelings of joy and peace. In Mormon terms, it is a testimony. They have the same experience when they go to Confession. I sometimes wish I could ask couples how they felt when they fell in love. Did God suddenly come close? How did they feel with the birth of their first child? Was it a wonderful discovery of the presence and blessing of God? How did they feel when they brought their baby to church for baptism? Or ask what they feel during their time in the Adoration Chapel. Or, how did they feel when they were struggling and God helped them with an answer to their prayers? If you are a parent, give these kind of testimonies to your own children.

What to do when the missionaries will not go away

I received an SOS from a young woman who was attending Utah University. A couple of "sisters" had dropped into her dorm and she reluctantly agreed to listen. After two lessons, she was not convinced, but she did admit that she felt good about some of the things the missionaries said about Jesus as our redeemer. Based on that, they began to tell her she had received a sign from the holy spirit and began to push her hard to prepare for baptism. She did not want to say yes, but was frustrated and frightened because, when she said no, the sisters would not take no for an answer, and followed her all over the university.

We talked for a while and I asked her if she kept saying no in different ways, without much conviction. She agreed she did. I told her that, like me, she was a people pleaser. She would have to practice saying no, maybe with the help of an understanding friend. The next time the "sisters" came around, she would have to be a broken record, saying no in the same polite but forceful way, over and over. I promised to keep her in my prayers. A few weeks later, I got a card from her telling me the missionaries finally gave up and went away.

7

Testimony, A revelation from God himself

Mormons build their lives around the religious story I explained in our second chapter. The experience of testimony is the anchor that keeps Mormons solid in their belief. If the missionaries can help a Catholic experience a testimony, he will often become a Mormon. And so we need to explain to Mormons, and to ourselves, that Catholics have their own testimony about the truth of their faith.

Mormonism: A faith grounded on testimony

Some people consider a religious testimony an emotional account of a personal religious experience. But for Mormons, it is much more profound than that. A testimony is *a personal revelation from the Holy Ghost*, offering a Latter-day Saint unshakeable proof that what he believes is true. I am not talking about the Holy Spirit (or Holy Ghost) of Catholics. I am talking about the Holy Ghost of the Mormons, an exalted human being without a material body who inhabits the lowest drawer in the Mormon Godhead. Receiving a testimony from the Holy Ghost is a vital and distinctive part of LDS life.

I saw the impact of testimony on Mormon young people when I was giving an account of my Catholic faith to the members of a class at the LDS Institute at Idaho State University. Also present was a young couple from a local

Evangelical church. I gave what I imagined to be a thoughtful presentation of Catholic history, authority, doctrine, and worship. As I talked, a couple of kids in the back of the room rolled their eyes and went to sleep.

Then it was that young couple's turn. They gave an account of their religious journey. They shared some of the times when they felt touched by God and called to religious growth. From the very beginning, the LDS students gave them their rapt attention. I watched their eyes grow wide with discovery and then even wider with a kind of alarm. The Evangelical couple had managed to tune into the Mormon wave length. They were giving testimony. And this was a frightening shock to those young Mormons, because they thought they were the only ones who ever experienced such a thing.

Mormons pin their faith on testimony. As one Mormon writer put it, "Response to personal revelation (testimony) is seen as the basis for true faith in Christ, and *the strength of the church consists of that faithful response by members to their own personal revelation.*"[16](My emphasis) If a person loses his faith in the Mormon Church, it is said that he has "lost his testimony." The *Encyclopedia of Mormonism* describes testimony as "the core of LDS religious experience." Youthful Mormons are instructed to pray for a testimony to prove the truth of Mormon teaching, and their parents pray that the Lord will "amplify" their testimony. Boasting about the power of testimony, the *Encyclopedia of Mormonism* tells us "It reaches beyond second hand assent, notional conviction, or strong belief. *It is knowledge buttressed by divine personal confirmation by the Holy Ghost.*"[17] (My emphasis)

---

[16] . *Encyclopedia of Mormonism*, Vol 3, under "Revelation."
[17] Op. Cit. Vol 4, under "Testimony."

Once a month, LDS members gather in church and listen while people stand and share their testimony about some aspect of their religious lives. However repetitive or clumsy, testimonies have a powerful effect on the other members of the congregation. The Mormon faithful are reminded once again that they are a people whose beliefs are buttressed, not by eloquent argument or some kind of "proof," but by rock-solid personal revelations from the Holy Ghost himself.

What does a testimony look like?

A better question would be, what does a testimony feel like? In April, 1829, Joseph Smith gave this revelation:

> *Behold, I (God) say unto you, that you must study it out in your mind; then you must ask me if it be right, and if it is right, I will cause that your bosom shall burn within you; therefore, you shall feel that it is right. But if it be not right you shall have no such feelings, but you shall have a stupor of thought that shall cause you to forget the thing which is wrong...* [18]

Even though this revelation urges the seeker to "study it out in your mind" first, Mormons put most of their emphasis on testimony as a "feeling." It is a feeling of calm certainty...a burning in the heart...a peaceful sense of conviction...a clear awareness of truth. And so, they pray for a testimony about the president of their church, about Joseph Smith the Prophet, about Jesus as savior. But they also give a testimony about more mundane things that happen in their ordinary lives.

---

[18] Doctrine and Covenants, Section 9, 8-9

A Mormon grounded in his testimony is invulnerable to non-Mormon attacks, even if those attacks are based on verifiable historical facts. *Joseph Smith lived a questionable moral life?* A Latter-day Saint blessed with a personal revelation about Smith's status as prophet of the Last Dispensation will dismiss the evidence. *No identifiable remnants of the wondrous Nephite cities described in the Book of Mormon have ever been found?* A Latter-day Saint with a burning in his heart has evidence superior even to the discovery of actual ruins in the jungles of Central America. *Joseph Smith and his closest followers practiced polygamy and lied about it under oath?* A Latter-day Saint with peaceful feelings in his heart knows that the name of Joseph Smith can still be mentioned in the same breath with the name of Jesus Christ.

An ordinary part of life

LDS people believe that, beginning with their Prophet and the Twelve, their leaders can claim the revelations they need in order for them to fulfill their tasks. On the local level, people called to lead the Priesthood Quorums, Relief Society, or other ward organizations can pray for a guiding revelation or testimony. In the family, parents, and especially the father believe that they will receive testimony from the Holy Ghost when it is needed. When wisdom comes in the middle of a crisis or struggle, it is a testimony. A testimony will also come when a person needs insight or has to make a choice. Or, when a person feels at peace in the midst of life, that is also a revelation from the Holy Ghost.

In appreciation

Some people believe that Mormons live in Satan's darkness, but they are mistaken. Your average Mormon tries hard to live a virtuous life, close to the heart of the Christ they know. I have the wonderful example of my own LDS family members. As one young Mormon told me, "I have tried all my life to be closer and closer to my Savior." Pope John Paul asked us to look with love at other religions, trying to discern how God works among people of different faiths. From a Catholic perspective, I know that their good lives can only be the work of the Holy Spirit.

A Catholic perspective

My experience of testimony over a lifetime

I was seven years old. I heard the radio announce that the US had just dropped an atom bomb on Nagasaki, Japan. 100,000 civilians were killed in a single blast. With extraordinary moral insight, my father looked past the faces of our enemy and grieved loudly over the death of so many men, women, and children. I was suddenly weighed down by the dread of cosmic evil. I could not sleep. In the morning, I got up before dawn. My heart still shaking, I went outside and watched the sky slowly turn blue. We lived in a slum with shacks all around us. When the sun rose, I felt its growing warmth and watch gold light touch those shabby roofs. As I stood in the sun-drenched silence, my spirit lifted. Even though I couldn't put it into words, I believed in God's goodness in a world where people could do such evil. It was a defining moment in my life.

I was sixteen years-old when I asked a priest how to pray. He taught me the Benedictine way of prayer, called Lectio Divina. *I said a prayer to the Holy Spirit and began to read a psalm. A passage struck me. The monk had told me to stop when this happened, because the Holy Spirit was speaking. I pondered the passage, letting it guide and question me. Suddenly I was caught up in joy and ecstasy. The presence of God surrounded me. My heart was on fire. For a long time, I sat still in the presence of God. I continue to pray* Lectio *and have this experience to this very day.*

I was thirty-two and had just made an eight day Ignatian retreat, which is a long experience of God's love and presence, with a spiritual director who helped me hear and taste what God was saying. Along the drive home, I was listening to a tape by a spiritual master. He was talking about the love of God the Father. Suddenly, I experienced what some call the Baptism of the Holy Spirit. God's love and joy burst in me and around me. I had to pull my car to the side of the road, or I was going to get in a wreck.

This often happens when I have stopped in front of a traffic light and I have a few seconds on my hands. I breathe in, saying the name "Jesus." I breathe out slowly and say the name again. Jesus…Jesus…Jesus. A sense of Jesus' loving presence surrounds me. Peace fills my heart.

This experience happens when I am celebrating Mass and the Body of Christ is in my hands. "Behold the Lamb of God," I say. The space between Jesus and my heart is thinner than my two fingers pressed together. When I receive Communion, Jesus is an abiding, uplifting presence. Even as I describe those moments, Jesus and his love come close again.

Those are examples of how the experience of what Mormons call testimony fills my ordinary life. What follows is a testimony corresponding to the kind of testimony the missionaries give during their lessons. I use words like comfort, joy, and heart-felt witness as I express my belief in deep Catholic truths. As I write this, I feel the Holy Spirit coming very close.

As a Catholic I feel the comforting presence of Jesus in my heart. God is my father, and the Holy Ghost is the companion on my journey. I realize with joy that I live within the life of the Trinity, one God in three persons. I also know by the clear witness of the Holy Ghost that the true Church subsists in the Catholic Church, and that God will support and sustain that Church until the end of time. This is my peaceful, heart-felt witness, and I give thanks to God in the name of Jesus Christ.

I have given all these examples because I want LDS people to understand that devout Catholics also have a testimony over the course of their religious lives. We will discuss the implications of this in this chapter.

Finding the Spirit in your life

A Catholic who is trying to live his faith without asking the Holy Spirit for light and wisdom is living a bone-dry religious life. They settle into a narrow box fashioned out of laws, doctrinal statements, and the dutiful but unenthusiastic fulfillment of spiritual obligations. As loyal members of the Church, they go to Mass, go to confession, and say the rosary. But they might not have a deep sense a loving, healing God. They might not have the confidence that comes to those who believe that life is a gift from God. When they meet a problem or personal crisis, they might not ask the Spirit to give them the mind and heart of Christ. As is happening at this frightening moment in history, they might follow the heart and mind of some yammering political figure more than the heart and mind of Jesus Christ. As I give them the sacred Body of Christ in Communion, I can see that their thoughts are often far away, already busy with the details of life after Eucharist.

But when we choose to look with the eyes of faith, the Holy Spirit will appear all over our spiritual landscape. It is by the power of the Holy Spirit that we learn in the depths of our hearts to call God our Father. It is only through the witness of the Holy Spirit that we are able to know that Jesus is the Christ, the Son of God, our Savior. It is the Holy Spirit who helps us taste the Word of God in Scripture. Unless the Holy Spirit gives witness, we do not recognize the Body and Blood of Jesus in the Host and in the Cup. With the witness of the Spirit, we walk back to our places after receiving Communion, hearts afire. By the wisdom of the Spirit, we meet Christ present in His Church.

The Holy Spirit is the living creative Love of God at work in the world and at work in our lives, calling us to a deeper and deeper relationship with God and with each other. St. Paul tells us, "But the fruit of the Spirit is love, joy, peace, patience, kindness, goodness, faithfulness, gentleness, and self-control." (Gal 5:22) And so, wherever we savor these fruits in our own lives, we are tasting the abundance of the Holy Spirit. Whenever we see these fruits in the lives of other people, we are walking on holy ground.

Can we trust our spiritual feelings?

Wait a minute! you say. There is too much emotion here. Truth is based on facts, not good feelings. Feelings are not trustworthy. But the heart knows in ways that the head does not, and it can grasp spiritual realities that escape rational explanation. Our life with God is an affair of both the head and the heart, and it is usually the heart that first feels his loving touch. "The Lord is my strength and my shield," prays the Psalmist, "my heart trusts in him, and I am helped. My heart leaps for joy." These feelings from the Spirit can alert us to the presence of God, and they can validate the truth of our religious beliefs.

The need for balance and caution: the discernment of spirits

But we have to be careful. As St. Paul warns us, not every spirit is from God. The "wind" or "breath" of good feeling could be a destructive force, instead. We need the discernment of spirits because feelings encountered even in the midst of prayer can be mistaken. The history of religion shows us that there is a blurry line between authentic religious enthusiasm and delusion. Not all feelings about the world of faith and religion come from the Holy Spirit. Our inner world echoes with unhealed wounds and painful memories from the past, and they can stir up distorted feelings about the voice of God and the meaning of our religious journey.

Some advice about discernment from St. Ignatius of Loyola

The Catholic tradition says we have to practice "discernment of spirits" to determine if our good feelings come from God, self-delusion, or the Evil One. This discernment begins when we put a spotlight on our lives and decide whether we are living by the spirit of the world, or by the spirit of Christ. Life is a battleground where God and Satan both try to win our minds and hearts. God wants us to live as his sons and daughters and as brothers and sisters of Jesus his Son. Satan wants to make us enemies, not only of God, but even of each other. A glimpse of light and a feeling of peace might not be the best answer to our questions. So St. Ignatius offers us some tools for discernment.

--- We have to be aware of what the world wants. The world wants pleasure. The world wants wealth. The world wants power and control. The world despises the poor. The world dreads sacrifice. Pride, covetousness, lust, anger, gluttony, greed, envy, and sloth help define the attitude of the world.

— We have to make the conventional effort to discover the truth. This means a clear understanding of our faith and the effort to sort out its deepest meaning.

— This means that a person truly desires to know what the Lord wants. He truly hopes to accomplish God's will. His deepest wish is to be a faithful child of God.

--- We have to face our inner wounds. We have to be aware of anger, fear, the lack of forgiveness for others, the refusal to grow intellectually, morally, or emotionally.

— Implied in this desire is the decision to be taught by, and led by, the Lord. So often in my own life, I am really looking for what I want, and hope that God can squeeze it into his agenda. So often, I fail to let God truly be the boss.

— In order to accomplish the first two goals, I must have a loving personal relationship with God. This is the great task of the spiritual life, a task that can only be accomplished through prayer, discovery of the living God in Scripture and worship, and in loving service of neighbor.

— If we seek to know God's will, we must be *humble* because the spiritual walk is always down a shadowy path and our judgment is always clouded to some extent by our sinfulness. The great saints tell us that we need to have a healthy self-doubt. We have to act with ordinary prudence. We have to seek spiritual guides and to respect the teaching voice of the Magisterium of the Church. If we seek to know God's will, we must be *honest*, recognizing our weakness, sinfulness, and tendency toward self-deception. We also have to be *courageous* because not everyone we meet is an angel of light. Paradoxically, sometimes we have to be willing to step out in trust, walking by the certitude of faith and not by reason.

Catholic growth points

Culture is like a pair of green sunglasses with smears and spots. We get used to looking through them, and we begin to think we are seeing reality as it actually is. Our modern era teaches us to evaluate everything in terms of money. It teaches us to believe that our five senses and science are our only valid contact with the world. Anything that cannot be explored by our senses or studied in a laboratory is an illusion. This view also insists that feelings have little value and religious feelings are private experiences which possess no larger meaning. Some people collect postage stamps they say, and some people are religious. But in the real world, money, pleasure, logic and objective science are all that count.

Some Catholics cannot understand that the journey to a vital faith life usually begins in our hearts. They shut those feelings off. But God does touch us through our feelings, as we see with saints like St. Francis and St. Theresa the Little Flower. Other saints testify that religious doctrines are only a door to the deeper world of a love-affair with God. As Catholics, we should pay attention to the feelings that move through the experience of our faith. So, when you experience God in your world, do a gut check and take your feelings seriously. When you go to Communion, let your spirit rejoice in the presence of your Redeemer. When you return to your seat, let the Spirit of Christ rest peacefully in your heart. Pay attention to the beauty of your faith. Know the story of the saints. Let the good people in your life lead you to a deep sense that the Lord is present. Religious art, like a cross or a picture of Mary, is more deeply understood by the heart than by the mind. If you have no crosses or spiritual images in your house, your children are suffering spiritual malnutrition, and so are you. Buy the thoughtful books that help you meditate on, and rejoice in, your faith.

8

Can we believe Joseph Smith?

Joseph Smith insisted he had seen Heavenly Father and Jesus. He claimed to be a prophet, seer, and revelator. He insisted that the revelations he published in the Doctrine and Covenants had come word by word from the mouth of Jesus himself. And so, for better or for worse, the moral integrity of Joseph Smith is more important than any of his doctrines.

Our survival kit asks serious questions about Smith's integrity and moral character

If you listen to the missionaries, they will give you very little information about their prophet. You will have a three page pamphlet and their own well-practiced testimony. They will not help you ponder Smith's controversial life. Instead, they ask you to read your pamphlet and then ask God to tell you that Joseph Smith is a true prophet. The way this question is phrased is pure manipulation. They should have said, Ask God to show you *whether or not* Joseph Smith is a true prophet. The missionaries will challenge you to pray in their manipulative format, trusting that warm feelings will arrive in your heart that will provide all the proof needed.

And so, as I proceed with this book, do I simply offer a discussion of the differences between LDS and Catholic beliefs? Or do I go deeper, touching the questions raised, not by the raving of anti-Mormons whose writings I ignore, but by faithful LDS historians and even by Joseph Smith himself?

Once upon a time, I decided to write a long chapter about Smith's controversial life. I wanted to describe his career as a treasure digger, how he started a fraudulent bank, and how he began the secret practice of polygamy. I wrote long and hard, but I became more and more uncomfortable with my effort. I am not a good muck-raker.

I finally decided to ask my readers to go to a library or a bookstore and do some serious reading for themselves. I recommend two biographies by respected historians, and an historical novel that has been written from a non-judgmental perspective. But as you read, I do ask you to keep an eye on Smith's *moral* character and decide for yourself. Consider this passage from the *Doctrine and Covenants when you finish.*

> *Joseph Smith, the Prophet and Seer of the Lord, has done more, save Jesus only, for the salvation of men in this world, than any other man that ever lived in it. (* D & C 135:3)

When you have finished your reading, would you agree? Here are my three books.

No Man Knows My History, by Fawn Brodie. Fawn Brodie was an historian who authored a prize-winning biography about Abraham Lincoln. As a Mormon with strong family connections to the Mormon elite, she decided it was time to write a biography about Joseph Smith. Not long before his death, Smith gave a speech teaching that God was a human being. At the end of the speech he shouted, "No man knows my history!" Brodie decided to take him up on the challenge. Church authorities gave her access to well-guarded church records. Maybe they were expecting another hagiography so prevalent in Mormon bookstores.

As an accomplished historian, she was bound to the ethics of her craft. And so she used the critical standards serious historians use to tell the story of the Mormon prophet. The result is considered a masterpiece. Stunned by the story she was forced to tell, she left the Mormon Church before the book was finished. Mormons were dismayed when the book was published. One of my distant relatives wrote a clumsy rebuttal called *No, Ma'am, That's Not History*. To this day, *No Man Knows My History* remains the gold standard for anyone who wants to write a credible biography about the prophet. Anybody who makes this attempt will have to match her scholarly and un-blinking effort.

Richard Bushman is such a man. In his **Joseph Smith, Rough Stone Rolling**, this faithful Mormon and famous historian produced a well-written book which meets the demands of good scholarship. Like Brodie, he was forced to face the good, the bad, and the ugly of Joseph Smith. It is interesting to compare the way Brodie and Bushman explain some of the more unsettling events in Smith's life, including the Kirtland Safety Anti-bank and his marriage to at least thirty-three girls and women.

And finally, those who find detailed biographies too boring might read a two volume historical novel called **Joseph Smith, the Prophet King**, by yours truly, who writes under the clever pen-name Robert Taylor. After a lot of research, I took several years to write a book that is respectful, entertaining and challenging. Despite what some Mormons might say about my effort, I bent over backwards to avoid sarcasm and judgment. I simply tried to tell one of the more interesting tales in all American history.

Now that you have finished

Maybe you chose Fawn Brodie and found her book to be a good read. Or maybe, oh joy, you read my spectacular novel. Now let us go back to that passage from the *Doctrine and Covenants*::

> *Joseph Smith, the Prophet and Seer of the Lord, has done more, save Jesus only, for the salvation of men in this world, than any other man that ever lived in it.* (D & C 135:3)

Can you agree? Can you imagine Jesus living the way Smith lived? Can you imagine your father doing some of the things did? If he displayed such behavior, what would you think?

The survival kit has asked you to ponder Smith's moral character. Now it comes to another question we might consider fair game. What about his honesty?

People who have visions

As we have seen, Joseph Smith claimed to be a new Moses, a modern prophet, a seer and revelator. Latter-day Saints boast today that the presidents of their church continue his legacy. Catholics do not sneer at such a claim, because the history of Catholicism is filled with men and women who had amazing religious experiences. But because Mormon claims depend on the integrity of Joseph Smith, we have the right to ask him to show his credentials.

A precautionary note: The full story of the Catholic Church is not just the story of saints and the celebration of its profound moments with God. If a Catholic tries to tell the story of his Church without acknowledging its dark side, the first person he is deceiving is himself and he does not understand the real meaning of salvation. If I can look with an honest eye at the church I love, it seems fair to use this same measure on Joseph Smith, the man who claimed to have founded the one true church on earth.

Problems about honesty presented by Joseph Smith himself.

First problem: One vision, but which version?

> *It was nevertheless a fact that I had beheld a vision....I felt much like Paul, when he made his defense before King Agrippa, and related the account of the vision he had when he saw a light, and heard a voice; but still there were but few who believed him; some said he was dishonest, others said he was mad, but all this did not destroy the reality of his vision....So it was with me.*[19]
>
> —Joseph Smith

With these words, Joseph Smith testified to the reality of a vision he received when he was only a teenager.

Another precautionary note

The Catholic Church is no stranger to visions. St. Joseph heeded angel messengers in his dreams and St. Paul heard the voice of Christ on his way to Damascus. Throughout Catholic history, saints like Julian of Norwich, Joan of Arc,

---

[19]*Joseph Smith—History* 1:24-25

Margaret Mary Alacoque or Bernadette have heard voices or witnessed visitations from Jesus, Mary, or one of the saints. Some visions have born fruit in Catholic devotions, such as the Rosary, the wearing of a scapular, or the devotion to the Sacred Heart of Jesus. The places where visions have occurred are now places of pilgrimage, such as Lourdes, Fatima, or the shrine of Our Lady of Guadalupe, in Mexico City.

But the Church always approaches such incidents with great caution. Was it a real event, she asks, or some kind of spiritual pathology? After two thousand years, the Church has learned to be very skeptical about such experiences and accepts them as authentic only after a careful and prayerful evaluation. Even when officially accepted–as with the appearance of Mary at Fatima–they are not considered public revelations for the whole Church. As St. Pope John XXIII said, a Catholic is free to accept them or not.

A thoughtful search into Smith's first vision

I had actually seen a light, and in the midst of that light I saw two Personages, and they did in reality speak to me....I have actually seen a vision; I knew it, and I knew that God knew it, and I could not deny it, neither dared I do it.[20]

So Joseph Smith solemnly testified about an account of his famous vision, written in 1838. But a serious investigator quickly discovers that the prophet gave *different* renditions of this astonishing vision. Two previous versions appeared in a book called *The Personal Writings of Joseph Smith*,[21] while

---

[20] Ibid.

[21] *The Personal Writings of Joseph Smith*, compiled and edited by Dean C. Jessee, Deseret Book, Salt Lake City, Utah, 1984. The Deseret Book Company is surely the most important publisher of books written from an LDS perspective.

the 1838 account appears in the *Pearl of Great Price,* a book Mormons consider scripture. Each version was authored in one way or another *by the prophet himself.* And each version is different. In the passage I just quoted, Joseph Smith is swearing that the 1838 account, which Mormons consider scripture, is what really happened.

The first vision, *Take One,* 1832

In 1832, the young prophet revealed for the first time the vision that marked the beginning of his career. None of his family ever mentioned it in their letters or memoirs. Smith penned the account himself, *in his own distinctive handwriting.* It was vintage Joseph Smith: The spelling and grammar were poor, the phrasing clumsy, but the ungainly account contained a dramatic tale of wonders.[22]

Smith testified that, at the age of sixteen, he was caught up in his own religious search. After thoughtful study of the scriptures, he concluded that all churches and all institutions were corrupt. Worse, he was desperately concerned about the state of his immortal soul and the possibility of damnation. As he put it:

> *...for I become convicted of my sins and by searching the scriptures I found that <mankind> did not come unto the Lord but that they had apostatized from the true and living faith and there was no society or*

---

[22] Op. Cit. The book provides photostatic copies of the original, and carefully shows the reader which sections were written in Joseph Smith's own hand-writing and which sections were written and polished by secretaries.

denomination that built upon the gospel of Jesus Christ as recorded in the scriptures....[23]

This was not a new thought. Many people on the American frontier, including Smith's own father, were disillusioned about organized religion. Many worried about damnation. Filled with despair, the youth *"cried unto the Lord for mercy for there was none else to whom I could go."* In the sixteenth. year of his life:

a piller of light...come down from above and rested upon me and I was filled with the spirit of god and the <Lord> opened the heavens upon me and I saw the Lord and he spake unto me saying Joseph <my son> thy sins are forgiven thee. go thy <way> walk in my statutes and keep my commandments behold I am the Lord of glory I was crucifyed for the world that all those who believe on my name may have eternal life....

As we can see in the photostat of the original, Smith's ink-spot blemished handwriting ends in mid-paragraph and someone else takes over. But the story is clear. Like many a young Protestant of h9is day, Smith was agonizing about the sinful condition of his soul and the uncertainty of salvation. The reader should note that only *one* person appeared to the young Joseph. When the visitor said he was "crucifyed" for the world, he was clearly identifying himself as Jesus Christ. Jesus forgave Joseph his sins and promised–without mentioning anything about corrupt churches–to return in judgment.

---

[23] . Ibid. p. 5. The reader will note that in this testimony, Smith has already emphatically decided that all the churches have apostatized from the true faith. His concern is the state of his soul and fear of damnation.

The first vision, *Take Two*: Angelic visitors-1835

Three years later, Smith dictated this rendition to a secretary on November 9, 1835. By that time, his church was prospering and converts were coming from near and far. In this new version of the story, he tells a visitor that he was fourteen at the time. He says he had a basically positive attitude toward the churches but, troubled by their conflicting claims, he longed to know which church to join. Again, this is pure Joseph Smith, full of dramatic agony and a desperate search for the truth:

> determined to "call upon the Lord for the first time" about the name of the one true church. I made a fruitless effort to pray, my toung seemed to be swolen in my mouth, so that I could not utter, I heard a noise behind me like some person walking towards me...I looked around but saw no person or thing...I kneeled again my mouth was opened and my toung liberated, and I called upon the Lord in mighty prayer.[24](Misspellings are part of the original)

The young Smith saw a pillar of light, and again, a "personage" appeared before him. But this time the personage was joined by another, who was "like unto the first." Instead of telling him which church to join, "he said unto me thy sins are forgiven thee, he testifyed (sic) unto me that Jesus Christ is the Son of God."[29] The two personages disappeared without telling him which church to join.

---

[24] Ibid. p. 75 [29] Ibid.

114

The first vision, *Take Two: Supplemental Notes*–1835

Who were these personages? In the 1832 account, a single personage clearly revealed himself as Jesus, but this second version leaves us in doubt about the two mysterious visitors. Smith himself identified them in a notation appearing in his diary only six days after telling the story cited above:

> *A Gentleman...called to make enquiry about the establishment of the church of the latter-day Saints and to be instructed more perfectly in our experience while in my...juvenile years, say from 6 years old up to the time I received the first visitation of Angels which was when I was about 14 years old.*[25] (*My emphasis*)

A visitation of angels. In this brief paragraph, there is no mention of the Jesus who died on the cross, or the spectacular appearance of Jesus or his Father. Somehow, Smith had suffered a staggering loss of memory and had forgotten that he had seen Jesus face to face

The first vision, *Take Three:*
The Father and the Son–1838

Three years later, a highly polished account dictated to a secretary appeared and, among Mormons, it has the status of scripture. It is found in "Joseph Smith–History," included in the *Pearl of Great Price*. In complete contrast with the first telling of his story, Smith, a sincerely religious

---

[25] Ibid. p. 84

fifteen year-old youth,[26] was no longer in agony about the sinful state of his soul or grimly convinced about the corruption of all the churches. Instead, he was a sincere seeker attracted to the Christian churches but utterly confused by their differing claims.

As in the second account, Smith was unable to decide which church to join. This time he heeded the Epistle of St. James and went to a glen in the woods to "ask of God." Again, the drama is pure Joseph Smith. Seized by darkness, unable to speak, he called upon God for deliverance. Again, a pillar of light descended from heaven and fell upon him. Againhe saw two personages, but now they are in human form. One pointed to the other and said, "this is my Beloved Son. Hear him." Clearly, Smith was face to face with the Father and Jesus, who were two separate individuals. He immediately asked which of all the sects was right. He was told to join none of them, for they were all wrong. After repeating the command, the divine figures left, and the youth awoke, dazed and exhausted, in the forest clearing.

We go back to the quote appearing at the beginning of this discussion. Smith swears that the Father and the Son had actually appeared to him when he was fifteen. *"It was nevertheless a fact that I had this vision...I felt much like Paul,"* he said. Did he fail to remember that six years before, it had been a vision of Jesus by himself, that three years before, the visitors had been angels? Would Smith have called some other would-be prophet a liar if he had offered three different versions of what should have been the same story We come to that challenging question asked by Mormons

---

[26] In the version told by the missionaries, Smith was fourteen. But in the account appearing in the *Pearl of Great Price*, Smith says, "I was at this time in my fifteenth year."

when they are telling us about Joseph Smith: Was he a con-man, a mad-man, or a saint?

Mormons respond

Forced to admit the confusion that exists in these three accounts, Mormons point out that there are four different versions of the gospels and two different accounts of the conversion of St. Paul. But the gospels were written by four *different* individuals in four *different* Christian communities across the span of at least two generations, while the story of Paul's conversion was described first by Paul himself, and then, almost forty years later, by St. Luke in the Acts of the Apostles. When different persons tell the same story in separate places over a period of time, we do not expect their versions to match. But Joseph Smith *himself*, over a period of just six years, gave three dramatically different versions of one of the most amazing experiences ever recorded in religious history.

What I have just explained is news to most Mormons. But LDS historians know. They usually try to weave these differing accounts into a single narrative. In *The Mormon Experience*, Arrington and Bitton argue that the first story represents Joseph Smith as a youth with little insight, while the last version represents the mature Joseph who had time to reflect on his experience. They tell us:

> *As a teenager Smith had probably seen the experience primarily as a relief from anxiety about his sins and concerns about the jarring claims of the different sects. By 1838 Smith was head of a church, his prophetic status challenged both from within and*

without. His shift of emphasis...*was natural.*[27] (My emphasis)

Non-LDS historians are not satisfied by this explanation. They point out that the Joseph Smith who wrote the 1832 account of his first vision was not a bumbling teenager, but a very confident twenty-eight year old prophet who had published the Book of Mormon...founded a church...moved with his disciples to Ohio...established "Zion" in Missouri...started a revision of the Bible...and had received and was preparing to publish forty-five revelations which drew church doctrine into a coherent whole and created an organizational structure that would withstand the attacks of an ever more hostile world.

Conclusion

If we take each story literally, we have three different stories. The reader can take his pick. Shall he decide there was one Jesus, or two angels, or the Father and the Son? In the first version, Smith's is agonizing about his sins. His sins are forgiven, and Jesus says he will come again. In the second version, Smith is agonizing about which church to join, but the angel visitors declare that Jesus is the Christ, tell him his sins are forgiven, and say nothing about a church. In the third version, Jesus is called the Beloved Son and all churches are declared false, while nothing is said about forgiveness. Would this be an obstacle for a discerning reader? Could someone fairly conclude that none of the three stories are true? That they are tales told by a man not clever enough to fabricate a single coherent lie?

---

[27] . Leonard J. Arrington and Davis Bitton, The Mormon Experience, Vintage Books, New York, 1980) p. 8.

Or can we see behind each story the effort of a half-educated man trying to describe an experience that is beyond describing? In this case, we could call them a kind of Frontier midrash,[28]imaginative stories springing from Smith's confused memory of alternate reality experiences which included some kind of discussion about sins and churches. If that is the case, we can conclude that the stories are not factual, but we can't exactly call them lies. The reader will have to place this puzzle into the middle of all the other questions and conundrums presented by Joseph Smith.

Next problem: **Joseph Smith's seer stone.**

> *Every man who lived on earth is entitled to a seer stone."* Joseph Smith[29]

Precautionary note

Within Catholic history, we find fragments of the true cross, the shroud of Turin, relics of saints, weeping statues, mysterious paintings of Mary, scapulars, medals, and etc.. Catholics bear witness to the role these objects play in their journey of faith. They know that relics, statues, pictures and medals are only signs pointing to the redemptive and healing presence of Jesus Christ, who sends the Holy Spirit into our hearts. They are not cherished for any special power they magically possess, and some of them are surely fakes. They have value only because they are like doors

---

28 Modern biblical scholars tell us that the Bible contains fictional stories called "midrash," which were often used to teach an inspiring lesson. Read the Book of Tobit.

29*Millenial Star 26* (1864), 118-19. These words were remembered by Brigham Young

which open us to the presence of the Sacred, and to an encounter with the God who loves and saves us.

The amazing career of Joseph Smith's peep stone

A shiny, black and orange-yellow stone plays a key role in our story. Many people all over the American Frontier believed that, just beneath their feet, there was a vast and mysterious underworld. Its nooks and crannies were full of hidden treasures there for the taking. But you had to find them first. When he was in Vermont, Joseph Smith, Sr. belonged to a group of true believers who dug in vain for swag buried by Captain Kidd. Smith owned a seer stone, or peep stone, which he used to search for the treasure. When Smith moved to Palmyra, he was still on the hunt. Neighbors gossiped about the low-lifers and loose women who gathered on the Smith farm to help him on his moonlight journeys.

Teenager Joseph Smith Jr. soon owned his own peep stone, which he used to find lost things and tell fortunes for a small fee. He earned some fame as "Joe the Peeper." As his reputation grew, a gang of much older money diggers hired the youth to use his peep stone to spy out the buried riches. In his *History of the Church*, Smith took pains to include a story that is very important for this part of our discussion. Still only sixteen:

> *I hired with an old gentleman by the name of Josiah Stoal...He had heard something of a silver mine having been opened by the Spaniards...and had, previous to my hiring to him, been digging, in order, if possible, to discover the mine.* (Joseph Smith— History, 1:56)

He then informed the reader: "*Hence arose the very prevalent story of my having been a money-digger.*" (1:56) With these words, Smith tried to explain away an embarrassing part of his past, blaming it on gossip mongers and character assassins. But he actually made us pay attention to what really happened.

When he was at work as a peeper, Smith followed a ritual familiar to the world of folk magic. He would drop the peep-stone into a hat, put his face at the opening to block out the light, and see visions of lost silver mines or chests full of gold and jewels. Smith would then use a steel knife to draw a circle over the location of the hidden treasure, plunge his knife into the ground directly above the spot, give a signal, and the dirt would fly. The sweating money-diggers never found a single coin or jewel. But Smith had an explanation which made perfect sense to anyone enmeshed in the fever of money-digging. Pesky guardian spirits watching over the treasures had moved them further into the earth, out of reach.

A spectacular vision

On the fateful night of September 21, 1823, seventeen year-old Smith led his money-diggers to a nearby place called Robinson Hill. Unsuccessful as always, he came home to find his parents in the middle of a religious argument. Sighing with frustration, he went to bed full of doubts and turned to God in "prayer and supplication," begging for some kind of "divine manifestation." In the midst of his prayer, a light appeared in his room which became lighter than mid-day, and a personage stood at his bedside.

The visitor called the youth by name and identified himself as Moroni. God had a work for him to do, Moroni said.

121

There was "*a book deposited, written upon gold plates, giving an account of the former inhabitants of this continent...he also said that the fulness of the everlasting Gospel was contained in it.*" (History, 1:34) Smith was called to translate the book and bring it forth to the world.

Where did the vision take place, what did Moroni look like, and who was he?

If you go to Palmyra, New York, there on the edge of what used to be the Smith farm, you can visit a full-sized replica of the little cabin where the young Joseph met Moroni. A bedroom and dining room/kitchen occupy the lower floor. Above is a storage loft under a low ceiling. Joseph and his five brothers slept thereon two corn-leaf filled mattresses laid on the rough-plank floor. A smaller room next door was occupied by Smith's two sisters. Mormon art often depicts a startled Joseph lying in bed in a light-filled room of his own. But anyone who has visited the cabin knows this is fantasy. When the vision occurred, Smith was lying next to two of his brothers under the cover of a ragged, shared blanket.

Mormon art also depicts Moroni as an angel in shining white. But Smith's earliest descriptions, recorded by relatives, portrayed the visitor as an old man with a beard, or an ancient Spaniard whose throat had been cut. Mormon biographies mention this fact and quickly hurry on. They do not stop to explain that this description matches the traditional folk description of the guardian spirits hunched over the treasures in the underworld, the ones who had frustrated Smith's efforts as a treasure peeper. Only later did Moroni become an angel.

Smith said that Moroni appeared three times, each time repeating his message. In the morning, he informed his father of the vision. Again, he climbed Robinson Hill. There, half buried on the hillside, he discovered a stone box and within, found two stones in silver bows called "the Urim and Thummim,"[30] a breastplate, and the precious gold plates. Moroni appeared and refused to let Smith take the treasure home because the sight made him greedy. He wrote that four years would pass before he was allowed to remove his discoveries from their hiding place. In the meantime, Smith married and worked to support Emma, his young wife.

The peep stone helped Smith locate his gold treasure

Smith never shoveled dirt alongside the money-diggers. He was busy stooped like a crane, his face covering the opening in his hat, studying the stone. The effort would end with a moan and a curse as the guardian spirits frustrated the money diggers. But on that fateful day in September, for the first time in its career, the peep stone actually helped Smith uncover a buried treasure. We have only his say-so, of course.

Willard Chase, the man on whose property the golden plates were discovered, remembered that, in 1827, Joseph Smith's father remarked, "If it had not been for that stone, he (Joseph Smith Jr.) would not have obtained the book."[31] Martin Harris, who served briefly as Smith's secretary and then financed the printing of the *Book of Mormon*, wrote that Smith found the hidden location of the golden plates "by

---

[30] The ancients had no concept of what Smith seems to describe as eyeglasses. Biblical scholars tell us that the urim and thummim were actually a set of dice used by the priests in the earliest days of Judaism to decide God's will.

[31] William Chase Affidavit, 1834, quoted in Eber Howe, *Mormonism Unvailed* (Painesville, OH: E.D. Howe, 1834)

looking in the stone found in the well of Mason Chase. The (Smith) family told me the same thing."[32]

Bringing the treasure home

It was September 22 again, and this time Smith had high hopes. He had married Emma and she waited in a carriage while he climbed Robinson Hill and confronted Moroni again. Because of Emma, the spirit relented and the plates were his. He came back with his discovery wrapped in an old coat, and for whatever reason, he hid the plates in a hollow tree. But his cider-addicted father blared the news in the ale-house and the word quickly spread. Members of his former money-digging crew demanded their share of the booty. When Smith refused, they used another peep stone to track the treasure, and they were getting close. It was time to fetch the plateshome.

According to Smith, it was a near thing. Battling his enemies along the way, he ran across fields and jumped over fences with the gold plates tucked under his left arm. As he arrived at the Smith homestead and slammed the door, Smith shouted that he had the golden plates at last. But he refused to let anybody look. God would smite them dead, he said. He wrapped the plates in his mother's pillow case and stuffed them into a wooden box used to ship window glass. Finally, witnesses were allowed to heft the plates in their box. Different disciples picked up the box with its plates, including three women. They guessed it weighed from thirty to sixty pounds. Some were allowed to touch the plates through the pillowcase. They said it felt and sounded like a real book with metal pages. Its dimensions were about six inches by seven inches by eight inches.

How much does a 6x7x8 bundle of gold plates actually weigh?

Once more, we are walking in the murky mist where Smith and his family found their home. He told parents and friends that the plates were made of pure gold. They lifted the box full of plates and took him at his word. Unfortunately, a gold book with those dimensions, allowing for a loss of weight because of the individual pages, would have weighed more than one hundred twenty pounds. By coincidence, a book made of tin sheets with similar dimensions would have weighed forty pounds. Without admitting that this might be a fishy story, Mormon apologists have tried to find substitutes for gold which would have been lighter, including plates made out of a gold alloy from Central America called matanga. Some Mormons are not really comfortable in Smith's shape-shifting world.

The peep stone finds an even higher calling, and helps Smith translate the plates

Modern Mormon artists like to show the young seer studying one of the golden plates, which he holds in his hand. I discovered a recent painting with Smith running his finger along the characters inscribed there. Artists portray a thin little man named Oliver Cowdery sitting behind a screen, quill pen in hand. As Smith translates the mysterious characters phrase by phrase, Cowdery writes them down.

But within Joseph's blurry universe, fact and fiction run together like oil on water. Our first witness is Emma Smith herself, who was his first scribe. If her husband had examined the plates openly, she would have seen them for herself. But the plates sitting on the table were always covered with a cloth. Filled with fear of God's fury, she never peeked. But when she was dusting the table, she had to lift the concealed stack of plates. It was not too much for her to manage. She ruffled the pages through the cloth covering and heard the sound of metal.

By the witness of everyone who ever served as a scribe, Smith left the cover on the plates and did not study a single golden page. The basically illiterate young prophet did not have to sort out the syntax and grammar of the "Reformed Egyptian" language supposedly etched on the plates. He returned instead to his world of myth and magic, and reached for his hat and the peep stone. According to Mormon historian Donna Hill, "She (Emma) said that she wrote for her husband hour after hour as he dictated, *sitting with his face buried in his hat, which had the stone in it.*"[33] (My emphasis)

When disciples Martin Harris and Oliver Cowdery took Emma's place as scribe, Smith's method did not change. The golden plates sat on the table, covered by their cloth. The young translator stared into the darkness at the stone in his hat. Martin Harris, who served as Smith's second scribe, described the process. Sometimes, they sat face to face at the same table. At other times, the Prophet was on the other side of a cloth hung between them. At still other times, Harris was upstairs in the small attic. According to Harris, the translation of the plates would appear before the prophet's eyes. He would dictate the words and Harris

---

[33] Donna Hill, Op. Cit., p. 73

126

would write them down. "Written!" Harris would call out, and Smith would continue dictating the story.

Emma's family considered Smith's efforts a fraud. Smith did not have a job and their store of supplies had run out. The pregnant Emma was going hungry. Her father told Smith to get some work and support his wife, or else. In the nick of time, disciples from New York came with food supplies and money, and so the translation continued. When Emma's family threatened to steal the plates and reveal the scam, Smith got up in the middle of the night and hid them in the nearby mountains. But even though the plates were now in a ravine guarded by rattlesnakes, the translation went on. Apparently the peep stone was more important than the plates. Smith continued with the comfortable ritual of folk magic. He would put the peep stone in his hat, cover the opening with his face, and dictate the new words appearing on the stone. "Written!" new scribe Oliver Cowdery would shout from the other side of the screen.

A pattern left over from the money-digging days

What we discover in all this is *the continuation of the pattern observed during Smith's money digging days.* 1) Smith followed a folk ritual handed down by the practitioners of folk-magic. He would put his peep stone into a hat, block out the light with his face, stare into the dark, and discover gold buried in the ground. 2) Following the same ritual, Smith used the peep stone to search for and then discover the gold plates, also buried in the ground. 3) The stone helped Smith locate invisible treasures. 4) The stone helped him translate the invisible gold plates.

After generations of denial, LDS Church authorities now agree that Smith had a peep stone and used it to translate the *Book of Mormon*. They argue that God used traditional folk ways to bring the book to simple people. They are reluctant to admit that he used the stone during his previous career as peeper for a gang of money diggers. The black and orange-yellow peep stone is still in the possession of the church. A picture of the stone recently appeared in the *Ensign*, a church publication.

Did the gold plates actually exist?

Some might point to the testimonies at the beginning of the *Book of Mormon* by three of Smith's closest collaborators, who said they had seen the plates, even though Smith had left them far behind in Pennsylvania. This happened in the middle of an intense religious experience. An angel held up the plates before the witnesses, and turned the pages. Eight other witnesses, most of them friends or family members of the Prophet, also testified that they had seen the plates. Historians do not give much weight to those witnesses.

Did the plates actually exist, like the coffee cup sitting on my desk? I would use a term created by some sociologists and call it the experience of an "alternate reality." I witnessed alternate reality for myself when I attended a class conducted by an expert in black magic. Such experiences happen in other cultures, and routinely happened in early America. But our modern scientific culture looks at alternate reality with great suspicion.

I think alternate reality experiences really happen, but they are ambiguous and a strong personality can induce them in suggestible people. When Smith's three disciples saw an angel turning the golden pages, they were true believers in the middle of an intense religious frenzy, and he had them under his emotional thumb. They were feeling tremendous pressure to see the plates for themselves. Martin Harris was in an especially agitated state. The reader will have to place this story within the larger context of Smith's behavior.

Next puzzle: Revelations to fit a new theology

Joseph Smith claimed to govern his church by divine revelation. As his fascinated followers looked on, Jesus would speak directly through the Prophet's mouth while a chosen secretary took careful notes. Parley Pratt said Smith spoke each sentence slowly and distinctly, with a pause between them long enough to allow the words to be taken down. There was never any hesitation, never any reviewing or reading back, never any revision or correction.[34]Once, the elders present tried to correct Smith's grammar. He angrily rebuffed their effort, insisting that every word spoken had been dictated by Jesus Christ himself.[35]

The *Book of Commandments*

At a church conference held in November, 1831, those present agreed that the carefully transcribed revelations were "the foundation of the church in these last days."[42] The first forty-five revelations were then reviewed by Joseph Smith, Oliver Cowdery, and Sidney Rigdon, and prepared for publication as *The Book of Commandments*. In a letter dated July 31, 1832, Smith warned W.W. Phelps, the printer, *"not to alter the sense of any of them (the revelations), for he that adds to or diminishes the prophecies must come under the condemnation written therein."*[36] The *Book of Commandments* was printed in Independence, Missouri, in1833. Most of the books were soon destroyed by a mob, but some crudely

---

[34] Donna Hill, op. cit., p. 141

[35]*History of the Church*, I, 226, quoted by Donna Hill [42] Ibid., 235

[36] Ibid, 270

bound copies survived. I have a copy of the Book of Commandments on my bookshelf.

The *Doctrine and Covenants*

The *Book of Commandments* was replaced in 1835 by another book called *The Doctrine and Covenants*. A modern copy of the book contains one hundred thirty-five divine messages given to Joseph Smith, including detailed instructions about the foundation and organization of his new church. This book is also on my bookshelf.

Additions and deletions

Again, we tread the mushy turf trod by Joseph Smith. Here begins another puzzle which the missionaries never mention and which Donna Hill and other faithful LDS authors do not really explore. When the reader compares certain revelations contained in the *Book of Commandments* with the same revelations printed in *The Doctrine and Covenants*, he discovers that, without a footnote or any other explanation, they *have undergone some very considerable alterations*.

For instance, Chapter IV in the *Book of Commandments* contains an eleven paragraph revelation "given to Joseph and Martin, in Harmony, Pennsylvania, March, 1829." The same revelation appears in Section 5 of *The Doctrine and Covenants*, also "given to Joseph and Martin, in Harmony, Pennsylvania, March, 1829."But the revelation appearing in the *Doctrine and Covenants* has experienced eighty-nine changes, including the addition of more than one hundred fifty words and the deletion of two paragraphs. The changes in the original revelations coincide with changes in Joseph Smith's evolving theology.

Other troubling alterations appear in the *Doctrine and Covenants*, Section 27, which was supposedly given to Joseph Smith at Harmony, Pennsylvania, in August, 1830. Again, the reader is not informed that changes have been made. Verses five through eighteen contain a revelation which speaks about the power of the keys, the ordination of Joseph Smith and Oliver Cowdery to the "first priesthood" by John the Baptist, and their subsequent ordination by Peter, James, and John, which made them Melchizedek priests possessing the power to act in God's name.

But when we compare Section 27 with its original, which appears in Chapter Twenty-eight of the *Book of Commandments*, we discover nothing about keys or ordination to any priesthood. Comparing the two texts, we learn that more than *four hundred words have been added to the original revelation*, including all the verses describing Smith's ordination by John the Baptist to the Aaronic priesthood, and his ordination by the three apostles to the Melchizedek Priesthood, which included possession of the power of the keys of the Kingdom. Because the two different forms of priesthood play such a key role in Mormon life, this is not a small issue.

Mormons argue that a prophet can surely change his own revelations. But why make it appear that subsequent changes were part of the original? The path Smith chose—adding and subtracting words in the original without advising the faithful that changes had been made—sounds like deliberate deception. When some of Smith's earliest disciples noticed the changes, they left the church.

Final puzzle: The Book of Abraham

The *Book of Abraham* is part of a small volume called the *Pearl of Great Price,* and is considered scripture. It is important because it contains doctrines unique to the

Mormon Church. For example, the book teaches that Abraham possessed the Melchizedek Priesthood...gives us the name of the great star Kolob, which is "nearest unto the throne of God"...teaches about the eternity of matter and introduces the concept of "eternal intelligences"...and says that not God, but "the gods" were responsible for the creation of the world.

The most amazing Biblical discovery of all time

Once more we enter the dreamy world of Joseph Smith. In July 1835, Smith announced an astounding discovery which should have been the most dramatic moment in the entire history of Biblical archeology. He claimed to have in his possession "The writings of Abraham while he was in Egypt...*written by his own hand*, upon papyrus." (My emphasis)[37] Historians do not possess original copies of any ancient manuscript. The most ancient copy of the Old Testament is found in the Dead Sea Scrolls, which were written a little before the time of Jesus. If Smith truly possessed something actually written by Abraham in his own hand, his name should be enshrined in Biblical history.

How did this marvelous event take place? A man named Michael H. Chandler had inherited four mummies and several papyri scrolls plundered from a tomb in Egypt. Hoping to make a little money, Chandler brought his collection to America for display. When he heard of Smith's amazing accomplishment with the *Book of Mormon*, he traveled with his treasures from New York to Ohio and asked the prophet if he could translate the Egyptian writing. Smith immediately took up the challenge. He wrote in his diary:

---

[37] Forward note in the Book of Abraham

With W.W. Phelps and Oliver Cowdery as scribes, I commenced the translation of some of the characters or hieroglyphics, and much to our joy found that one of the rolls contained the writing of Abraham.[38]

With his usual flamboyant energy, Smith used his mother's inheritance to purchase the collection, and we flounder deeper into Smith's wonder-filled universe. He proudly displayed his acquisition to any interested visitor, including tourist Quincy Adams, who noted in a letter that the "cheeky" prophet had boldly identified one mummy as the ancient Pharaoh Necho himself. Smith made some notes on a small part of one scroll, but when it came time for translation, he did it through the gift of revelation, without his peep stone.[46] When he performed this feat, Smith and the scrolls were not even in the same city.

After Joseph Smith was murdered, the Egyptian scrolls passed into the hands of Emma, his wife. Somewhere along the way, they disappeared, and it was assumed that they had perished in the great Chicago Fire. The only vestige remaining were the three drawings called "facsimiles" that are routinely published today by the Mormon Church as a part of the Book of Abraham. Under each facsimile is an explanation written either by Smith himself, or by an associate with Smith's approval.[39]

A blessing or an embarrassment?

In 1966, the story took a twist and Mormons found themselves in another uncomfortable place manufactured by their prophet. The Metropolitan Museum of New York

[38]*History of the Church*, II, 236, quoted by Donna Hill, *op. cit.*, p. 193. [46] Ibid.

[39] The reader can find these facsimiles in any Book of Abraham, which appears as part of the *Pearl of Great Price*.

discovered the lost scrolls in its vast collection, and returned them to the LDS Church. Attention focused on the small scroll where Smith had written some notes. That, Mormon historians argued, was the source for the *Book of Abraham*. The LDS Church handed the scroll over to competent scholars, confident that Joseph Smith's skill as a translator would finally be proven to a doubting world.

But scholars proved instead that the scroll Smith claimed was "from the hand of Abraham himself"[40] was written sometime around the birth of Jesus and had absolutely nothing to do with the old patriarch of Israel. The document was merely part of an ancient Egyptian funeral rite for a man named Hor, whose mummified body was accompanied by the scroll. It testifies that Hor was embalmed in the approved way, allowing him to continue his life in the after world. This was called a "breathing permit." The other scrolls told the same story about the other mummies.

We are back in that foggy world of Joseph Smith, wondering what is real or an illusion. Mormons now admit that the scroll "containing the writing of Abraham" was an Egyptian religious document written almost two thousand years after Abraham died. Joseph Smith repeatedly called his work a "translation," but modern Mormons are now forced to offer other explanations. For instance, this is Donna Hill's complicated effort to find a reasonable answer to the dilemma created by her prophet:

> *The evidence so far accumulated suggests that Joseph Smith had no need of the Egyptian papyri to produce The Book of Abraham, but he found them stimulating.*

---

[40] Mormons themselves discovered this manuscript while they were examining the recently returned scrolls. It was a fragment labeled "XI.
Small "Sensen' text."

Feeling in direct communion with the Lord, through the workings of his mind, he believed that he had done a translation.[41] (My emphasis)

Hill wants us to see a confused prophet who thought he was translating the words of the great patriarch. So, what is the *Book of Abraham*? A book of scripture in spite of it all? A mirage seen by someone hiking the desert of self-delusion? A deliberate fraud? A problem that can be spun away by those who try hard enough? The reader will have to ponder this odd story and decide one more time if Smith was a mad-man, a liar, or a saint.

---

[41] Ibid.

9

A Look at the Book of Mormon

In the eyes of many, the publication of the Book of Mormon established Joseph Smith as God's prophet. In this modern era, the missionaries still consider the Book of Mormon *a key to conversion. They ask potential converts to pray to know that the* Book of Mormon *is real scripture. They are confident that the warm feelings in their hearts will cause them to accept Joseph Smith as God's true prophet and become faithful Saints. Last year, a couple of young missionaries came to my house. With their usual confidence, they asked me what I thought of the Book of Mormon. This is an expanded version of my response.*

A brief summary of the book

Joseph Smith claimed that it all began when he was only 17 years old. The angel Moroni told him about golden plates buried in a stone box on what is now called Hill Cumorah. Moroni told him that the plates contained *"the fullness of the everlasting gospel…as delivered by the Savior to the ancient inhabitants."*

The *Book of Mormon* tells a story that covers almost a thousand years. The narrative begins around 587 B.C, a fateful date marking the destruction of Jerusalem by the Babylonians, and the beginning of the Babylonian Exile. The *Book of Mormon* opens with two books called First and Second Nephi, which are narrated through the voice of a prophet named Nephi. He introduces us to his father Lehi, a "visionary man." Neither Lehi nor Nephi are mentioned in the Bible.

Lehi had a series of visions about the Messiah which have no parallel in the writings of any biblical prophet. His son Nephi had similar visions. The Messiah would be born of a virgin, gather twelve apostles, start a church, and die on the cross for the sins of the world. This sets the theme for the *Book of Mormon*, which is basically a story about waiting for the promised Savior of the World. That is why the LDS Church advertises the *Book of Mormon* as "another testimony of Christ."

God told Lehi in a dream to flee with his sons to escape the destruction of the city by the Babylonians. Guided by a mysterious round ball called the "Liahona," Lehi and his family started out on their long journey. After eight years in a place called Bountiful by the edge of the sea, God instructed Nephi to build a ship. Undaunted by the opposition of his brother Laman and his other brothers, Nephi mined and refined ore, forged the extracted metal into tools, singlehandedly built the ship, and convinced his quarrelsome family to climb aboard. Directed by the *Liahona*–now clearly described as a compass—the exiles made their perilous way half way around the world to America. Modern Mormons believe that the refugees came ashore in Central America or southern Mexico. There, Lehi and his sons found refuge on an unpopulated coast.

When Lehi died, the children of Nephi and Laman split into two warring factions called the *Nephites* and the *Lamanites.* The Nephites were faithful believers in the prophecies about the coming Christ. The Lamanites, following the example of their evil patriarch Laman, refused to believe the prophecies and fell into violence and corruption. Because of their sinful disbelief, the Lamanites were cursed with dark skins. This explains the presence of Native Americans, who are called Lamanites to this very day by many faithful Saints.

The Lamanites haunted the wilderness, but the Nephites built prosperous cities, which waxed during times of belief, and waned when the people fell into sin. Throughout the *Book of Mormon,* a series of kings and prophets repeated their belief in the prophecies about the Messiah. They preached the same message: Confess your sins, believe in Christ, listen to his prophets, and prepare for his coming. The Lamanites were used as the scourge of God whenever the Nephites proved unfaithful. The lapses were frequent and times of peaceful belief short-lived. Much of the Book of Mormon wallows in murder or brutal warfare.

The coming of Jesus

In Third Nephi, the long expected Savior finally appeared in America after his death and resurrection in Israel. He immediately established his church among those who had waited so long for his coming. He appointed apostles and established a detailed system of worship and belief. For a little while, both Nephites and Lamanites were at peace in Jesus' New World church, but inevitably they fell away from the Gospel and warfare erupted once more.

Tragic defeat

The *Book of Mormon* ends with a book written by Mormon, the last great general to lead the Nephite people. Mormon made a pact with the Lamanites to fight a final battle to the death. The two nations traveled at least three thousand miles to Hill Cumorah, in New York state. There, the enemies clashed for the last time. The Nephites were defeated and massacred.

At several points in the *Book of Mormon,* we learn that the gold plates were written for the Lamanites in a last effort to achieve their conversion. With the fateful battle formations gathering on Hill Cumorah, Moroni addressed any Lamanite who might discover the golden plates. He explained the proper organization of the true church and, in a long essay, warned about the evils of infant baptism. In the final chapter, Mormon's son Moroni sealed the golden plates inscribed by his father and given to his care. He then gave a final word of testimony to the victorious Lamanites, begging them to come to Christ. With this plea, the book abruptly ends, sometime around 421 AD.

A general reaction to the Book of Mormon

Compared to the Bible,
the *Book of Mormon* lacks color and interest

On the surface, *The Book of Mormon* sounds like the Bible...or rather, like the King James Version of the Bible. But despite the use of "thee" and "thou," the differences are obvious from the very beginning. First and most obvious are its detailed prophecies about the Messiah, which have no parallel in the Old Testament. Even though the book contains fifteen smaller books, it lacks the literary complexity of the Old Testament. One looks in vain for anything like the Psalms, which express the prayer of faithful Jews, or the Proverbs, which express their wisdom. There are no gems like Ruth, Judith, or Jonah. The exalted, anguished poetry of Job and the Psalms is missing. Women play a prominent role in the Bible. But in the *Book of Mormon,* only three women are mentioned by name, and they quickly vanish from the story without playing a real role. The magnificent Sarah, Rachel, Deborah, Judith, Esther, Ruth, Mary, and Mary Magdalen find no counterpart among the Nephites and Lamanites.

The *Book of Mormon* does repeat the prophetic poetry of Isaiah, but these beautiful words come somehow straight out of the *King James Bible,* including some of the mistakes that were printed in the particular version of the *King James* that belonged to Joseph Smith. As I write this, I think of the times when Martin Harris the scribe was in the attic of the house, while Smith was downstairs, shouting his translation through the ceiling. Why? Did he have that *King James Bible* on his lap, afraid that Harris might see him turn the pages?

There are some stirring sermons in the *Book of Mormon,* along with long quotes from the Prophet Isaiah. But mostly, there are monologues which simply numb the mind, along with battles and persecutions in a style that outdoes Samuel and Kings. We have murder and patricide. People are tormented for their belief in Christ, and the Nephites fend off endless Lamanite invasions and defend themselves against a mysterious secret society called the Gadianton Robbers. The book is also the story of perpetually fragile faith and the harsh judgment of a merciless god.

The Book of Mormon makes sense only to someone who follows a "literalist" interpretation of the Bible

Modern copies of the *Book of Mormon* contain a subtitle: "Another testimony of Jesus Christ." For the Bible reader of Smith's day, it was not too difficult to believe that Lehi and Nephi knew in miraculous detail about Jesus and his messianic mission almost six hundred years before the Savior was born, or that Jacob could plead with his people, "Come to Christ." In those days, people read the Bible without wondering about its historical, cultural, or literary context. The thought didn't cross their minds. As we will see, such people are called literalists. The only enlightenment they needed was from the Holy Spirit. But for modern scripture scholars, the literalist interpretation fails to answer an important question: Isn't the Bible at least as complicated as a newspaper?

When I read an old newspaper, I need to know something about context. I have to be aware of the history and culture of the times during which the paper was written. For instance, a New York Times published in the 1930's would make little sense to a young adult today who knows nothing about the Great Depression. When I read a newspaper, I also have to recognize that it contains several different "literary forms." This means that a news story contains the facts while an editorial contains opinion. It is important to know the difference. Imagine if someone took a sports page literally. Eagles defeat lions, and giants are laid low by red sox. And the comics? What if someone thought Garfield was a real cat?

The Catholic Church believes that a modern reader of the Bible must understand its context if he is to look deeply into its message. He has to study the history, culture, thought patterns, and literary style of the ancient Semitic world. An understanding of context gives a lot of insight and avoids a lot of confusion. The *Book of Mormon* simply falls apart when we ask it to be consistent with the ancient history and culture within which it was supposedly written.

Some examples of a lack of context in the *Book of Mormon*

An "anachronism" is something out of place and out of time–like a picture of George Washington scrolling the Internet. The *Book of Mormon* is famous for anachronisms which throw the whole book into serious doubt. For instance, in one place, Nephi stole the "steel" sword of

141

Laban and, in another place, he broke a "steel" bow. A pretty good feat for a man who lived in the Iron Age. When Lehi and his family landed on the shores of America, they found "the cow and the ox, the ass and the horse." (I Nephi 18:25) Scientists inform us that these creatures did not exist in America at that time. The armies of the Nephites wore metal armor and wielded metal swords. Metal can rust away and vanish, but archeologists have never found a trace of the massive foundries needed to make iron or steel. The Nephites went to war in chariots. We find this in several places, including the book of Helaman. Archeologists have never found a trace of such a thing in all of ancient America.

Out of time, out of place:
The entire focus of the Book of Mormon

The Old Testament focuses on great moments in the past

The big difference between the Old Testament and the *Book of Mormon* has to do with their frames of reference. The Old Testament focuses on overpowering events that occurred in the past. The five books that form the Law...the books of Judges, Samuel, and Kings...the Psalms and the Wisdom Books...all the words of the Prophets have only one purpose: To teach the people how to remain faithful to the creator God who made covenant with his people at Mount Sinai and promised David through a prophet that his kingdom would last forever. As their nation slowly lost her power and prestige, the Jews remembered God's power revealed in creation and his mighty deeds when Joshua conquered the Canaanites, The Jews never forgot the covenant at Sinai, and the kingdom David founded. The Old Testament speaks and dreams within that tradition.

Her prayers for a messiah were expressed in terms of a new creation, a new Moses, or a new David.

When Jesus preaches the Sermon on the Mount, Mathew is portraying him as a new Moses. We hear children cry, "Hosannah to the son of David!" Even after the death and resurrection of Jesus, we see this expectation in his disciples. In the beginning of the Acts of the Apostles, for instance, two of them ask, "Now are you going to restore the Kingdom to Israel?"

The Book of Mormon focuses on the Redeemer to come

The *Book of Mormon* abandons this point of view. Its prophecies are about Jesus, six hundred years in the future, and they are more and more specific. He is a crucified redeemer, the Lamb of God who will take away the sins of the world and then found a church. The church becomes the central institution in the Book of Mormon long before the risen Jesus comes to establish his church in America. The constant call is to "come to Christ."

And so the reader finds a puzzle: In the Old Testament, God speaks through Elijah, Isaiah, Jeremiah, and the other prophets, always emphasizing creation, the Sinai Covenant made with Moses, the expectation of a new David and the restoration of the Kingdom to Israel. But in the *Book of Mormon*, God asks his people to believe in a religious message that matches the Protestant vision of the nineteenth century, with detailed prophecies that focus all their attention on the coming of a Messiah, his atoning death, his church, and the need to walk by faith. For instance, in Jacob, the next book after I and II Nephi, we find this gem:

Wherefore, beloved brethren, be reconciled unto him through the atonement of Christ, his Only Begotten Son, and ye may

obtain a resurrection, and according to the resurrection which
be in Christ, and be presented as the first-fruits of Christ unto
God, having faith, and obtained a good hope of glory in him
before he manifested himself in the flesh. (Jacob 4/11)

This passage appears in the middle of a long-winded sermon that is one passage extracted from St. Paul after another. None of this would make any sense to someone living within the world view of the Old Testament. Every phrase in this paragraph would have caused Isaiah and Jeremiah to scratch their heads.

New Testament theology in an Old Testament context

Should we be startled when we find these New Testament ideas in Old Testament places? This might not bother a literalist, but for someone who believes that something calling itself scripture should fit the world within which it was supposedly written, it is an obstacle. For instance, *Book of Mormon* prophets abound, but again, their message would have confused Isaiah and Jeremiah. We ponder another example.

For the natural man *is an enemy to God, and has been, from the fall of Adam, and will be, forever and ever; but if he yieldeth to the enticings of the Holy Spirit, and* puts off the natural man, *and becometh a saint, through the atonement of Christ, the Lord....* (Mosiah Ch. 1, p. 161, 1830 Edition. My emphasis)

In the Bible, the "natural man," "putting off the natural man," and the "enticings of the Holy Spirit" are not found in the Old Testament. But they are found in different places in the New Testament, especially St. Paul. Joseph Smith probably heard these phrases as a young man during Methodist camp meetings in the woods, or read them in his

New Testament, and they sprang naturally to mind as he was writing the Book of Mormon. Witnesses said he was an accomplished "exhorter" who stirred up enthusiasm for the message that had just been preached by a Methodist minister. But what are these expressions doing in the mouth of someone whose ancestors left Jerusalem and fled to America around 587 B.C.? Brigham Young, who could barely read a book, was a literalist who would have been amazed and inspired by these passages. For a contextualist, such anachronisms put the whole text into doubt.

A scandal to diminish any other scandal: the Jesus who finally appears in the Book of Mormon

In the Gospels, we meet a gentle Christ

For me, nothing is as difficult as what I am about to discuss. I am especially troubled by the Jesus who finally shows up in Third Nephi, late in the *Book of Mormon*. In the Gospels, Jesus comes as a child born in a manger. This is our first encounter with Jesus. Later, when James and John ask him to call down fire from heaven on the unbelieving Samaritans, Jesus rebukes them severely. And when he dies on the cross, it is with forgiveness on his lips. After he dies, there is no divine vengeance. Yes, there is an earthquake and the veil of Temple is rent. But Peter denies Jesus without being hit by a thunderbolt and the apostles who had shared Jesus' Body and Blood slip away safely into hiding. All in all, Jerusalem, which saw Jesus face to face and then rejected and crucified him, is at peace.

A scandal to diminish any other scandal: the Jesus who finally appears in the Book of Mormon

Let's do a thought experiment and imagine that everything in the *Book of Mormon* is true. I want to ponder the obstacles that would have made it difficult for the average Nephite or Lamanite to believe that the Messiah was coming.

As our thought experiment begins, it has been 600 years since Lehi, Nephi, and Laman fled Jerusalem. The compass called Liahona has led them more than half way around the world, to the shores of El Salvador in Central America. There, the Nephites live prosperous lives in large cities. Even though they still had sacred books written in Hebrew, they no longer wrote, and maybe they no longer spoke, that language. Even when they were still in Jerusalem among the Jewish people, the language of Lehi, Nephi, and all their descendants seems to have been the mysterious "Reformed Egyptian" etched on the gold plates discovered by Joseph Smith. The Lamanites, cursed with black skins and still a dangerous enemy, live in the wilderness. But some of them have mixed with the Nephites and have come to believe in the coming of Christ.

During those six hundred years, kings and prophets have demanded loyalty to Christ. But he is a figure in the vague future. And when he does arrive, Christ will live in the midst of a people on the other side of the world. No Nephite will ever hear John the Baptist call him the Lamb of God. He will never walk the streets of any Nephite city. Nobody will witness his sermons and his miracles. Nor will they ever boast to a neighbor, "I just made a pilgrimage to Jerusalem and Jesus was in the Temple!" The Nephites and Lamanites are asked to put their faith in an abstraction.

We turn to the Book of Helaman Around 6 B.C.. A prophet named Samuel the Lamanite predicts that, in five years, the Son of God, the redeemer will be born. His birth will be accompanied by a night without darkness. At this point we have to ask some questions. How far does Samuel's fame extend? In the ancient world, news had to be spread from city to city by word of mouth. Are his prophecies posted in the public square of every city or town? Or is it only local news for the local population? Is it some family's fault if they never get the word?

We turn to the next book, called Nephi III. The great prophet Nephi, the son of Nephi and keeper of the records of the people, hears a voice. At long last, the Messiah has come! True to prophecy, Jesus has been born of his mother Mary, in Bethlehem, in place completely beyond the experience of any citizen of Central America. Nephi wants to trumpet the good news, but again we ask, how far does the message get? Are the people of all the Nephite cities anxiously waiting for the latest message from Nephi? How many will take him seriously?

Nephi realizes he needs some kind of proof that the long awaited birth has really happened. He cannot invite his neighbors to do what the shepherds did, and go to the stable to see for themselves. And so the Lord gives his people a sign. In fulfillment of Samuel's prophecy, the sun sets, but there is no darkness. There is light when it should be night.

Some people glimpse a star. And then the sun rises at its appointed hour. Unfortunately, a night without darkness is not accompanied by a sub-title in the sky, explaining the meaning of what has just happened.

Again, we have to ask about the extent of Nephi's influence. Is his name a household word, and are the Nephites and the newly converted Lamanites anxiously waiting for him to say that it all happened because the Messiah had just been born half way across the world? Are his revelations discussed and prayed over in every public square and in every household? Or are the Nephites and Lamanites like the people of Jerusalem when the Magi arrived looking for the newborn king? Who was supposed to suffer because they did not understand what it was all about?

III Nephi continues and thirty-three years go by. Anthropologists tell us that, during those ancient days, thirty-five years is a lifetime. Disease and malnutrition are rampant. Those who were adults or older youth during that night without darkness are mostly dead. Half-remembered rumors are all that is left.

Nobody watches a Messiah preaching and performing miracles.

His disciples do not go out two by two in his name. Nephite and Lamanite life goes on. The merchants count their money and farmers head out to their fields. The women are busy raising the kids. But unknown to them , on the other side of the world, the mission of the Messiah was coming to its climax. On the first month, on the fourth day of the month, and thousands of miles away, Jesus is being nailed to a cross.

A contrast between the Gospels and the Book of Mormon

In the Gospels, there is no divine revenge

We ponder the scene around Calvary. Hearts broken, the tiny band of women look on from a distance. Only Mary, John, and the other Mary are close. Pilate is having a glass of wine and maybe a siesta. Herod is doing whatever. At Calvary, the chief priests jeer while the soldiers toss dice for a dying man's clothes. It grows dark. And then Jesus calls to his Father and dies. There is an earthquake and the veil in the Temple is rent. The dead walk the earth. ***But there is no divine retribution.*** Judas perishes after tying the noose around his own neck. Peter is not blasted by a lightning bolt. The apostles who abandoned Jesus scuttle safely into hiding. There is no news about a high priest struck down by God's wrath. Jerusalem, which had welcomed Jesus and then crucified him, seems to be at peace. For Juda and Galilee, it is just an ordinary day at the beginning of an ordinary week.

Catastrophe on the other side of the world

While the people of Israel lived peaceful lives while Jesus was dying on the cross, on the other side of the world it was a different story. Without warning, the whole population of Central America is suddenly throttled by the grip of a brutal God. Nephite and Lamanite alike are ravaged by tempest and earthquake, tornado, landslide, and fire. For as long as

Jesus is on the cross, land forms vanish beneath the sea while whole cities disappear into the earth. Husbands reach for their wives and mothers reach for their children, but hell opens and sucks them all in.

When the slaughter is finally over, a mere 2,500 survivors tremble together in the shattered ruins of a temple. The world still rings with the sound of their despair. The text describes howling and weeping and mourning. Why? And who?

In the midst of tarry gloom a grim voice thunders: "Wo, wo, wo unto this people! The great city of Zarahemla have I covered with earth, and its inhabitants. Morniah, Gilgal, Onihah, Jerusalem, Gadiandi, Gadiomnah, Jacob, Gimgimno, Jacobugath, Laman, Josh, God, and Kishkumen—all obliterated in blood and fire!" The boasting goes on for most of a chapter. Three days of darkness descend, a darkness so thick that the text calls it a choking vapor.

In the midst of that darkness, the speaker finally identifies himself: "And behold, I am Jesus Christ, the Son of God." (III Nephi 9:15). The voice cajoles and threatens while the earth continues to quake and shatter. Numb with horror, knees knocking with shock and the cold, the survivors huddle in the darkness for seventy-two endless hours. Finally, there is silence and light, just in time for the Jesus of the *Book of Mormon* to give a long justification for what he has just done.

The Gospel and the *Book of Mormon:* two stories that occurred in darkness

Turn your attention to two stories that unfolded in darkness. The first story is told in the Gospel of St. Luke. There are shepherds there. The song of angels. A young mother caresses her tiny child. In love and wonder the shepherds stare at the infant Jesus, the image of God's mercy made human flesh.

This is *their* first encounter with Jesus.

Now look at the story we have just read. Blinded by darkness, the wounded and the terrified cling to each other. All around them is the stench of the dead. And then an angry voice shrieks like a war trumpet. Wo! Wo! Wo!

This is *their* first encounter with Jesus.

The Jesus of the *Book of Mormon* meets a traumatized people

The survivors hear the voice of Heavenly Father: *Behold my son in whom I am well pleased…hear him.* A man dressed in white robes descends from heaven. He introduces himself as Jesus Christ and, after explaining what he has endured on the cross, lets the trembling crowd examine his hands and side.

Our eyes can't turn away from the wide-eyed mothers and children at the back of the crowd. Their faces are still slack with shock. But this Jesus of mass destruction has no time for wailing women and wounded little ones.

Instead, it is business first. After a preliminary set of instructions about proper ritual and formula, he picks out certain men in the crowd and gives them power to baptize for the forgiveness of sins. This involves the solemn laying on of hands, and takes a while. Jesus then chooses twelve apostles and solemnly ordains them to their task. Another while goes by. This is followed by a longwinded sermon at least six chapters long. It contains most of what Jesus ever said in the Gospels, and more. Only then, after shedding some tears, does this Jesus *finally* comfort the shattered children who have endured the doom of their families and the loss of everything they have ever known.

I finish writing these words and tremble. I can only call the Jesus of the *Book of Mormon* a brutal monster. What had the Nephites and Lamanites done to deserve a fate so much more horrible than the fate of the people of Israel? If the Mormons call the *Book of Mormon* "another testimony of Christ," it is the testimony of a Christ without mercy. The reader needs to ponder again the Christ of the Gospels and the Christ of the *Book of Mormon*. Which Christ do you want to encounter after giving in to sin and temptation? Which Christ lives in the hearts of broken people in a broken world?

A crucial question: Did the Lamanites really become the American Indians?

According to the *Pearl of Great* Price, the Angel Moroni told Joseph Smith,

> *There was a book deposited, written upon gold plates, giving an account of the former inhabitants of this continent, and the source from whence they sprang."* (Joseph Smith –History, Verse 34, my emphasis)

As we have seen, Mormons believe that the Jewish Lamanites became the American Indians. *Meet the Mormons*, a beautifully illustrated book explaining LDS belief and practice, makes this clear:

> *Following the extermination of the Nephite civilization, the Lamanites continued to inhabit the Western Hemisphere. Their dark skinned posterity, along with some supplementary groups found nowhere else in history, constituted the many aboriginal tribes, now known as the American Indians, that were found by European discoverers of the New World.*

But archeologists tell us that the American Indians actually came to America by way of Siberia and Alaska

The discoveries of modern science have challenged this story. Archeologists have determined that the American Indians did not arrive in America a mere1600 years ago, as Lamanite-to-Indian story would contend. Old traces found in the Alaskan wilderness show that Asians crossed from Siberia to Alaska during the last Ice Age, 12,000 years ago. They became the American Indians. Traces of Indian inhabitants have been found in caves in the American west that are almost that old. In my state of Idaho, scientists just found a trove of ancient weapons about thirteen thousand years old, the oldest weapons ever found in North America. Mormon apologists finally admit that the American Indians came from Asia thousands of years before Nephi and Laman fled from Jerusalem. But they then argue that their presence did not endanger the story told in the *Book of Mormon* because the Asian immigrants did not get as far as Central America. Mormons breathe a sigh of relief. The

Jewish origin of (at least some) of the American Indians stands battered but intact.

But we descend again into the murky world of Joseph Smith when we come to the end of the *Book of Mormon*. Mormon, the last great Nephite general, challenged the Lamanites to a battle to the death. For whatever reason, they chose Hill Cumorah as their battle field. It was a mere 3,000 miles away in upper New York State.

Smith loved things military, but when it came to logistics and geography, he was only a half-educated youth in a frontier backwater. We have to imagine Nephite and Lamanite armies marching side by side, burdened by their wives and children. It would have been a years' long journey by anybody's measure. People accustomed to the tropics encountered snowy winter more than once, finally arriving in the ice and snow of New York State. They traveled over mountains, crossed deserts, traversed endless plains, forded mighty rivers, and survived fever swamps. Along the way they finally collided with those Indian tribes who had arrived in America via the Bering Strait, including the Mound Builders, whose ruins testify to a mighty empire. Surely it was hunger, thirst, disease, exhaustion and battle every step of the way. A death march. No wonder some Mormon historians argue that Hill Cumorah was really located in Central America. They even point to a certain place. And then I watched a Mormon tour guide in Palmyra speculate that the Nephites and Lamanites might actually have arrived in New York State instead of Central America. Archeologists who have spent generations unearthing Mayan cities find no glimpse of the people who populate the *Book of Mormon*. Despite all the dirt thrown around by the archeologists from Brigham Young University, the prosperous Nephite cities described in the *Book of Mormon* have never been found. With each new discovery of a lost city in the jungles of Central America, LDS hopes rise. But inevitably, the city belongs to Native American people and the ancient writings on ruined walls tell of kings, pagan deities, and the events of Mayan politics, religion, and commerce.

An even greater woe: the comparison of DNA

The Mormon explanation of the Jewish origin of the American Indians hangs by a really thin thread. DNA fingerprinting has snipped that thread and the whole idea lies shattered on the ground. Molecular biologists and molecular anthropologists–some of them with LDS backgrounds–studied five thousand American Indians from different tribes all over North, Central, and South America. Their study tracked Y chromosome DNA, which is passed on intact from father to son to son, and Mitochondrial DNA, which remains intact as it is passed on to sons and daughters from their mothers. They were able to trace these DNA markers through hundreds of generations to determine ancestry. They then compared their results with the Y chromosome and Mitochondrial DNA found in other groups of people, especially people from the Middle East, where Judaism had its origins. If the Lamanites become Indians were really refugees from Israel, it should show in American Indian DNA. Sadly for the *Book of Mormon*, these researchers conclude that the ancient American Indian DNA does not contain the smallest glimpse of Middle Eastern ancestry. As one LDS scientist put it, "We are in a dilemma."

A furious counter-attack

Neck deep in Smith's imaginary world, LDS apologists now admit that a huge Mayan Indian population was already present when Lehi and his family supposedly came ashore in Central America. The Nephites and Lamanites were a very small drop in a huge bucket. When the Lamanites joined that gene-pool, their DNA with its Jewish base was altered to a state unrecognizable today.

An obvious and devastating question: Where was everybody?

But this ingenious argument simply begs a new question which never gets discussed. Let us suppose that–despite the huge numbers of people repeatedly mentioned in the *Book of Mormon*–the Nephites and Lamanites actually were only a small population in an area dominated by vastly more numerous Mayan neighbors. If this was true, then we are compelled to ask: *Where was everybody?*

Even Mormon archeologists now agree that the whole area was controlled by city-states whose famous monuments are scattered across the whole area. The *Book of Mormon* does not mention a single cultural, commercial, or military contact with the Mayans or any other Native American people. It asks us to believe that the sons of Nephi and Laman expanded their territories and wandered throughout the area for almost a thousand years without ever confronting a nation whose numerous citizens were fierce about trade and territory.

But this defies human history. If an area has a good climate, a source of water, or safe access to the sea, people move in for commercial and agricultural reasons. When they encounter weaker people already there, they either dominate or exterminate them. When they encounter stronger people, they submit or flee.

So, where was everybody? We contrast the absence of other people in the *Book of Mormon* to the Israelite Exodus from Egypt to the Promised Land. Even though it was a short journey of less than two hundred miles, the Jews had to battle the petty kings who controlled the road and, in the end, had to conquer the Canaanites who inhabited the Promised Land. Conflict with neighboring peoples was a major part of the Old Testament story. Imagine what the Bible would be like if it failed to mention the Amalekites, Edomites, Moabites, Canaanites, Egyptians, Hittites, Syrians, Assyrians, and Babylonians, Greeks, and Romans? They were not just part of the story. God turned them into players within the drama of Salvation.

It gets much worse. According to the *Book of Mormon*, the Nephites mined ore, smelted it into steel, and fashioned weapons. They had metal swords, metal tipped spears, and were protected by metal armor. The Mayans, in the meanwhile, had spears and arrows with stone points and wore armor made of thick pads of cotton. By all the logic of history, the Nephites and Lamanites should have used their chariots and metal weapons to mow the Mayans down. Like the Spanish *conquistadores*, the descendants of Lehi should have become a super power sweeping like an unstoppable tide throughout all of North, Central, and South America.

The phenomenon of parallel universes

If I want to believe that the *Book of Mormon* contains real history, I am forced to conclude that, in some way, two parallel universes existed side by side, each universe invisible to the inhabitants of the other. One universe was populated by the Nephites and Lamanites, who created a mighty civilization, yet left no trace behind. The other universe was populated by the Mayans, whose vast cities and temples are visited by tourists today.

The value of the *Book of Mormon*

Joseph Smith insisted the *Book of Mormon* was true history, but we have seen that it turns history into a shambles. And yet, we can appreciate the book if we place it in the literary genre called fantasy fiction. I am not mocking the *Book of Mormon* when I say this. Books of fantasy fiction are often quite serious and successful in their purpose, which can be profoundly moral or religious. We think, for instance, of C.S. Lewis and his *Chronicles of Narnia*, or J.R.R. Tolkien and his *Lord of the Rings.* Even though Joseph Smith could not begin to match those skillful writers, his book is an epic in its own way, successfully influencing the lives of millions.

The best parts of the *Book of Mormon* are contained in long sermons preached by figures like Alma and Mosiah. Sounding like St. Paul and St. John, they proclaim a message that might remind an historian of sermons preached at the Methodist camp meetings attended by Joseph Smith. He became a famous exhorter whose on-the-spot sermons drove the message home. The sermons in the *Book of Mormon* inspire people to this very day. Sincere Mormons have followed the Christian teachings contained in the *Book of Mormon* with considerable spiritual success for generations. This is an accomplishment that has to be recognized, even by those who do not believe the gold plates ever existed.

PART THREE

What Kind of God

I hope I helped you in the previous section. Now we will look much more deeply into Mormon and Catholic belief about the Father, the Son, and the Holy Spirit.

10

Who is God the Father?

Our profession of faith begins with God, *for God is the First and the Last, the beginning and end of everything.*
                                    - Catholic Catechism

How Bill Sarto found God in the Cosmos

"I will always remember the moment I chose to open my heart to the reality we call God. I had been driving for hours into a dark moonless night, following U.S. 95 across Nevada, with only the faint lights of a small town on the horizon. Growing sleepy, I pulled over by the side of the road for a stretch. I turned off my headlights, stepped out of my car, looked up, and gasped. The Milky Way flowed overhead, a sparkling river of white winding between a staggering display of stars. I felt my heart expand toward infinity, and spoke God's name into the spangled silence."–
Bill Sarto

Different ways of understanding God

God turns out to be a very difficult three-letter word. Many modern people, including some Catholics, say God exists, but they are thinking about a beneficent but impersonal energy that fills the universe. Maybe like the "Force" in *Star Wars*. While they would advise their children to yield to the kindly flow of this power, they would never imagine that it has any kind of personal love for anybody.

But others think of God as a personal reality who has revealed his name. For some, he is an ever-watchful judge, a stern old man in the sky, an avenger who will afflict those who violate his commandments. Or he can be a cosmic Santa Claus–who lives only to make us happy, satisfy our every desire, and keep us safe from any sorrow. I think of the actress with her life of wealth and pleasure who spoke fondly of "good old God." For others, including myself, God is a Father of both love and justice, a mysterious abiding personal presence at the very heart of life, who calls us to live faithfully with him and with each other.

The Mormon understanding of God

Mormons quote Joseph Smith, who said, *"If men do not comprehend the character of God, they do not comprehend themselves."*[42] A few generations later and humbled perhaps by their own experience, modern Mormons soften Smith's boast a bit, using such expressions as "to master *somewhat* the mystery of God."[52] (Emphasis added)

A god made known through modern revelation

According to the *Encyclopedia of Mormonism*, the *basic* source for LDS teaching about God is *Joseph Smith* himself.[43] Mormons teach that the defining moment of revelation occurred at the very beginning of Smith's career, when the young prophet was only fifteen years old. The *Encyclopedia of Mormonism* calls this First Vision "pivotal."

> *In Church theology, the doctrine of the nature of God is established more clearly by the First Vision of the Prophet...than by anything else. Here, Joseph Smith*

---

[42] Joseph Smith, *The King Follett Discourse*, Eborn Books 1994, p. 5 [52] Ibid. A footnote by the editor

[43] #546, under "God.."

saw for himself that the Father and the Son were two separate and distinct beings, each possessing a body in whose likeness mortals are created.[44]

Written sources for the uniquely LDS belief in God as an exalted male human being are Joseph Smith's "King Follett Discourse," a funeral sermon based on revelations received by Joseph Smith now found in the *Doctrine and Covenants,* the "Book of Moses," and the story found in the "Book of Abraham." As I noted above, I believe that Mormons are modern *Gnostics* whose beliefs stem from visions, modern revelations, and the rediscovery of long lost books. These non-biblical sources are the real foundation for the uniquely Mormon understanding of God.

Mormons and the members of the "Godhead"

As we have seen, even though Mormons use the terms Father, Son, and Holy Ghost, they do not believe in the Trinity. But like Catholics, they do use the term "Godhead." The Mormon Godhead is made up of three separate and distinct divine beings who are unequal in stature: Heavenly Father, and his literal sons Jesus and the Holy Ghost. Someone unfamiliar with Mormonism will be startled when he reads:

> *The Father has a body of flesh and bones as tangible as man's; the Son also; but the Holy Ghost has not a body of flesh and bones, but is a personage of Spirit"* (D&C 130:22)

Remember, even though Mormons use the word "spirit," they are materialists. Spirit seems to actually be some kind

---

44 # 545-548, under "God the Father."

of refined matter. With this description, the Christian understanding of God vanishes.

Heavenly Father

> God...was once a man like us: yea...God himself, the Father of us all, dwelt on an earth, the same as Jesus Christ himself did...God himself was once as we are now, and is an exalted man...I say, if you were to see him today, you would see him like a man in form—like yourselves in all the person, image, and very form as a man. —The Prophet Joseph Smith[45]

As I have already pointed out, the Mormon god is a material being in the midst of an eternal, material universe. Heavenly Father and all other human beings belong to the same species and are at different points of the same process of eternal progression. Heavenly Father is following the journey that every male Latter-day Saint can follow in turn.

Godhood is a self-made position. If a man wants to become a god, he must learn the things that Heavenly Father has learned and do the things that Heavenly Father has done. Heavenly Father is the son of an unknown and unnamed father-god, who is preceded by an endless chain of father-gods who go back forever. By following certain eternal laws and principles set down by his divine parent, Elohim raised himself to the level of godhood. According to one Mormon writer:

> God...Has fought his way from the depths up to the position He now occupies...He has won that position

[45]*Teachings of the Prophet Joseph Smith*, p. 345-6

*by His own exertions, by His own faithfulness, by His
own righteousness.*[46]

The whole purpose of Mormon life is to progress by
following a disciplined plan, "line upon line, precept upon
precept, a little at a time... learning from the past, planning
for the future, and living for today."[47][48] All this is summed
up by a couplet written by Lorenzo Snow, the fifth
president of the LDS church: *As man now is, God once was; As
God now is, man may be.*

Heavenly Father is not a creator, but an organizer

Try to imagine an eternally existing cosmos filled with
eternal, self-subsisting realities, such as Eternal Law, the
energy called the holy spirit, tiny particles of gross and
spirit matter, primal intelligences, and the eternal
priesthood. In a discourse contained in Joseph Smith's
History of the Church, the prophet taught that God was one
"intelligence" in the midst of other "intelligences."

> *Finding that he was in the midst of spirits and glory,
> because he was more intelligent, he saw proper to
> institute laws whereby the rest could have a privilege
> to advance like himself.*[49]

---

[46] *Journal of Discourses* 26:24

[47] Gordon Allred, "Our Father," taken from *God the Father*, edited by Gordon
Allred, (Deseret Book Company, Salt Lake City, 1979) pp.
[48] -16

[49] *History of the Church, VI, pp. 310-312* Hyrum Andrus, *God, Man, and the Universe*,
(Bookcraft, Salt Lake City, 1968) p. 146

Living in space and time, Heavenly Father became "the great Organizer of self-existing matter and things."[50] He used as building material the "gross matter" that fills every corner of the cosmos. Each tiny particle possessed an independent, eternal existence. Other refined material particles, called spirit element, were organized together in some kind of divine sexual activity by Heavenly Father and his queen companions in pre-existence. They became their spirit-children.[60]

Heavenly Father is supreme, absolute...and limited

Mormons tell us God is supreme and absolute. But, as usual, this familiar description is confusing. The *Encyclopedia of Mormonism* teaches that Heavenly Father is not the highest of all the gods, but is preceded by his own father and his father's father in an eternal line backward into infinity, all of them further advanced than the one who follows, because a father is always superior to his son. Like all the others, the god we call Heavenly Father is on the way of eternal progression, which means he is not perfect or complete, and never will be.

And so, if the God of Mormonism is supreme, it is not in relation to his divine father and the other gods. It has to be in relationship with the limited area in the universe under his power and influence, the worlds he has organized, and the spirit-children he formed with the help of his heavenly spouses. If his will is absolute, it can only be through the power of the holy spirit or light of Christ and through the laws he imposes on lesser beings. These lesser beings would include Jesus, the Holy Ghost, and the rest of his spirit-children. If Heavenly Father is perfect, it also can only be in

[50]*Mormon Doctrine*, op. cit., under "Intelligences." [60] Ibid.

comparison to his spouses, his spirit-children and his children on earth.

A clinching word of testimony

The last chapter of the Book of Mormon tells is readers,

> I would exhort you that ye would ask God, the Eternal
> Father, in the name of Christ, if these things are not
> true; and if ye shall ask with a sincere heart, with real
> intent, having faith in Christ, he will manifest the
> truth...by the power of the Holy Ghost.
> (Moroni.10:4-5)

As we saw in our second section, Smith is talking about testimony. A Latter-day Saint who has received a peaceful feeling or a burning in the heart has a sure witness by personal revelation that someone of his own species has risen to the level of godhood and truly lives as the Father of us all. Like him, his faithful sons will one day be upon their own journey of eternal progression.

In appreciation

Joseph Smith reacted against an emphasis on the transcendence of God which moves God so far away from the world of human beings that he is totally beyond our grasp. Mormons feel a deep personal kinship with their Father God. God is their father in the most literal way, and Mormons address their prayers to him with love and respect. A young female missionary asked me, "How can you pray to a God who is far away?"

The Catholic understanding of God

I am the Lord your God who brought you out of the land of Egypt…. You shall have no other gods before me. (Exodus 20:2-5)

We plunge into mystery. Any Catholic talk about God begins with this humble admission: We who live within the world of nature being believe that God is outside of nature itself. We, whose vocabulary has been formed on a tiny speck swirling around a star lost among the countless galaxies in the cosmos, can't throw a net of words which will trap God for our inspection.

We are tempted to forget this. At Mass, we recite together the Creed which expresses our belief in our God who is a Trinity of Persons: "Light from light, true God from true God, begotten, not made, one in being with the Father" The Mormon theologian James Talmage sneered when he read these words because, to a common sense hard-headed materialist, they made no sense. But Catholics realize that these words are poetry meant to describe the indescribable. We call such language "God-talk."

The puzzle of God-Talk

Catholics need to ponder what I am about to say. Mormons might find it helps understand Catholics a little better. My little brother, who married a Mormon and joined her church, agrees with Joseph Smith. *If you don't understand God, you don't understand yourself.* This is because, for Mormons, God is an exalted member of the human race and their literal father. But I agree with St. Augustine. *If you think you understand God, then the god you worship is not God.*

167

Catholics use the word *mystery* a lot. To most of us, mystery means a puzzle I can't solve. For instance, I wash three pairs of socks, but get only two and one half pairs back. Where did one sock go? It is a mystery.

But when Catholics use this word, they mean realities on the deepest level of life that we will never explain. Why? Because we live *within* those realities and cannot step away from them and view them from the outside. We encounter natural mysteries every day. A perfect example would be our minds. We cannot open up our heads and look around until we find a mind in some corner. All the different psychological schools of thought show that nobody has the final definition of mind. I was on the Internet yesterday and there was one more long article by somebody trying to figure it out. We try to make a box out of words and scientific experiments, but our mind slips past, like wind through cheese cloth.

The paradoxes we encounter in life frustrate us. When Catholics talk about the mystery of God, they tumble into paradox at its deepest level. We say that God is a spiritual reality who exists *outside* every other reality. I think of the LDS missionary who asked, "How can you pray to somebody so far away?" True enough. We say that God exists outside our universe, and outside of natural being itself. But then we say that God lives around us and within our hearts.

Catholics by the multiple millions describe this experience: Infinitely greater than the universe with its thousand billion galaxies and uncountable trillions of stars, God is as near as our deepest breath, found personally present in the beating of the humblest human heart. I explained my own experience when I discussed the idea of testimony.

We come to know the mystery of God by living *within* the mystery of God. We reach out with our minds and with our hearts. We find glimpses of God in the world he created. We come to know God when he reveals himself to us as he did in Jesus. Then we deepen that knowledge by serving, loving, and worshiping him. And so we probe God's mystery.

While praying my breviary, I came across these words from Catherine of Sienna, which are a perfect expression of what I trying to say:

> *You are a mystery as deep as the sea; the more I search, the more I find, and the more I find the more I search for you. But I can never be satisfied; what I receive will ever leave me desiring more.* --Catherine of Sienna

And so we understand that the words we use to describe the experience are poetry and metaphor. This is a disturbing thought for Americans steeped in science who imagine everything can be boiled down to natural laws and precise definitions that can be researched in a laboratory. But how does science explain why a sunset is beautiful and why love is the greatest of all gifts? Actually, poetic words give us great freedom because they are open-ended. Poetic words mean this, and this, and much more.

How Catholics talk about God

Catholics agree that no creed can ever capture or tame the unknown God. As Augustine said, "*God is more than can be uttered, and exists more profoundly than can be thought.*"[51]

---

[51]*De Trinitate*, 7.4,7.

And yet, Catholic experience has discovered at least *four ways* into the mystery of God.

The way of the mind

This is the way of so many great saints, like St. Thomas Aquinas. Using the best tools of his intellectual world, he probed the meaning of God's self-revelation, climbing the high mountains of human thought until his mind was staggered by vast landscapes still stretching over the farthest horizon. Stunned by the beauty and power of a Wisdom so much greater than his own, he could only drop to his knees and call everything he had ever written "mere straw".

The way of the heart

This is the way of saints like Francis of Assisi or St. Theresa of Lisieux. As Augustine says, the unknown God lives in the heart as Love itself. By loving we embrace God. By loving we taste God's goodness and trust in God's faithfulness.

The way of analogy

The way of analogy begins with the experiences which take place in this world. It selects concepts and images born from our daily lives and uses them to talk about God. We can do this because creation gives us a tiny glimpse of our infinite Creator.

The way of analogy follows three related steps. *The first step* builds on a similarity between our world and God's world. Thus, for instance, the fact that the prophet Hosea calls God "the Spouse of Israel." The Bible uses this expression because it helps us see that God's love for us is like a faithful husband's love for his wife.

In the second step we understand that even though there is a similarity between God and a loving spouse, there is an even greater difference. Spouses are creatures while the infinite God is their creator who called them out of nothing and holds them in the palm of his hand.

In the third step, we return to the original comparison, understand its limits, and then realize that whatever is profound and beautiful about the love and forgiveness between spouses reaches the loftiest possible level when we talk about the love between God and God's people. Theologians call these three steps a moment of affirmation, a moment of negation, and a moment of transcendence.

In the way of analogy, the Bible calls God a rock, a fortress, a hovering mother bird, a betrayed husband, a forgiving father, a mother who nourishes her child, a redeemer, a savior, and a judge. We let each image resonate within us, and God is close. Each image gives us an insight into God's presence and action in our midst and leads us to praise and adoration. But at the same time, each image fails. Once we admit that our words and images don't explain God's unexplainable mystery, we can permit them to carry us to new heights of awe and worship. As the songs say, God bears us up on eagle's wings...God holds us in the palm of his hand...God is the potter and we are the clay. These images lead us to silence and the sweet, sweet taste of God's loving presence.

The way of sacrament

The Catholic Church is a church of sacrament. I am not simply talking about the Body of Christ received in Communion or the rest of the seven sacraments. I am talking about the way earthly realities can be bridges bringing the world of God and the world of human beings together. This is what the word sacrament really means.

The way of sacrament is a powerful way to know and love God. There are so many things in an ordinary life that are bridges crossing over to God's world. For instance, I look at a sunset and praise the beauty of our Creator. Or, a young couple rejoices in the birth of their child and breathe a prayer of gratitude. Or, in a time of suffering, a woman looks at a crucifix, feels herself touched by the compassionate heart of God, and breathes a prayer of hope and trust. Or parents bring their child to be baptized. Or a person receives Holy Communion and welcomes the living Christ into his heart.

A Humble and Incomplete Summary of What Catholics Say About God

We believe in one God

The only God we know is the God who revealed himself to us as *one* to the people of the Old Testament. "Hear, O Israel: The Lord our God is one Lord; and you shall love the Lord your god with all your heart, and with all your soul, and with all you might." (Deut. 6:4-5) As a pious Jew, Jesus repeated these words as part of his morning prayer.

We believe in the Trinity

Mormons, as we have seen, are polytheists, which means they believe in countless gods. Catholics are monotheists, believing in one God. But within our Tradition, our experience with God revealed in Jesus teaches us that the one God is a trinity: *One divine nature, three divine persons*. This is a problem for modern thinkers, who envision a person as a self-existing reality separate from other self-existing realities. And so the Mormons speak of a godhead made up of three separate, unequal

172

entities they call Heavenly Father, Jesus Christ, and the Holy Ghost.

In order to help us glimpse of the meaning of the one God in three divine persons, Catholics have turned to metaphors found in nature. "God from God," the ancient Creed says, "light from light, true God from true God." As I said, the Mormon theologian James Talmage reacted to those words with contempt and frustration. But he had stumbled across God-talk and didn't know what to make of it. This poetic glimpse of the Father, the Son, and the Holy Spirit revolves around the image of light. Seething light bursts forth from the sun. We cannot explain where the sun ends and its light begins. The sun's blinding light candles the whole earth. A single sunbeam brings morning light into a room. Light is one, but three, three, but one. Thus I have a glimpse of God as Trinity, who is infinitely more than my words can ever say.

I like the metaphor seen in a perfect triangle. It is made up of three equal sides that form three equal angles that make up a single reality. Angle "A" sweeps out the entire area of the triangle, but it is not angle "B," which sweeps out the same area, or angle "C," which also sweeps out the same area. Three different but equal angles exist together within a single reality. They live *within* each other. I like this image because it helps explain a word theologians use when they talk about three persons in one God. They use the term "mutual inexistence." As one of my favorite theologians put it:

> God's relatedness to the world in creating, redeeming, and renewing suggest to the Christian mind that God's own being is somehow similarly differentiated. Not an isolated, static, ruling monarch, but a

173

relational, dynamic, tripersonal mystery of love.
(Johnson, 192)

This brings us to the explanation attributed to St. Augustine. God is Love. The Father is Love who pours all that he is into a Word of love. Love speaks Love, and we call Love Spoken, the Son. The Word that is Love Spoken contains the fullness of God, and responds to his Father with his own shout of Love. And so we have Love shared, the Holy Spirit. And from that furnace of love speaking, love spoken, and love shared, creation bursts forth.

We believe in a personal God

One of the highest moments in Old Testament revelation occurred when God revealed his name to Moses:

> *Moses said to God, "When I go to the Israelites and say to them, 'The God of your fathers has sent me to you,' if they ask me, 'What is his name?' what am I to tell them?" God replied, "I am who am." Then he added, "this is what you shall tell the Israelites: I AM sent me to you." (Ex 3:13-14)*

In the Jewish culture, people revealed their name only if they were willing to be involved in a personal relationship. The God of Jews and Christians is a God who makes himself known to us as a loving presence. God hands himself over to us. We can address God in a personal way, face to face, and ask for God's blessings.

We believe in one God, who is Lord of history

Along with creation, *Human History* is the place where God has revealed himself. God is the God of Israel because

174

God revealed himself to their forefathers during their wandering from Ur to Haran to Canaan to Egypt. Israel called itself "God's son" because it stood with Moses at the foot of Mt. Sinai and then, with God in its midst, marched on to the Promised Land. God was the Father of Israel because of God's faithful love, which means mercy and forgiveness. (Hos. 11:9, Isa. 63:16; Jer. 31:20) God was with his people through the up and down journey of their lives, and they still remembered the experience. It was in the midst of that historical journey that God revealed who he was, who his people were, and what they would be.

We believe in a God who reveals himself to us as our lives unfold

God also writes his word on the pages of our personal lives. Birth is God's welcome. The fragrant breath of a morning dawn is God opening his arms. The birth of a child is God's challenge to a young man and young woman who find themselves parents. The smile of a child or loved one is God's smile. The struggles and blessings of life are God's invitation to trust and thanksgiving.

We believe in one God, the Father of our Lord Jesus Christ

The God in whom we believe has revealed himself above all through Jesus Christ. In the New Testament, the word "Father" or "the Father" becomes *the* name for God."[52] In the Gospels, this term is used by Jesus more than 170 times. Jesus calls God "Father" whenever he is speaking about God's reign. He teaches us to pray to the Father, and say, "Thy kingdom come." Only through Jesus do we know that God is "Abba," a word that is one part child's babble and another part an expression of a deep and trusting

[52] Walter Kasper, *The God of Jesus Christ*, (Crossroad, New York, 1984) p.

relationship. The God of the Big Bang and the galaxies has drawn close to us in unconditional love.

We believe in one God, the creator of heaven and earth

The Encyclopedia of Mormonism repeatedly describes the human person as "self-subsistent." As male human beings, it is our job to "fight our way from the depths" as God the Father did, and make ourselves into gods. When we reach that goal, we will stand alone, grounded only within ourselves, depending on nobody or nothing for our continuing existence.

In contrast, a Catholic will say there is only one God and, at the unfathomable core of our deepest selves, we are *creatures*. "Creature" comes from the word "creation," and Catholics use that word with all its deepest implications. Let me repeat myself. We are fashioned by God *"ex nihilo."* From nothing. And held in His hand.

What does it mean to be created from nothing?

Creation *ex nihilo* is a religious way of saying that the cosmos and everything in it burst forth in utter mystery from the heart of God, I have explained that creation *ex nihilo* is a process that never ends. Day by day, second by second, the power of God grounds the expanding universe and anchors the inner core of the subatomic puzzle. Day by day, second by second, God calls us into life from out of the void.

When we say we are created from nothing, we admit that every particle of our being and our every deepest secret thought is rooted completely in the love and life of God and his dream for us. Our need for God is total and never stops. Grounded in God who is Love, we can face the struggles and disappointments of life with confidence. Quoting the Vatican Council, the Catechism begins with a statement no Latter-day Saint could ever make:

For if man exists, it is because God has created him through love, and through love continues to hold him in existence. He cannot live fully according to truth unless he freely acknowledges that love and entrusts himself to his creator.[53] (My emphasis)

I have already used the image of words written on a blackboard. If the blackboard should suddenly vanish, the words would be dust on the floor. We are living words written in the love of God's heart. If God should ever forget that he loves us, we would instantly be less than dust. But when we recognize this, we have no fear, because our loving God is faithful. We will live forever in a cosmic dance, bound to each other and bound to the astonishing love and mercy of God.

Catholic growth points

— Enjoy the world of nature, which reveals God as creator.

— Get up in the morning and think of your life flowing *now* from the heart of God. Look out the window and see a world bursting forth. Take a deep breath of love and gratitude.

— Look at your spouse and children, at your parents and siblings. They are living sacraments. God's presence comes to you through them, even when they are difficult to be around. When this happens,

[53] *Lumen Gentium* 8, #2

they become God's question, can you love and forgive?

— At the end of the day, imitate St. Ignatius of Loyola and ponder how God has touched your life. Think of things you have seen, people who came into your life, and things you have discovered in your thoughts, in your reading, or even things that have revealed God on something as secular as television.

— Ponder God as Trinity: *Glory be to the Father, and to the Son, and to the Holy Spirit. As it was now, and ever shall be, world without end. Amen*

11

Who is Jesus Christ?

People who enter the Visitor's Center next the Mormon temple in Salt Lake City will see a soaring statue of the risen Jesus carved in pure white marble. The sight is stunning. But the LDS Jesus is not the Catholic Jesus.

THE MORMON UNDERSTANDING OF JESUS

L ike the Protestants before them, Latter-day Saints pick through the Bible, piecing together their own version of Jesus and his relationship with his Father. But as we have discovered, they consider the gospels corrupt and incomplete. And so, for a deeper understanding, they let "modern revelation," expressed through their prophet Joseph Smith paint a final portrait of a savior and redeemer ordinary Christians will not recognize.

> *In the beginning, the head of the Gods called a council of the Gods; and they came together and concocted a plan to create the world and people it.* –Joseph Smith, Jr.

As we have seen, Jehovah, the first-born of Heavenly Father's spirit-children and the god of the Old Testament, entered the body formed by the union between Heavenly Father and Mary his daughter, and became Jesus. Jehovah-become-Jesus belongs to the "Godhead," but is a lesser god who is the literal first-born son of Heavenly Father. In the pre-existent world, he had attained "that pinnacle of intelligence which ranked him as a god, as the Lord Omnipotent."[54] But Lord Omnipotent or not, his time of probation was not finished until his resurrection, and he will forever remain inferior to Heavenly Father on the ladder of eternal progression.

Jehovah: the Volunteer Who Became the God of the Old Testament

We review the Mormon story. When Heavenly Father explained the great Plan of salvation to his spirit children, he warned them that their time of testing on earth might trap them in sin and death. Constrained by what Mormons call "the eternal Law of Justice," the only way to this trap was through an atoning bloody sacrifice. Without this sacrifice, the Law of Justice would not be served and there would be no journey toward exaltation and godhood. The noble Jehovah volunteered to die this atoning death on a cross, thus opening the door to salvation for his brothers and sisters.

The Plan began when Jehovah and Michael the Archangel "organized" the earth. Michael then became Adam, while Jehovah was appointed God of the Old Testament—the God of Adam, Abraham, Moses, and all the people of Israel. The Jehovah of the Old Testament was *not* God the Father, but his First-born Son, a lesser god with an iron fist who ruled the earth in the Father's name.

Jehovah becomes Jesus

As I have also already explained, Mormons describe Heavenly Father as a god with "body, parts, and passions." In the fullness of time, Heavenly Father came to earth and, in some way, had a child with Mary, one of his spirit-

---

[54]*Mormon Doctrine*, under "Christ," p. 129

daughters now living a mortal life. *Jehovah entered the body of the child they somehow conceived, and was born as Jesus of Nazareth.* Thus, Jehovah/Jesus was the fruit of a union between a mortal mother and an immortal father. He was Heavenly Father's "firstborn son" in premortal existence, and his "only-begotten son in the flesh"[55] in earthly existence.

Since Jehovah/Jesus was still going through his own time of testing on earth, he could have chosen to sin, but he led a perfect life, a man of compassion who taught his followers how to love and serve each other. He gathered disciples, ordained them to the Melchizedek Priesthood, and restored his church. When the time came, Jesus went to his atoning death so that the great Plan of salvation could continue.

While his body lay in the tomb, Mormons say that Jesus went as a spirit to "Spirit Paradise," where he organized an LDS-style church among the disembodied righteous spirits awaiting the reunion of their bodies and spirits. I remind the reader again: When the LDS use the term "spirit," they are still talking about material realities. On the third day, Jesus took up his body again and became the first person to be resurrected. It was only *then* that Christ himself achieved complete exaltation and a level of godhood one step less than his father. Because of his atonement, everyone born on earth–the good and bad together– will also be resurrected. For Mormons, this is part of the word "grace."

The Mormon love for Jesus

As I have emphasized, Latter-day Saints have a wonderful love for Jesus as they understand him. Their reverence for Jesus appears, for instance, in a book of

---

[55] James E. Talmage, *Jesus the Christ*, p. 104

instruction for young women called a *"Laurel Manual."* In the middle of an instruction on Jesus, the manual quotes deceased President Marion G. *Romney:*

> Only through *"Jesus Christ"* were revealed the *"gospel,"* all *"saving truths,"* *"ordinances,"* and *"covenants."* Only through him do human beings achieve *"immortality"* and *"eternal life."* All *"redemption"* and *"salvation"* come through him. All prayers to the *"Father"* are directed through him.

I have used quotation marks to remind the non-Mormon that not one of these words has a traditional Christian meaning.

It would be inaccurate to say Jesus founded the church

As we noted, the Mormon "Gospel," which includes the church, its teachings, and its authority structure, goes back to Adam, who presided over a church overseen by Jehovah from the very beginning of time. Because Jehovah became Jesus, Mormons call their church the Church of Jesus Christ.

Over the centuries, the true church, wracked at least six times by apostasy, was repeatedly taken back into heaven to await a new restoration and a new dispensation. Jesus accomplished the restoration of the church in "the fullness of times." But even that church quickly fell, and waited until Joseph Smith could restore it again in these final days.

The cross in the LDS Church

High school students who wear a cross can experience scorn from their LDS classmates. Apostle Bruce McConkie derides the display of crosses on church towers, in church buildings, or worn as jewelry for "dwelling on the personal death struggle of our Lord." The gesture called a sign of the cross is "without scriptural or divine warrant." McConkie tells us that any display of the cross is "inharmonious with the quiet spirit of worship and reverence that should attend a true Christian's remembrance of Our Lord's sufferings and death."[56] The LDS do not observe Good Friday. In fact, when I was young, at least, that day was often marked by a social celebration called the "Green and Gold Dance."

But at the same time, Latter-day Saints see the cross as the key to salvation. By offering his life in sacrifice, Jesus restored immortality and opened the door to eternal life. Saints accept their afflictions or trials as crosses sent to test their patience or virtue. They are commanded by their faith to bravely take up their crosses and follow Jesus. Below is a quote from an LDS authority describing his discovery of Jesus and the role he plays in that man's life.

> *During my early teens, a small book titled, "what would Jesus do?" came into my hands....The title has been in my mind ever since....Countless times as I have faced challenges and vexing decisions I have asked myself "what would Jesus do?"*[57]

The first chapter in that little book tells the reader that "Turning to Jesus brings strength and inner peace." The students are advised to turn to the Savior—not by the words of personal prayer directed to Jesus—but by studying his words in Scripture and by listening to "the voice within." (ie, listening for a testimony). The teacher is asked to bear her testimony about her own experience of the love of Jesus, and the fact that "each young woman can gain strength and

---

[56] Ibid., under "Cross," pp. 172-3
[57] Laurel Manual 2, pp. 2-3

peace by learning about Jesus and living as he showed her to live."[58]

Jesus Christ, our personal Lord and Savior?

The LDS have begun to use this Christian term. But their relationship with Jesus differs from the intimate relationship that exists between Jesus and a traditional Christian. Because Jesus is an organized material being living within space and time, the Saints do not believe that Christ dwells personally in the hearts of his disciples. The Doctrine and Covenants calls this a "false doctrine of the Sects." Nor do they pray to Jesus. Apostle Bruce McConkie tells his readers,

> *Prayers of the Saints are expected to conform to a prescribed standard...they should fit into the approved pattern of proper prayer. They are to be addressed to the Father; should always be made in the name of Jesus Christ....*[59] (My emphasis. See Doctrine and Covenants 14:8; 18:18-25,40; 42:3; 49:26).

If a Latter-day Saint claims a personal relationship with Jesus, it is with Jesus as a teacher or example and Jesus as the long distance mediator who keeps in touch with him through that mysterious impersonal power Mormons call the holy spirit or light of Christ. And yet a good Mormon can talk about his struggle to become ever closer to his Savior.

A Catholic understanding of Jesus

---

[58] Ibid. P. 4
[59] *Mormon Doctrine*, p. 581, under "Prayer"

The most dangerous thing we can do in this discussion is forget that we are dealing with mystery. When we use the term "mystery" to describe our experience with God, we are saying that his love and wisdom confound our best efforts at a simple explanation. We are also talking about the corresponding mystery of the human condition: our freedom, weakness, and profoundest longing. The words we use to explore mystery belong to the world of poetry. But somehow, such language can bring us deep into the heart of God. I can say this from my own experience: when we reach that point, we don't need an explanation at all.

We believe in Jesus Christ, God's only Son, our Lord

> *God has visited his people. He has fulfilled the promise he made to Abraham and his descendants. He acted far beyond all expectation–He has sent his own Beloved Son.* (Catholic Catechism, #422)

The Catholic understanding of Jesus is based on the witness of men and women who knew him face to face. Those first disciples discovered that God's love, mercy, and forgiveness had come to them in the very person of Jesus Christ. Given life in Christ by the Holy Spirit during Pentecost, the apostles went forth to proclaim this good news. Those who accepted their witness and received baptism then experienced through the power of the Holy Spirit their own personal and community relationship with Jesus Christ. They found light, inspiration, healing, love, peace, and life–beyond anything they had ever known before.

The ancient Catholic understanding of Jesus Christ was a two- step process that began in the New Testament and continues to this day.

First—They experienced God acting through Jesus and God giving himself to us through Jesus.

Second—They began to recognize God united with Jesus, and God living in Jesus, and then they discovered Jesus as the divine Word of God made human flesh. In the midst of both steps, they had to find words to explain what they were coming to understand. In the beginning, they turned to words already found in the Old Testament: Rabbi, Teacher, Prophet, Messiah. As their shared experience and understanding deepened, the Spirit-guided Christians turned to other words: Son of God, Son of Man, Lord, Savior, Redeemer. Each name carried the believer deeper and deeper into his into his encounter with God the Father through and in Jesus Christ.

Jesus (Catechism of the Catholic Church, #430-435)

In Hebrew, "Jesus" means "God saves." This was the name Mary gave her son. When we use this term, we are usually referring to the humanity of the Savior. We think of Jesus born in a stable, walking the roads of Galilee, preaching and working miracles. His compassionate human heart expresses God's love for us.

Christ (#436-440)

Taken from the Greek for oil, "Christ" means the "Messiah" in Hebrew and in English, the "Anointed One." When we say "Jesus is Christ," we confess our belief that Jesus, anointed by the Spirit, is the long awaited Messiah or Anointed One who brought about the beginning of the

Kingdom of God. Often, when we use the term "Christ," we are also referring to the divinity of the risen Savior.

The only Son of God (#441-445)

God the Father is the source of all existence, the ultimate ground of the Holy Trinity itself. The Creed tells us that the Second Person of the Trinity was "begotten, not made." This means that, in the eternal 'NOW' that has no beginning or end, God the Father pours his entire being into a single living Word of Love which is the perfect expression of his divinity, containing all that he is. This divine Word of Love spoken forever by God, has entered human history, taking upon itself a human nature. Jesus of Nazareth is the Father's Word of Love with a human face. Following the example of Jesus himself, Christians call Jesus the "Son."

Lord (#446-451)

In Catholic Bibles, the term "Lord" is used to translate the term "Yahweh" in the Old Testament, which is the name God revealed to Moses. The New Testament bears witness that the "Lord" of Moses was the God of Jesus, whom he called "Abba," or Father. The New Testament also bears witness that the ancient Church called Jesus "Lord." And so we learn that in the ancient Church, the power, honor, and glory belonging to God the Father also belonged to Jesus Christ. Jesus sent the Holy Spirit, and only God can send God. This led to the Church's teaching about the Trinity, one God in Three Divine Persons.

The Word Become Flesh (#456-463)

For us men and for our salvation he came down from heaven; by the power of the Holy Spirit, he became

incarnate of the Virgin Mary, and was made man.–
The Nicene Creed

At the split nano-second of Jesus' conception, the eternally existing person we call the Son united himself to the human nature being formed in the womb of Mary by the power of the Holy Spirit. Because of this, Catholics believe that the Second Person of the Holy Trinity now has two natures, one divine, the other human.

Why did the divine Word enter this world and join the rest of us in the toil and struggle that comes with the mere fact of our common human nature? The Catechism gives us several reasons: To teach us to call God our Father....To reveal, by his life and death, the depth of God's love for us....To reconcile us to the Father....To unite us to his humanity so that we could be adopted as sons and daughters and so share in his divinity. But I can also say this, again from my personal experience: Jesus on the cross made himself one with each of us, all of us, no matter how lost, lonely, little, or forgotten. This was the discovery that saved my faith when I was lost and broken among all the dying children in a slum in Latin America.

True God and true man,
the firstborn of a new creation (#464-470)

Catholics believe that, from the first second of its existence in the womb of Mary, the human nature of Jesus was united to the divine nature of the Son. Through his human nature, the Word became one with the human race. And so Jesus became the bridge between God and humanity. Jesus possesses the absolute fullness of divinity that can belong only to the Father's Living Word, and he also possesses the fullness of humanity. By the power of the Holy Spirit, the humanity of Jesus united to our humanity draws us into the life of the Trinity itself, and this union is the key to our salvation.

Savior and Redeemer (#599-679)

For Catholics, Jesus Christ is our Savior and Redeemer only because of his divine/human nature. To paraphrase the Catechism: As Jesus, the Son of God became one with our wounded, sinful race. While on the cross, he drank to its dregs the cup of human darkness. Lost in anguish, he cried: "My God, my God, why have you forsaken me?" Tortured and nailed, the body of Jesus of Nazareth sagged lifeless on the cross...a brutal scar, as some poet once said, slashed into the face of a darkened sky.

The sacrifice had been poured out, drained to the last bitter drop. Faithful in obedience to his Father and faithful in his love for us, Jesus laid down his life. But God's love was stronger than death. From the broken obedient heart of the God-Man, life spilled forth into our dying hearts. In his resurrection, a new creation began to spread through the earth, like flowers in the desert after the rain. Jesus lives and, through him, God pours out his powerful, healing love on people of every age, including our own.

The resurrection stands at the center of the way a Christian knows God and the world. Through the event of the resurrection, God pours forth his Spirit upon all people of faith. Filled with the Spirit, the disciple is transformed. He or she sees Jesus in a new way, feels within his or her heart the hope and love that come from the presence of the living Jesus himself, and is transformed by the gift of the Holy Spirit.

Our personal Lord and Savior

Protestants like to ask: have you accepted Jesus as your personal Lord and Savior? Catholics say this is more than a once in a lifetime decision. It is an ongoing relationship, like a marriage vow. It begins with a yes that involves new giving, again and again. Through the power of the Holy Spirit, Jesus Christ lives ever more deeply in our hearts.

Jesus Christ, Son of God, Have Mercy on me, a sinner

This is the "Jesus Prayer," one of the oldest Catholic prayers. A Catholic says this prayer like a kind of mantra, a repetition of the same simple words. The person saying this prayer learns to rest in the love and life of Jesus and is taught by the Holy Spirit to live with the heart and mind of his Savior. This awareness of Christ, fostered by prayer and meditation, reaches its high point in the reception of the Eucharist, when a person welcomes the living Jesus into his or her heart, and sits still and grateful in his presence.

Always a relationship lived within the Church

But this is not the solitary experience of an isolated individual clutching his Bible. We come closest to Christ within in the community called Church. The people of the Bible did not experience life first of all as an individual, but as part of a family, part of a community. If we are to know Jesus as they did, we have to go to that place. As Paul said, we are his Body. If we are one with him and faithful to him, we will be faithful to our brother and sister, our neighbor, the weak and powerless, the stranger, and even our enemy.

All of this is an ongoing process. We have to discover and treasure our own experience of God...the difference Jesus Christ makes...and how he is present in our lives today. To explain this mystery to ourselves, we use the ancient poetry of the past, but we also have to find words within our own culture and tradition. The process begins when we meet God and Jesus in the Church and its body of beliefs. It continues when we meet Jesus in Word and Sacrament, in the present, personally, prayerfully, and when we begin to frame our own answer his question: who do *you* say I am?

Catholic growth points

Christ loved me *first*. This is the beginning of our life in Christ. It is the thing we have to discover and accept. Some of us learned this from our parents and the experience deepened as we continued our religious education. But sooner or later, we have to make it our own truth. As I will point out in my chapter on Sacrament, we stand before the crucified Christ until a door opens, until our own eyes meet the searching eyes of Jesus Christ, the Son of God.

This is a lifelong process. Life flickers. Our discovery of Christ is the work of the Holy Spirit, and our responding love can be focused, or it can disappear. All this can happen in a single, busy day.

— Is a prayer to Jesus part of your day?
— Does the name of Jesus touch your lips and your heart every single day?
— Have you read one of the Gospels, pondering the Christ you find there?
— Do you have a crucifix in your home, above your bed, and above the bedsof your children?
— Is the Sign of the Cross a frequent, thoughtful gesture?
— Parents, do you bless your children with the Sign of the Cross?

12

Our Experience of the Holy Spirit

Mormons speak often about the Holy Spirit. This is a surprise to non-LDS people, who equate a focus on the Spirit to the emotional Pentecostal Christian churches. Post-Vatican II Catholics are learning to listen more intently to the Spirit, but, as usual, they do not share a common meaning with Latter-day Saints.

A Latter-day Saint perspective

The term "spirit"–a complicated concept

As I have taken time to point out, Mormons consider themselves materialists. But then they confuse non-Mormons by using the word spirit. They speak of spirit in a number of different ways, based mostly on latter-day revelation to Joseph Smith.

God is not a spirit in the traditional Christian sense

An official church textbook for fledgling LDS Aaronic priests tells us about Ev, a black youth who became a faithful Saint.

When Ev was about fourteen years old, he began to question some of the teachings of his church. He was especially confused by its description of God. Ev had a hard time picturing in his mind a God without body, parts, and passions, who could be everywhere at the same time and yet nowhere in particular.[60]

And so Ev left his church for the LDS belief in a god who is an exalted human being, a god who is limited by space and time.

The Doctrine and Covenants teaches that "all spirit is *matter*, but it is more fine or pure." (Doctrine and Covenants 131:78) Confused enough? What about spirit-matter or gross and refined matter? According to Joseph Smith, spirit-matter "existed before the body, can exist in the body; and will exist separate from the body...and will in the resurrection, be again united with it."[61] During life and even after the resurrection, the body (gross matter) and the spirit (refined matter) will remain two separate, if joined realities.

Good and evil spirits

Mormons tell us that good and evil spirits are "Intelligent, self-existent, organized matter...governed by eternal laws."[62] Catholic confusion continues. Spirits are "organized matter" that is somehow, at the same time, "self-existent." This means that spirit is rooted only within itself and exists forever without being rooted in anything else. In the Catholic world, "self-existence" *can only be applied to God.*

The Holy Ghost

Again, we have to pay close attention. *For Catholics,* "Holy Spirit" is the default term for the Holy Ghost. Holy

---

[60]*Priests*, Part B, official LDS publication, Salt Lake, p. 1

[61]*Teachings of Joseph Smith*, p. 207

[62]*Encyclopedia of Mormonism*, #1403

Ghost is a name for the Third Person of the Trinity that is rooted in German and old English. It is now going out of style. *For Mormons*, the Holy Ghost is the third person of the Mormon Godhead, a being completely separate from Elohim (the Father) and Jesus (the Son). According to Joseph Smith, the Holy Ghost is "God the third, the witness or Testator."[63]

McConkie tells us that the men and women of this dispensation know nothing about his origin or destiny. Smith described him as a personage of spirit, a male being without the exalted body possessed by the Father and the Son. His power and influence can be felt throughout the universe through the impersonal power of the holy spirit. Mormons teach that the Holy Ghost can be in only one place at one time. And then, confusing gentiles like myself, they talk about the "indwelling of the Holy Ghost" and the constant companionship of the Holy Ghost.

The LDS teach, as Christians do, that the Holy Ghost is the one who reveals the truth of the gospel about Jesus Christ, the sanctifier, teacher, and comforter. The Holy Ghost will lift the burdens of someone thus blessed, giving him courage, deeper faith, hope, and light. This is given only to worthy Mormons by laying-on of hands by someone with priestly authority, after baptism. If a Saint proves unworthy, he will lose the companionship of the Holy Ghost.

The holy spirit

Here, Catholics must pay special attention. For Mormons, the holy spirit is the *impersonal instrument of God's will in the universe.* Some Mormon writers have chosen not to capitalize the words holy spirit and the light of Christ,

---

[63] *Teachings of Joseph Smith*, p. 190

and I have done the same. When new converts join the LDS Church, the missionaries inform them that they have been led by the holy spirit to accept the gospel. Catholics mistakenly conclude that they have been touched by the Third Person of the Trinity. As I said, I know a man who felt that touch and decided that God himself had told him to become a Mormon. But as I have also said, that feeling can be manipulated.

The holy spirit or light of Christ is *not a person*. It *is an impersonal force or power*. The concept of the holy spirit (or light of Christ) flows by necessity from the Latter-day Saint belief that the Father, Jehovah, and Holy Ghost are beings of the human species, bound by the laws of space and time. If they are so bound, how can they be all knowing, all powerful and omnipresent, as Mormons believe? How can they hear a thousand prayers rising from a thousand hearts at the same instant from all over the world? How can they accomplish their will throughout the universe? The answer is the holy spirit. As Bruce McConkie writes, "This spirit fills the immensity of space, is in all things."[64] Through this omni-present, impersonal reality, Christ is present in and around all things.

But I repeat, it is not the *personal* presence of Christ. In an airport, a man behind the ticket desk gave me a free lesson in Mormon faith by comparing the holy spirit to electricity and the power of the Internet that was keeping simultaneous track of people all over the system. Maybe today, a Mormon might compare it to an algorithm. This impersonal force brings insight and wisdom. As McConkie tells us, "The spirit which is the light of Christ is sent to strive with men, and to give the guidance that results in the great inventions and discoveries."[65] The Saints see these

---

[64] McConkie, under "Light of Christ," p. 446

[65] Ibid. P. 753

days with all their scientific accomplishments as a special time for the outpouring of the spirit. They would also include great documents like the Declaration of Independence and the U.S. Constitution to be the result of this impersonal power of light, sent from God. I think about the Constitution and remember that it defines a black as 3/5 of a human being, thus opening the door to slavery.

Good and evil spirits, as eternal as the Mormon gods

When Mormons talk about spirits, they talk about good and evil spirits. *Both are as eternal as God*. Here, a Catholic would see a glimpse of a heresy that goes back as far as ancient Persia. There, the forces of good were in endless conflict with the forces of evil.

The essential role of Satan and the eternity of evil in Mormon thinking

When I discovered what I am about to write, it felt like a whack on the side of my head. It begins with a concept appearing in one of the books of Nephi, called the "law of opposition." Traditionally, the force pulling us toward evil is called "Satan." In the LDS perspective, Satan is an *essential* character in the story of salvation. When Satan tempted Adam and Eve, he was unwittingly performing an *essential* role. Without his temptation, the journey toward godhood would have stopped in the Garden of Eden. Without Satan's continuing temptations today, faithful LDS would not prove themselves and proceed victoriously toward celestial glory and exaltation. And so, even though the Saints despise Satan, they need him and the evil choices he offers. Christians say, "without Christ there is no salvation." Mormons seem to add, "without Satan, there is no salvation."

In the final battle after the Millennium, Satan will be defeated. But this will happen only in that scrap of the infinite cosmos under the personal control of Heavenly Father. When his sons become gods, they will rule over their own sons and daughters who live on some new planet a couple of them helped organize. When this happens, the relentless struggle between good and evil will go on. The eternal spirit of evil will inevitably stir tumult among new generations of spirit-children, and the conflict will continue, forever.

Spirit children

It is LDS doctrine that human spirits are the literal offspring of exalted parents, a Father and a Mother in Heaven. That would include you and me. Since Mormons emphasize that their Heavenly Father and his eternal companions have "body, parts, and passions" some kind of deity level sexual activity must have been involved to bring billions upon billions of spirit children into existence. In our premortal life, we had freedom and were capable of love, anger, hate, envy, knowledge, obedience, rebellion, repentance, etc. During all that time, we have undergone intellectual growth and maturation.[74] Jehovah, the Father's oldest son, reached the highest level of them all. As spirit-children of an eternal God, some of us might be billions of years old.

A spirit child's journey

When a human spirit-child made of refined matter comes to earth, he enters the body of crude matter provided by its human parents and becomes a mortal being. The body and spirit united together are called "the soul." (Doctrine and Covenants 88:15). He lives in an "embodied" state and no longer remembers life with his Heavenly Father.[75] At death, his physical body is separated from his spirit and his spirit lives in a "disembodied" state in the post-mortal spirit world. This world is split into two parts: "Spirit Paradise," where good Mormons will go, and "Spirit Prison" for everyone else. At the resurrection, spirit and body will be reunited and never separated again. Depending on the way they lived their earthly lives, they will go on to telestial glory, terrestrial glory, or celestial glory and possible exaltation.

The spirit of Truth

This title belongs to Christ, a title first given to him in preexistence by the Father when, exceeding all the efforts of his brothers, he rose to the level of godhood and became the creator of worlds. But the title also belongs to the Holy Ghost, whose mission is to guide the Saints to all truth.

A CATHOLIC PERSPECTIVE

The Holy Spirit within the life of the Trinity

Let me repeat myself. God is a mystery. I do not mean a divine puzzle, but a reality that cannot be placed in a box. Joseph Smith said that a person who cannot describe God has not found God. St. Augustine said that a person who thinks he can describe God is worshiping a false god. Catholics believe that God, the maker of an infinite universe, will always escape our efforts to catch him in a net made out of our humble words. We have to turn to poetry and metaphor, which give us a glimpse, like the flashing glimpse of a meteor. Thus: *God from God, light from light, true God from true God.* (The Nicene Creed)

Catholics believe that, in baptism, the Holy Spirit comes into the heart as "God's pure abundance, God as the overflow of love and grace."[66] By the power of the Holy Spirit, the Risen Jesus is closer to us than he ever could have been in Galilee. Each new Christian generation is as close to Jesus as the first, because the Spirit is the link between Jesus and his faithful people. The bond is so close that St. Paul can say that we are Christ's Body. And because Jesus Christ is as close as our hearts, so is his Father. In the Spirit, everything is united to Christ and returned to the Father. "It is this experience named Spirit, this conscious experience of the living relationship with God that is the center of Christian reality."[80]

The Spirit of God stoops over us in Baptism and Confirmation

Holy Chrism is the sacramental sign of the Holy Spirit. The priest makes a sign of the cross with this oil on our foreheads when we are baptized. With this simple gesture, he calls the Holy Spirit into our lives. In Confirmation, the bishop marks another sign of the cross with the Holy Chrism and prays that the Spirit will come in his fulness and bring to maturity the anointing of our baptism.

As I write this, I have to ponder my own experience. I was six years old when I was baptized and anointed with the Spirit with the rest of my family, and twelve when I received Confirmation. But it was not magic. Like any Catholic, I had to hear the witness of the Church and, in faith, discern the work of the Spirit in my life. I had to

---

[66] John J. O'Donnell, *The Mystery of the Triune God*, (Paulist Press, Mahwah, New Jersey, 1989) pp. 78-9 [80] Ibid. P. 40

consciously immerse myself in the mystery of the Spirit's love and wisdom. It involved and continues to involve prayer, meditation, and repeated moments of repentance and conversion.

There are times in my life when the Spirit moves with great power, and there are times when I heedlessly surrender to sin and the empty promises of the world, the flesh, and the Devil. As I tell my people, the experience of Spirit flickers. What calls me back to the light? Sometimes it is the voice of conscience during a time of prayer. Or something I see or read. Or a time of spiritual retreat. But just as often it is the people who attend Mass in my little parish. I cannot celebrate well with them when I am a whited sepulcher. It is time for repentance, a good confession, and a new promise of conversion.

The Holy Spirit falls on the Church

At Pentecost, Jesus, crucified and risen, became the "Spirit baptizer" and God's Spirit flowed through him into the Church. His followers attempt the same surrender and, when they live in the Spirit, they live in Christ, and God's Spirit flows through them. They are his New Creation, his Body in this world. As our insightful theologian put it:

> *The people who are the church now mediate to one another what Christ mediated to them. When this happens, they become the Body of Christ, the visible offer of God's salvific love[67]*

Moments with the Spirit

---

[67] Ibid. P. 40

200

The *Catechism* offers a number of ways in which the Holy Spirit lives within the Church:

— *In the Scriptures inspired by the Spirit*
— *In the living Tradition of the Church*
— *In the Church's Magisterium*
— *In the Liturgy, through its words and symbols*
— *In prayer*
— *In the charisms and ministries which help us serve the Church and each other*
— *In the signs of apostolic and missionary life (Evangelization)*
— *In the witness of the saints*[68]

Savoring the Spirit, a meditation

The journey of Catholic faith includes a catechism full of doctrines and a church with its Magisterium, moral rules, and liturgical rituals. But those are only stepping stones. The goal of a Spirit-guided Christian faith is to catch us up into a living relationship with God that centers on Jesus and the Father, revealed to us by the light of the Spirit. God lives within our hearts and we live within the heart of God. Above all, the Holy Spirit bonds us to Christ, and we are his Body.

We meet God's Spirit in the midst of human experience, "With all its complexities, abundance, threat, misery, and joy."[69]When we are able to look at our own face in the mirror and recognize our goodness and accept our failings, God's Breath stirs within us, helping us live with honesty and courage. When we discover the goodness and beauty of another person, we are touched by the Spirit. People in

---

[68] #688
[69] Ibid.

love can understand better God's love for the world, and his desire to heal and forgive. They are carried along in the Spirit. The Spirit is the source of what makes us unique and what draws us toward community. Wherever we see stubborn endurance, joyful delight, courageous suffering met by compassion and shared life, we are witness to the bond between the Spirit of God and the world.

History is a sacrament where the Spirit breathes over the human struggle, calling us to our destiny. In our fragmented world wracked by suffering and sin, a peaceful world is more in the future than in the present or past. But we ask, why isn't the world completely dark? Why are there lights on the horizon? Glimpses of renewal escaping the cold grip of decay? Healing undefeated by sickness? Freedom breaking the bonds of slavery? Forgiveness in the face of hatred? Peace quenching the bonfires of war? It is because the Spirit is at work.

The Holy Spirit, giver of grace

Many believe the world is about to end. Grimly, they stare into the abyss. Some hope that the heavens will open, so that God's chosen handful can be raptured away from trouble into the world of God's eternal bliss. But St. Pope John Paul II had a different view, surely based on his confidence in the hovering Spirit of God. In his mind, we are at the beginning of the third great era of the Church. He believed that, somehow, the Spirit will bring it all together again. Nobody can say how it will happen or what it will look like. But he saw a blossoming, God's Springtime still to come.

The Holy Spirit is not the private possession of the Church

Some Catholics mistakenly believe that the Holy Spirit is encountered only through the proper Church authorities in the midst of the proper Church sacraments and ceremonies. But the Spirit is Freedom, and God's living Spirit blows where God wills. The Vatican Council acknowledges this when it writes:

> Those who have not yet accepted the Gospel are related to the people of God in various ways. The Council then includes Jews, Moslems, and "those who in shadows and images seek the unknown God...These too may attain eternal salvation. Whatever of good or truth is found amongst them is considered by the Church to be...given by him who enlightens all men and women that they may at length have life."[70]

It is for this reason that I can appreciate with joy and gratitude the good people and good lives I encounter within the faithful members of the LDS Church. Whatever I might think about Joseph Smith, I admire the goodness of the Mormon members of my family, and the staunch commitment of the Mormon Church to its high ideals.

Catholic growth points

Catholics believe that Jesus is alive with us and in us through the power of the Holy Spirit.

---A prayer to the Spirit should be often on our lips. The Holy Spirit helps us as we try to live the challenge of our Baptism, which has made us sons and daughters of God. So, take a deep breath and recognize the presence of the Spirit at this very moment. Let God's fire leap into your heart.

---

[70]*Constitution on the Church #12*

---Be a witness as God's creative power draws the entire universe from the abyss of nothingness. Reach out to others with love and understand that it is the Spirit who is directing your hand.

---Find the moments in the world around you when the Holy Spirit bursts forth as a roar or a whisper. When you live your life faithfully, thank the Spirit.

---*Come, Holy Ghost, creator blest, and in our hearts take up thy rest.*

PARTFOUR

Sources of Religious Truth

Where do our religious beliefs come from? Catholics and Mormons have the same answer: They have come to us from God, by divine revelation. But what do we mean by revelation? And what are the sources of revelation? For Catholics, our religious truths come from the Bible and from Tradition. For Mormons, from the Bible and three other scriptures called the Book of Mormon, *the* Doctrine and Covenants, *and the* Pearl of Great Price. *Above all, the Mormons have a living prophet, the president of their church, who is the source of ongoing revelation.*

As we come to this point, we will contrast Mormon and Catholic views about the meaning of revelation. We will then look at the issue forming the deepest divide in Christianity itself: how do we interpret the Bible? Finally, we will ponder Tradition, and why Catholics consider it part of the story of revelation.

13

The Concept of Revelation

The LDS boast that theirs is a church built on "prophecy and revelation." Catholics would say that Christianity is founded on God's self-revelation in Christ, the gift of the Holy Spirit, apostolic witness, and a living Tradition. As usual, each church has a different understanding of what the terms mean.

A MORMON PERSPECTIVE

A prophet visited by God and groomed by

angels

Mormons take great pride in what they consider the highpoint of their faith: the existence of modern day revelation proclaimed by a living prophet who is president of their church. Through him, God reveals his mind and will for the whole church. The first and greatest of these latter-day revelators was Joseph Smith. Through Joseph Smith, God revealed his true nature and the true destiny of the human race. He spoke with the voice of Jesus himself. The living presidents who guide the church today are also considered "prophets, seers, and revelators." Their voice is considered the voice of scripture.

The LDS definition of revelation focuses on what theologians call "propositional" revelation, which means carefully phrased divine teaching or instruction about true doctrine, legal authority structure, the correct order of worship, and rules of moral conduct. Also included would be orders to members of the church to perform certain actions. We see these kinds of revelation in the formation of the LDS Church, crystalized in the Doctrine and Covenants.

The Saints find their sources of revelation in the Bible and in other books of scripture revealed to Joseph Smith which we have already listed. Revelation did not end when Smith was murdered. The *Pearl of Great Price* was not considered one of the "Standard Works," a book of scripture, until long after Smith died. But above all, revelation comes to us through the mouth of a living prophet, beginning with the prophet Joseph Smith and continuing in the current president of the LDS Church. *"Ongoing revelation"* is a key phrase in Mormon statements of belief. An example of ongoing revelation would be the command asking all Mormons to create a supply of food that would tide them over in times of catastrophe.

Revelation at every level of authority

Although only the living prophet can give revelations for the whole church, Mormons also believe that their leaders at every level may receive revelation "for the benefit of those over whom they preside."[71] Included in this list are General Authorities, stake presidents, bishops, general presidencies, and even husbands and parents. This gives Mormon leaders an unmatched authority. They are "entitled" to revelations on questions of doctrine, church policy, programs, callings, and disciplinary actions.[86]

This raises questions in the mind of a non-Mormon. How do the LDS distinguish between a revelation and a mistake? Can the LDS faithful even talk about a mistake? Do they dare challenge their authorities in any way? Or is a Saint who questions an authority doubting the expressed

[71] Ibid. #1226 [86] Ibid.

command of God himself? We will return to this question when we compare the "restored authority" in the Mormon Church to the leadership of the Catholic Church.

Personal revelation

A key aspect of Mormon belief is the notion of "*personal revelation.*" Mormons teach that after baptism and confirmation, each worthy church member has a right to the "constant companionship of the Holy Ghost." As we have noted, the "Holy Ghost," the third and lowest god within the Godhead, must be carefully distinguished from the "holy spirit," which is an impersonal force filling the universe. Faithful Mormons believe this force–like the all-present Internet–is used by the Holy Ghost to give them personal revelation in the midst of all the noise of daily life. Personal revelation helps the sincere Mormon believe the gospel his church teaches, and helps him repent, avoid evil, and grow in his faith. We have called this Testimony.

In appreciation

Joseph Smith seems to have understood that the Protestant *Scriptura Sola*, or "Scripture Alone" principle can be a source of confusion. Added to that, for Protestant literalists, the Bible contains the answer to all of life's problems. It is the task of the Christian to ponder Scripture and extract the truth he needs as he lives his life today.

Mostly, I agree. But does the Bible contain the answers to every question we will ever encounter in human life and human history? This seems quite a stretch. For instance, the Bible has nothing to say about vaccination, stem cell research, nuclear arms, toxic waste, a global economy, or global warming, because they were simply not part of the biblical world. How does a Protestant fundamentalist solve questions posed by these modern issues? If he cannot somehow mine a solution out of an ancient text, he has nothing to say.

Joseph Smith and the Latter-day Saints solved this problem by appealing to modern revelation through new scriptures and a living prophet whose words can be considered new scripture. And yet, in the eyes of this observer, LDS leaders seem reluctant to use the powers they claim. The world faces desperate questions today and it could use a little divine guidance. The one man on earth who claims prophetic power to offer such guidance has spoken only within the framework of conventional Christian morality on traditional moral problems like abortion, homosexuality, and family values. When it comes to the mega-dilemmas of our moral universe, he has chosen mostly to be silent.

A CATHOLIC PERSPECTIVE

The *Catechism of the Catholic Church* begins its Prologue with a poetic vision:

> *God...in a plan of sheer goodness freely created man to make him share in his own blessed life. For this reason, at every time and in every place, God draws close to man. He calls man to seek him, to know him, to love him with all his strength. He calls together all men, scattered and divided by sin, into the unity of his family, the Church.*[72]

---

[72]*Ibid.* #1

We have already discovered that, for Catholics, revelation is, first and foremost, *God's self-unveiling and God's gift of himself to us.*

> *Through an utterly free decision, God has revealed himself and given himself to man. This he does by revealing the mystery, his plan of loving goodness, formed from all eternity in Christ.* —CCC #50

As Vatican II Catholics understand it, revelation is not just a divine cook book containing doctrines, moral rules, and correct religious practices that must be handed down intact through two thousand years of history. *It is God coming to meet us, and our relationship of faith, hope, and love.* In the midst of this meeting, our doctrines and moral rules, our traditional way of worship, and the authority structure of our Church have unfolded under the guidance of the Holy Spirit.

Where do we encounter revelation?

Creation: A basic place for meeting God

As we have already seen, Catholics believe that creation is humanity's first glimpse of God inviting us into community and filling us with grace and justice. As St. Paul said in Romans, even the pagans should know God through the world God has made. Today, God continues to meet us through the world and cosmos around us, because creation is an ongoing process. Modern science with its great discoveries offers us deeper and deeper insight into the wisdom, power, and beauty of God.

Revelation in history: The Old Testament

The *Catechism* talks about a "divine pedagogy," a step by step process in which God shares his life, presence, and dreams for us. As we have seen, God revealed himself first in creation. Then, beginning with Abraham, revelation unfolded within the history of the Jewish people and their encounter with God. The Old Testament is the *collected faith testimony of Israel.*

But as this story unfolds, we don't expect to find a single viewpoint. The story is told by different people from different places in space and time. In those echoes from the past, we hear the story of a people of God who lived their religious lives in good season and bad. We hear the Law, the challenge of prophets, faith testimony, the poetry of prayer, moral admonition, liturgical remembrance, and religious story.

Ancient Jewish communities decided which texts authentically proclaimed their experience with God and their life as God's chosen people. Within this framework and in a secondary sense flowing from the wisdom of the Spirit, we can say that, through the experience of our Jewish ancestors, God revealed himself to us and instructed us about doctrine, worship, authority, and moral rules.

In the *midst* of this process, the Old Testament became Scripture, a store-house of revelation where new generations can encounter God for themselves. Under the light of faith and with the guidance of the Spirit, the story of an ancient people and their relationship with God intersects our own faith, our own stories and our own relationship with the God who loves, heals, and reveals. It is from this story and witness of a faith-filled people that we draw some of our key doctrines and beliefs.

Jesus: the fullness of God's revelation

For Catholics and all Christians, the self-revelation of God that gradually unfolded in the Old Testament reached its peak in the person and mission of Jesus Christ. Because Jesus is God's Word of love made flesh in a human heart, *he is the absolute fullness of God's revelation of himself.* This is the great Christian truth that scandalizes all other religious believers. A recent document from the Congregation of the Doctrine of Faith summarizes Catholic belief:

> *In the mystery of Jesus Christ, the Incarnate Son of God, who is 'the way, the truth, and the life'(Jn 14:6), the full revelation of divine truth is given. By this revelation, the deepest truth about God and the salvation of man shines forth in Christ....For this reason, Jesus perfected revelation by fulfilling it through...his words and deeds, his signs and wonders, but especially through his death and glorious resurrection...and finally with the sending of the Spirit of truth.*[73]

Jesus Christ is the *living* Word of God, and the apostles and the others who walked by his side and followed him to Jerusalem were his witnesses.

The process we discovered in the unfolding of the Old Testament was repeated. The New Testament was born out of the lives of the first disciples who met Jesus in Galilee, followed him to Jerusalem and, after his crucifixion and resurrection, met him alive with them through the power of the Holy Spirit. The New Testament was born in ancient Christian communities which, by the guiding light of the Holy Spirit, experienced Jesus as the Messiah and the Son

---

[73] Congregation for the Doctrine of the Faith, *Dominus Jesus*, August 6, 2000 # 23

of God. The New Testament includes faith testimony, moral admonition, liturgical remembrance, religious story, letters, and a kind of literature called apocalyptic.

The ancient Christian community decided that certain books were an authoritative apostolic witness to their experience of Jesus as Messiah and God's Son, and their life as the community of God's people filled with the Spirit of Christ. These books were preserved by the Church for future generations. *Thus, the New Testament witness became Scripture, something for the future generations, an authoritative source of God's truth and God's revelation.* When we read the New Testament as Scripture, the ancient story meets our faith story in a way that changes our lives and the lives of our communities.

There are no new revelations that supplements or adds to revelation in Christ

As we have emphasized, revelation is not just a list of rules and propositions dictated by God. As the Vatican Council made clear, t*he primary meaning of revelation is God's gift of himself to the world.*[74] Through Creation, through the Old and New Testaments, through Tradition which involves our long encounter with Jesus Christ the living Word of God, we find revealed God's actions, God's purposes, God's mind, God's heart.

Catholics and other Christians never forget that Jesus Christ "is the Father's one, perfect, and unsurpassable Word."[75] Because Jesus is the "full revelation of divine truth" and because Jesus sent his Holy Spirit to guide us into all truth (Jn 16:12), *nobody will ever add to what Jesus said and did.* To put it in the terms of our discussion, there will be no

---

[74]*The New Dictionary of Theology*, (The Liturgical Press, Collegeville, Minn), p. 885
[75]*Catechism # 65*

modern prophet with new revelations that add to or supplement divine revelation in Christ.

But even if Revelation is already "complete," we will never totally grasp its depth and its meaning. Over the long centuries, Catholic faith comes to a deeper and deeper understanding of the message it has received in Jesus Christ.[76] We see the fruit of this reflection in the scriptures, in the creeds, in the Eucharist and the sacraments, in the deliberations of councils, in the teaching of popes, in the teaching of bishops in their dioceses, in the work of theologians, and in the prayerful lives of ordinary Catholics. We call this Tradition, and we will discuss Tradition in a future chapter.

We also see revelation lived out in the Christ-like lives of people who were not part of the Catholic Church. For instance: It was the Quakers who saw and challenged the evil of American slavery. Karl Marx denounced the evils of predatory capitalism long before Pope Leo XIII wrote his celebrated encyclical. Protestants have helped Catholics deepen their love and respect for the Sacred Scriptures. It was Ghandi who developed the tactic of non-violence in the face of structural evil. It was Martin Luther King who challenged racism in America.

Private Revelation

Catholic history is filled with men and women who had visions, received revealed knowledge, visitations by angels, or heard the voice of God. The Church calls this "private revelation." But what they learned and the experiences they shared have no binding authority on the rest of the Church. It is not the role of private revelation to "surpass or correct" the self-giving of God that is given to us in the revelation of

---

[76] See *Catechism*, #66

Christ. To accept such messages as binding would mean a fall into a modern form of Gnosticism.[77]

Inspiration, a divine gift

Inspiration is a gift of the Spirit which enabled the ancient biblical authors to faithfully record what God revealed to them in the midst of their faith communities. For Catholics, *inspiration is a community affair.* It was within the Jewish and Christian communities that God revealed himself and his will. Behind each writer we find a glimpse of the community within which he lived, with its questions and problems. God then called men from within these communities to begin the task of writing. The faith-message those authors put on paper was a message reflecting the faith of the body of men and women whose Spirit-filled life they shared. For instance, Paul lived in a mixed Jewish-Gentile Christian community in the great cosmopolitan city of Antioch. When he went forth as a missionary to proclaim what he called "his gospel," his proclamation of the gospel to the Gentiles reflected the God experience of the community he had left behind.

Inspiration, a human reality

The people who wrote those books were human authors who used their best skills as writers to write in a human way. Human means *human.* Some sacred authors couldn't spell and some of them didn't get their facts straight. At the same time, the Holy Spirit "breathed in them," acting in them and by them, so that their message revealed God present and spoke his truth. Because the Bible was written

---

[77] Ibid. #67

in ancient Christian communities under the inspiration of the Holy Spirit, the Church can teach that God is its author.

Inspiration and the modern reader of the Bible

We have to go further. The process of inspiration is not limited to ancient writers and the communities within which they lived. When we read any part of the Bible today, the Spirit guides us in our understanding. But we will never understand the Bible correctly if we read its words in solitary isolation. A lot of people try to do this today. They scorn the need for church community. They "learn from the Holy Spirit and their private interpretation of the Word." This has turned out to be the way to chaos. I say it again: Today, more than forty-three *thousand* separate Christian church denominations claim a foundation in the Bible. For the non-Christian world, this is a scandal. A Catholic understands that, if he is to truly understand the Bible and the revelation it contains, he has to understand it within the context of the biblical tradition, with an awareness of historical, cultural, and literary context, and with an openness to the Spirit-guided teaching authority of his church.

Inspiration, the pope, and the bishops

Thanks be to God! No pope or bishop ever dared to claim the gift of revelation. They are guided by the vision fashioned by the depth of their faith, but they are hobbled by their personalities, by their vices and weaknesses, the culture within which they live, and the wounded personalities that we all possess. I immediately hear someone ask, but what about the infallibility of the pope? I will discuss that later important topic when we come to Mormon and Catholic views of authority.

Catholics need to know their Church history because Catholic foes go there to search out our mistakes, blunders, and sins. The Church has never fared well when power, wealth, and prestige are involved. Some of those mistakes continue to haunt the Church, and no apology ever seems to be enough. I think of the Galileo affair, not forgotten or forgiven after five hundred long years. When I am challenged about Galileo, I always respond, yes, but give me a modern example of the Church scorning science. But we do have a modern example of the Church as broken and sinful. I think of the sex abuse scandal and the bishops who covered it up, and the pope who never quite realized its danger. This sin will burden us for generations.

But at the same time, I think of the holiness that has always existed within the Church, even in its worst times. Our best times have come when popes are holy and humble, when bishops are holy, humble, and honest shepherds of their flock, when there is true dialogue between Church authority, theologians, religious orders, and ordinary Catholics speaking out of the experience of Christ in their lives. As I write this, one of my heroes is a bishop who sat down with members of the Lesbian community in his diocese, and simply listened.

Catholics tend to use the term "guidance of the Holy Spirit" when they are talking about the saints, mystics, prophets, and theologians who have searched deep into the meaning of Christ. Catholics do not believe that their leaders receive new revelations from God, but they do believe that, as the centuries unfold, their Spirit-led Church will follow the way of truth.

As I said somewhere, the Church answered the great questions in the order they were asked. And so, in response to the Arian heresy, the question of Jesus and his relationship to his Father was answered at Nicea. Questions about the divinity of the Spirit and the relationship between the persons of the Trinity were clarified at Constantinople and Chalcedon. Then there was the matter of grace, the reality of Jesus' presence in the Eucharist, the role of Mary, the nature of the Church and its magisterium. In this present day, the questions seem to be about social justice, the role of women, war and peace, our sexuality, and global warming.

Throughout the ages, some leaders of the Church have stumbled. This is a moral disaster, but the Church does not depend on them for its existence. The Church depends on the Holy Spirit filling the hearts of all the faithful. And so, even when greedy or lustful leaders were wreaking their own brand of havoc, great saints were standing up, faithfully leading the Church closer and closer to the heart of Christ. Fast forward to today. Some of the recent popes have been great saints. But they do not always know how to best respond to the signs of the times. I think of the difference between Pope Pius XII and Pope John XXIII. And the people they lead can be wise or foolish. We only have to look at the Catholics who take opposite sides on the same moral and political issues. The Church inhabits the tumultuous hallways of history, and the way is not always clear.

But this much is clear. No Catholic has divine permission to gallop through life without listening to the voice of the Church. Church history is deep, carrying the witness of the saints. A person who tries to live with the heart and mind of Christ can expect the Holy Spirit to come with light, strength, and understanding. But, as instructed by St. Ignatius, he must learn "the discernment of spirits," which reminds me that I cannot live without the guidance of the Church.

Catholic growth points

Again, I am seated in the pews in a huge church, part of the restless People of God. It is not a hushed and reverent place. There is a lot of movement. Someone coughs. There is the rustle of missalettes. That little girl is standing on the pew in front of me, staring at me again.

The priest half my age is at the pulpit. We stand as he reads the Gospel. This awakens all the babies in the church and they wail in chorus. I start to understand what it costs parents to bring their kids to Mass.

We sit down for the sermon. The priest is only a fair preacher. He sings many parts of the Mass and has a wonderful voice. His style is solemn, his gestures so precise they seem mechanical, he spends huge energy celebrating a magnificent liturgy with all that gold and glitter so popular with the younger clergy. He doesn't realize it, but people who are short, including most women, the kids, and me, can't see him. Unless he is at the pulpit, he is a disembodied voice.

I have come to realize that we don't have the same vision of the Liturgy. He obviously imagines himself the star player in what liturgists call a glimpse of the Heavenly Banquet. All around him, he sees the four Creatures if the Book of Revelations, along with the saints in heaven in their white robes, choirs of angels, the Lamb Who was slain, the Father, and the Holy Spirit. He is not wrong. You can find illustrations of this on some of the churches in Rome.

For me, it is Jesus Christ among the folks, especially the children. He has drawn us all to himself, and we pray together to the Father. Instead of the Heavenly Banquet, we think of Jesus on the cross. We are standing there beside John and the two Marys. When we go to Communion, we are one with his sacrifice.

I just said that for short people, our priest is a disembodied voice. All his gold-threaded vestments are not that obvious. I discovered this in the middle of these folks and it brought me down a peg or three. That is why I love the small mission parish where I served until I retired. As I also just said, it was Christ in the midst of the humble folks with their joys and struggles. Maybe I let things get too informal, but I hope they don't get too rough at the edges. When Father and I celebrate Mass, we both try to be prayerful leaders of the people according to the vision that guides us. I am pretty sure we both are right.

In front of me is that family with little kids. It took a lot of energy for their parents, especially their mom, to round them up and get them ready for Mass. The kids bounce on and off the pews, but every once in a while, mom gives them a stern look. They quickly kneel or stand on the kneelers, and put their hands together in prayer. But it is too much for that little girl, who turns around and stares at me yet again. I can't resist. I wink at her and she whirls. Then shyly, she looks at me out of the corner of her eye. Unaware of the old mischief-maker behind her, her mom purses her lips at a little brother, and pulls him beside her. Her husband has his eye on still another brother.

To my left and behind me are some teenagers who are there without their parents. They poke each other, whisper, and giggle. Should I be upset with their antics? Shall I turn around and tell them they are supposed to be listening to the sermon? I am just glad they made the effort to come to Mass, even though they are doing it on their own terms. Some priests yell at these kids. I don't. They are still making up their minds about life, about Christ, about God and his church. I imagine Jesus being patient with the teenagers in Nazareth.

I see young men and women who are alone. I wonder, who helped them form their spiritual lives? What nourishment are they finding now? There are several single parents with their kids, usually the mom. I look again at the family in front of me. If getting kids ready for Mass was difficult for those parents, think of the challenge for that single mother. To the right are several old people, stalwarts whose long lives have helped anchor this parish. They ignore the noise and movement around them, and pray. I thank God for all of them, and I ask God's blessing on everybody.

People stand for the Creed, and the babies, newly disturbed, raise another howling chorus. I hope nobody humiliates their parents by pointing to the cry room. To me, they are a sign of life. In other parishes, there is no glimpse of any baby. Maybe it is the Saturday evening Mass attended mostly by older people Priests often call this somber liturgy "a Mass of the dead." But if it is a morning Mass, those parishes really are dying.

The Offertory has begun. Ushers are making their way with a basket. The choir begins to sing. Another thing I have learned in the pews: Even a mediocre choir is a blessing and a path to deeper prayer. I don't sing after a doctor cut my throat during a tonsil operation in South America. I just let the music carry me along.

Holy, holy, holy…. The Eucharistic Prayer has begun and most people are down on their knees. After two knee replacements and skin stretched over titanium knee-caps, I stay seated, maybe to the annoyance of the person behind me. A bell rings. The priest raises the host, the cup. For a moment, there is a great silence among the people of God.

The Mass goes on. Whether we think of all the saints and angels in heaven, or simply remember the little children, Jesus is in our midst. In our own way, we all bring our lives to God, even the antsy teens to my left, who made it to Mass when they could have skipped out and gone to the mall. I pray for the single mom behind me who admonishes her middle school kids, thanking God for her faith, begging his comfort in her heart.

I have come to see my time in the pews in the middle of the folks as something holy. These are the people of God. I wish every priest would step down from the altar once in a while and take his place where I am seated. It might shake his conviction that everything revolves around him. Christ is with us in the middle of all our imperfections. This is what it looks like, down here in the pews.

14

Mormons, Catholics, and the Bible:

A study in contrasts

Both Mormons and Catholics appeal to the authority of the Bible. But do they read the Bible in the same way? Before we proceed, we need to understand that the Word of God is not at stake here. The issue is how we interpret *the Word of God. For better or for worse, the Bible has fallen into our hands without a forward or owner's manual telling us exactly how we are supposed to read it. As a result, different churches use different styles of interpretation. How we interpret the Bible forms the deepest divide in Christianity today.*

The Bible is the foundation for Christianity, but we do not interpret it the same way

The Bible finds a place of honor in any Christian home because Christians believe that the Bible contains the very Word of God and, as Christians, we heed that Word and follow it. A skeptic hearing this might sneer, "If Christian faith is based on the Word of God contained in a single book, why are there so many different kinds of Christians?" I just talked about this painful reality.

Most of the fragmented Christian churches choose a *literalist*, or *fundamentalist*, style of interpretation. They stand on a cliff and look across a void at other Christian churches which use a *contextualist* style. It is important for us understand the difference, because Mormons interpret the Bible in a literal fashion, while Catholics interpret the

Bible in a contextual fashion This contrasting style explains some of the differences between the two churches.

The literalist approach

I emphasize again that the argument is not about the Word of God itself. It is about the way we choose to *interpret* the Word of God. The literalist assumes that all I need to do is pray to the Holy Spirit and start reading. Until about two hundred years ago, all churches were "literalist."

Literalists accept the Bible as something dictated by God himself to an author who was more or less a secretary. They consider it self-evident that the first five books of the Bible were written by Moses. The rest of the Old Testament is easily open to any prayerful reader. Everything written there happened exactly the way the Bible said it did. Readers who say a prayer to the Holy Spirit will clearly understand the Bible's inspired message. A person who follows this approach has a feeling of great power, because what he finds in the Word seems to come from the mind of God himself. He is more infallible than the pope. He is listening to the Spirit and does not need to bow to some pontiff or priest. A belief is considered true if it can be reasonably connected to any verse. "It is biblical" is the final proof for any question.

At the beginning of the Reformation, Luther rejected the authority of the Church and appealed to the authority of the Bible alone, and emerging Protestants everywhere followed suit. They imagined that the great leaders of the Reformation could get together with their Bibles, read wisely, and return as a united Protestant body to the true teaching and practice of the ancient Church. But when the leaders did get together, they quickly realized that they could not agree on the meaning of important biblical texts. Luther went off with his Lutherans, Calvin went off with

224

his Calvinists, and the Anabaptists went off in a dozen different directions. To repeat: By the year 1800, there were 500 different Christian churches. By 2017, the number had increased 800 fold.

The origins of contextualism: A journey into the past

When the nineteenth century began, scholars knew little about Israel and even less about the nations mentioned in scripture, such as Egypt, Babylon, or Assyria. Most people believed that the Bible was the world's oldest book. But when archeologists started to dig through the ruins of buried cities in the ancient Middle East, the fragments of a lost world began to emerge. They examined the remains of ruined cities, roads, pieces of pottery, and artwork. They found ancient libraries containing thousands upon thousands of clay tablets and papyrus rolls covered with writing which expressed the thoughts of vanished people.

Thanks to the discovery of the Rosetta Stone, linguists began to crack the language of Egypt. The silence of the past was broken at last and the world was deluged with information about the ancient Middle East. Building on discovery after discovery, scholars started to unravel the culture of that ancient time. Pious readers of the Bible were startled to discover that the Bible was relatively new on the scene. The world's oldest book actually belonged to the people of Sumer, who had their own alphabet, expressed via wedge-shaped characters on clay tablets in Mesopotamia more than two thousand years before the Bible appeared. Egypt and its hieroglyphics were almost that old.

Citizens of a larger world

The work of the archeologists uncovered a pattern of thought and behavior much different from our own world–but similar to the world of the Bible. Historians who pondered this evidence began to see that the Jews were part of the much larger Semitic culture that surrounded them. Clay tablets from Ugarit were written in a dialect very close to ancient Hebrew. The ruins of Mari contained a library that has thrown light on prophecy in the Bible, the nature of the Israelite tribes, and the political and economic interests of the nations who collided with Israel.

In other words, Bible scholars had discovered a new tool to help them see what the Word of God meant to the *original people for whom it was written.* Since the Bible contains 72 books, it was easy for them to call it an ancient library rooted in the religious experience of Judaism and ancient Christianity. Its books reflected a span of history covering at least 2000 years. They were written at another time, in another place, in another culture, and in the midst of a history quite different from our own. Their language was Hebrew and Greek, and represented all the kinds of literature known in the ancient world at that time.

All this is summarized in one word: *Context.* If we do not understand the historical, cultural, and literary context within which the Bible was written, we might misunderstand what we are reading. We might insert our own view of reality and our own religious presumptions into the pages we are reading. People who carefully take context into consideration are called *contextualists.*

Inevitably, the frightened conservative reaction

Most of us, including myself, are conservative about new things. We are tempted to fall into a flawed thinking process which proceeds as follows: If it is new, it must be wrong. If it is wrong, it must be bad; if it is bad, it must be dangerous, and if it is dangerous, we must attack. If it is a religious issue, we attack in the name of God.

By the middle of the 19th. Century, scholars had learned how to read history and literature with a critical eye. Inevitably, they turned their attention to the Bible. The emerging science of archeology began to peel it back, like an onion. The Bible was no longer the world's most ancient book. It had many things in common with the ancient peoples of its day. Conservatives, including leaders in the Catholic Church, shuddered. Could the Bible be dismantled like one of the poems of Virgil? Surely, it would erode Christian faith. How can we ask the Spirit to render account to some chunk of a clay tablet rooted out of a crumbled ruin? When would it all end?

Frightened by the work of modern biblical scholars who pondered the similarities between the Bible and the newly discovered surrounding world, the fundamentalist churches began to appear. These churches defiantly rejected modern biblical studies and made literalism a keystone to what they called Christian faith. The literalists live on today in a number of dynamic and growing churches whose black and white religious message appeals to a large number of American Evangelicals. They often consider themselves the only real Christians.

But many accepted the contextualist approach. They saw that modern scholars were shedding bright light on obscure places in the Bible. More and more churches were convinced that a good understanding of the *history, culture,* and *literature* of the ancient Jews and their surrounding world could offer a better understanding of biblical truth, a better insight into the story of salvation, and a better grasp of faith itself.

227

We apply the contextual approach to a problem passage in the Book of Genesis

Supposing you have just read the "First Creation Story" at the beginning of the Book of Genesis. (Gen. 1:1-31) On the surface, it seems to be an historical account of God's creation of the world over the space of six days. Six days? You are in a biology class. The teacher laughs at this story and tells you that life first appeared on earth billions of years ago. You feel a cold chill. Could the Genesis story be wrong? If you are a literalist, you argue that, since the Word of God cannot possibly be mistaken, it is the scientists who are wrong. And so continues an undeclared war between science and religion. Today, this war means the end of belief for many. Sincere religious people scorn the work of science; scientists scorn religion as an outmoded delusion. Both are giving the Bible a literalist interpretation.

Putting contextualist tools to work

But is the problem with the Word of God, or with the way the literalists and their scientific opponents have chosen to interpret the Word of God? Do we *have* to take this passage literally? A good Bible commentary can help us explore the context surrounding the Creation Story.

1) Our commentary explains that the Jews were a prescientific people. The questions and answers of modern scientists simply did not occur to them. It is the same with history. When they did write "history," they wrote about it in their way, not our way.

2) Drawing from the study of biblical anthropology, our commentary tells you that the Jews were a nation of *poets*. In their mind, a story that led to

growth and faithfulness could be profoundly true, even if it didn't happen in precisely the way it was told. This way of grasping the truth is still valid in our day. If not, adults would stop reading Shakespeare and kids would stop listening to rock stars.

3) When we read the creation story, we notice the repeated refrain, "And God saw that it was good!" We wonder, "Could the creation story be a poem or even a song? Was the author telling us how creation happened or celebrating the fact that it happened? The commentary tells us that this part of Genesis was written by a priest, and that rings a bell. We take turns reading the story aloud and imagine two choirs of priests in front of the Temple, chanting a majestic song of praise and thanksgiving for God's creation.

No quarrel between science and religion

Guided by the contextual approach of modern biblical commentators, we realize that the First Creation Story has no quarrel with modern science. The ancient Jews were poets, not scientists, and some of their poetry ranks among the best the world has ever produced. We understand that, for the Jews, truth was not so much about "the facts" as it was about insight into the meaning of life and God's love for us. Thus, the First Creation story is not a blow-by-blow account of God at work making the world in six days. Instead, it is a brilliantly designed poetic drama teaching the deepest of all truths about life. It was probably sung between two choirs, with a repeated refrain. In a few short verses, it teaches us that God the creator is the center of the universe and humankind is the crown of his earthly creation. It is up to scientists to try to explain *how* the world came to be, but the Bible is telling us *why* it came to be.

Liberated from the literalist trap, we marvel at the way the contextualist style of interpretation helped us solve a serious problem. There are times when a literal interpretation of the Bible can reveal the truth in a beautiful way, but at other times, a contextual interpretation is needed to get us past difficulties that would block a true glimpse of the Word of God.

MORMONS AND THE BIBLE

Latter-day Saints say in the "Articles of Faith," "We believe the Bible to be the word of God, *insofar as it is correctly translated*." This means that even though Mormons consider the Bible scripture, they imagine it has been badly corrupted.

But Mormons do quote and interpret the Bible and, when they do, their style is literalist. We see this literalist style when Mormons talk about the nature of God. Genesis tells us that man was made in the image and likeness of God, and Exodus tells us that Moses saw God face to face. From this, the Mormons conclude that God must have the appearance of a man, and is (as we have already seen) an Exalted Being with "body, parts, and passions." Dr. Hugh Nibley tells us in one of his collected works:

> But who's to interpret (the Bible)? Do I have a right to interpret the scriptures as much as anyone else? ...The story of the last dispensation begins with the Prophet Joseph reading the scriptures very much for himself, putting the most literal interpretation on them, belonging to no church at the time, without asking for anybody's opinion. So, we do that also. As

far as official interpretation of the scripture is concerned, the Latter day Saints scoff at the idea that one must study special courses and get a special degree....[78] (My emphasis)

Nibley's words are a perfect expression of the literalist position.

CATHOLICS AND THE BIBLE

(Based on *Dei Verbum*, Vatican Council document on Divine Revelation, and on the *Catechism of the Catholic Church*, 101-133)

The Catholic Church follows the contextual approach

The Catholic Church has a great love and reverence for the Bible and we can see this respect for scripture in the words of the bishops who attended the Second Vatican Council.

> *The Church has always regarded...the scriptures, taken together with Tradition, as the supreme rule of its faith. For since they are inspired by God...they present God's own Word...and they make the voice of the Holy Spirit sound again and again....It follows*

[78] . Hugh Nibley, *Collected Works*, Vol 9, Ch.4, p.88. Taken from the LDS Collectors Library '97

that all the preaching of the Church...should be nourished and ruled by sacred scripture.[79]

The *Catechism of the Catholic Church* contains an article on divine revelation, which also includes a loving discussion of sacred scripture. The *Catechism* tells us that the Bible is the place where God the Father comes to his children so that he can talk to them heart to heart.[80] This means that the Bible is not just the place where we can prove our doctrines or find our rules of conduct. A reader of God's word is involved in a dialogue of the heart where he can come face to face with the loving God who reaches out to us through its pages.

The Word of God made human words

As I have noted, the Church reminds us that the God who reveals himself to us in the Bible speaks to us in a *human* way. Human beings are born with inescapable limits: They live within a certain era, see reality through a window provided by their particular culture, and possess a unique combination of personal strengths and weaknesses. And so the words of the Old Testament reflect the ancient world of the Jewish people. The New Testament is built on God encountering us through Jesus, and on the reflection of the ancient Church on this good news. We meet *their* questions and problems, and not necessarily our own. The Bible manifests the strengths and weaknesses of the human authors who penned its pages. The Vatican Council tells us:

[79] . *Dei Verbum*, in *The Basic Sixteen Documents, Vatican Council II*, ed. Austin Flannery, O.P., Costello Publishing Co. Northport, New York, 1995, paragraph # 22.

[80] .*Catechism of the Catholic Church*, Liguori, 1994, I:101ff. *Dei Verbum 21*

Indeed the words of God, expressed in the words of men, are in every way like human language, just as the Word of the eternal Father, when he took on himself the flesh of human weakness, became like men.[81]

When the Word of God was expressed in the human words that make up the Bible, it accepted human boundaries. It was God's Word hemmed in by the realities of Semitic culture and Middle East history and politics. It was God's Word phrased in the sparse vocabulary of the Hebrew language, and in the rich complexity of even the simplest Greek. It was God's word expressed in all the different kinds of literature present in that day.

But we do not lose track of the divine

At the same time, the Church never forgets that those fragile words contain the presence of God. She venerates Scripture as much as she venerates Jesus' living Body and Blood in the Eucharist,[82] because "the divinely revealed realities, which are contained and presented in the text of Sacred Scripture, have been written down under the inspiration of the Holy Spirit."[83]

Reading the Bible: a dialogue

As we will see a little later, the Bible is the Church's gift to the world. When we read the Bible, we become involved in a dialogue that unfolds in two parts. 1) The Vatican Council tells us that "the truth is differently presented and expressed in the various types of historical writing, in

---

[81] .*Dei Verbum* 13

[82] .*Catechism of the Catholic Church*, Article 3, I, 102

[83] .*Dei Verbum* 11

prophetical and poetical texts, and in other forms of literary expression." This means that we need to use skilled biblical commentaries written from a contextualist point of view to help us understand each book. 2) But reading the Bible is a journey of faith, not just a mental exercise with biblical commentators. We need in the end to grasp its spiritual meaning. The Church instructs us to pray to the Holy Spirit for wisdom and discernment, and to ponder the words of great spiritual writers. Only in this way can we grasp the spiritual meaning of scripture. This led to the practice of "Lectio Divina," which nourished the faith of Benedictines a thousand years ago, and continues to nourish my faith today.

Logging in on the Holy Spirit's Web Page

But how do I know I am really in tune with the Holy Spirit? Some churches ask their members to be alert to the burning in their hearts. That is good advice but it needs a word of caution. What if two readers with the same burning in their hearts manage to come to opposite conclusions about the meaning of the same passage of the Bible? Can we have two infallible interpretations of the same text? Some people say we can, and this is one of the reasons why the Biblically based churches who follow a literal interpretation have divided again and again and again.

Understanding the true meaning of scripture

Quoting the Second Vatican Council, the Catechism offers three criteria to get us past this road block.

1) Scripture must be seen as a whole which fits within the unity of God's plan, with Jesus at the center. Several key themes weave their way through the Bible. We read the

Bible best when we are aware of those themes, and when we try to keep them in mind as we read.

2) The truths we discover in the scriptures must be in harmony with themselves and with the larger context of the scriptures and Tradition. When we discover a passage that seems to clash with the larger context of the Bible or Church Tradition, it is time for us to see what a commentary has to say about the passage, or find someone who has studied the scriptures more fully than we have. It is also time for that prayer to the Holy Spirit.

3) The final authority on the meaning of the Bible resides in the teaching power of the Church. The Church has this authority because the Bible grew out of her living Tradition. (We will discuss the Bible and Tradition in another chapter). This does not mean that the bishops and the pope want to micro-manage our prayerful study of the Bible. They have formally defined the meaning of only a few key passages, and only after listening to the best wisdom offered by biblical scholars. Official Church teaching about the meaning of scripture also has to be in harmony with the whole context of scripture and Tradition. More about that in the next chapter.

Catholic Growth Points

Since the Bible was written in another time and reflects another history and culture, we need some help if we are going to read it well. Buy a children's Bible with illustrations for your small kids. My little Bible with its black and white illustration stoked my Christian imagination when I was a kid. There are wonderful Catholic Bibles for teenagers. Buy a biblical commentary. The *Collegeville Bible Commentary* for the

Old and New Testaments would be a good help. Also, consider a Catholic Study Bible with its introductions to each book and insightful footnotes.

15

Tradition

Christian fundamentalists share a basic assumption about revelation: In the beginning there was a pristine Gospel of Jesus Christ which the first disciples knew in detail. The task of the Church was to pass this gospel down intact to following generations, through all the disruptions and changes of unfolding history.

The Catholic Church has its share of fundamentalists who believe that the reality of God is nothing more than a list of frozen truths. But since Vatican II, the Church has renewed its understanding of revelation as the self-unveiling of God. This gives a new understanding to Scripture and the role played by a living Tradition. The Church is a vital organism whose dialogue with God produces change even as it is careful to preserve continuity. Christ has released the Spirit upon his Church, enabling her to stand strong in the midst of a changing and sometimes difficult history.

Out of the matrix: The Bible and the Great Tradition

When Catholics speak of revelation, they are thinking of the Word of God carried in the flowing heart of a great spiritual river many theologians call the *Great Tradition*. The river flows broadly, communicating the presence of God in the experience of creation, in the struggles of human existence, and in our encounter with other people on a deep and mysterious level. Grace surges within this river, and the possibility of universal revelation.

The Bible and Tradition are about God revealing himself

As I have noted several times, what formed the heart of the Great Tradition was not so much *what* was revealed, but *who* was revealed. We see this clearly in the *Catechism of the Catholic Church*. In a chapter entitled "God Comes to Meet Man," – The *Catechism* tells us,

> *Through an utterly free decision, God has revealed himself and given himself to man. This he does by revealing the mystery, his plan of loving goodness, formed from all eternity in Christ*[84]

Riding on the waves at the center of the first chapters of the Great Tradition were the Jewish people. Their awareness of God began as a living conversation between the One God and faith-filled wanderers in the ancient Middle East. It was a conversation that took place in history, expressed in stories about creation and covenant, slavery and freedom, told by the old to the young. Those who heard the stories discovered in their own lives that creation continued and the Sinai Covenant lived on.

As the history of the people unfolded, God revealed more and more of himself through deeds seen in faith, and through his priests and prophets. At first, the Jewish awareness of the Great Tradition was expressed in an *oral* tradition handed on by word of mouth, which was natural in a culture where most people did not know how to read. But as the Jews became a settled people with a temple and a king, writing became more and more common. The oral traditions continued, but gradually, the Great Tradition

---

[84] # 50

gave rise to a *written tradition*. Thus the Hebrew Scriptures were born.

Scripture and Tradition, a mutual dialogue

Some writers say that revelation is contained in both Scripture and Tradition, as if they were two sources existing side by side. But I am talking about Tradition giving birth to the Scriptures which, in turn, gave life to Tradition, which in turn gave life to the Scriptures. Hinting at this, the *Catechism* tells us that Scripture and Tradition are linked together in "one common source." [85]

> *Sacred Tradition and Sacred Scripture, then, are bound closely together and communicate with one another. For both of them, flowing out from the same divine wellspring, come together in some fashion to form one thing and move toward the same goal.* [86]

They are "intrinsically bound up with each other and shed life on each other"[87] in what the Vatican Council document on revelation calls "a divine pedagogy." [88]

The Old Testament

Ancient Israel decided that their Great Tradition rested on a three part witness to the experience of the living God: the *Law*, the *Prophets*, and the *Writings*.

The Law

---

[85] # 80

[86] DV 9

[87] # 53

[88] DV 2

At the core of the story are the actions of God in the midst of his people. Beginning with the Book of Genesis and ending with Second Kings, the Old Testament summarizes the beginnings of the Jewish nation, the story of the Fathers and their wanderings, hardship and deliverance, call, promise, and covenant, infidelity and repentance, hope, promise, despair, and destiny. The five books that begin this part of their written tradition are called the *Law*.

The Prophets

By retelling their story from the beginning, the Jews were able to rediscover their sense of God's presence and will. But they also possessed the writings of the *Prophets* who spoke in God's name, demanding fidelity to the Covenant made with Moses and David. Among the prophets were Isaiah, Jeremiah, and Ezechiel. Also included were "Lesser Prophets," who wrote smaller books, and then books like Joshua, Judges, and the books of Samuel and of Kings We imagine they are books of history, but they were all written within the perspective of the Book of Deuteronomy.

The Writings

Then there was a mixture of books the Jews called the *Writings*, which contain the Wisdom tradition of the Jewish people. Here, we would include the Psalms, Proverbs, Song of Songs, and Ecclesiastes. Catholics have other books which were always part of the Greek version of the Writings, such as parts of Daniel, Sirach, and Wisdom. During Jesus' own day, the Jew were debating which books belonged in the Writings.

Words of salvation

When the Romans destroyed the Temple in 67 AD, the Jews lost the central focus of their faith. But their leaders did not allow their spiritual world to perish. They turned to their scriptures, realizing that the Law, the Prophets, and the Writings were the place where readers and listeners could hear again the Word, remember their Tradition, and encounter the living God. It became the key to their survival to this day.

An accidental controversy

The Jewish rabbis limited their scriptures to words written in Hebrew. This created a problem which surfaced under Martin Luther. A Greek version of the Old Testament existed during the time of Jesus and the early Church, called the Septuagint. The Septuagint possessed books not included in the Hebrew Scripture, like the Book of Wisdom and First and Second Maccabees. When Christians began to write the New Testament, they wrote in Greek. Every time they quoted the Old Testament, they used the Greek *Septuagint* as their source. We could call it the Old Testament of the ancient Christian Church.

As time went on, the Church included the *Septuagint* and all of its books in its official Latin version of the Bible, called the *Vulgate*. During the Reformation, Martin Luther and his fellow Protestants rejected all things Roman Catholic, including the Latin *Vulgate*. They wanted to translate the Bible into their own languages, and they chose as their source for the Old Testament the Hebrew version of the scriptures, with its fewer books. That is why Catholic Bibles have more books in its Old Testament than Protestant Bibles. Luther, who did not know the story of the Septuagint, charged the Catholic Church with adding books to the Old Testament for some evil purpose. Protestants call those books the *Apocrypha*, or the fakes. By doing this, they lose track of several hundred years of Jewish and Christian history.

Tradition and the New Testament

I have an old painting which portrays St. Luke at his desk, quill pen in hand, ears tuned to heaven, ready to take divine dictation. This is a good illustration of the literalist point of view. Until the birth of modern biblical scholarship, everybody assumed that the New Testament was written during the life-span of the apostles. That would mean that the entire New Testament was written over a brief period of about thirty years. It was easy to see it as a blue-print written by the apostles themselves or by people under their direct supervision.

But modern bible scholars give us a different picture.[89] They argue for good reason that the New Testament was written over a much longer period of time, flowing from the experience of ancient Christian communities living within the Tradition fulfilled now in Christ. At first, there were only oral traditions proclaimed by Christian missionaries. The writing began with I Thessalonians somewhere around 45-50 A.D., and ended with Second Peter, written around the year 120. The first of the four gospels was the Gospel of St. Mark, probably written around the year 65, while the Gospel of St. John was written around the year 90.

Catholics attack, and then accept, the contextualist point of view

---

[89] The *New Jerome Biblical Commentary* sums up the best scholarship on this subject, but the same information appears in a much more readable fashion in many other books. I found two books particularly helpful: Raymond E. Brown's *The Church the Apostles Left Behind*, and Frederick J. Cwiekowski's *Beginnings of the Church*.

Led by St. Pope Pius X, conservative Church officials rejected modern biblical scholarship out of hand, calling it part of a vague heresy they dubbed "Modernism." The hunt was on for heretics. Seminary faculties were gutted. Scripture scholars who accepted contextualism were fired. But there is a familiar pattern that causes some faithful Catholics to grit their teeth. After hammering something to smithereens, Church authorities will reconsider, think again, and then say, "As we have always taught and believed...." And so, in 1948, Pope Pius XII officially welcomed modern biblical studies into Catholic life in his encyclical *Divino Afflante Spiritu*. During the Vatican Council, the pope and bishops solemnly embraced those studies in a document entitled *The Divine Word, a Constitution on Revelation*.

How the understanding of Tradition unfolded

In continuity with the Council, the Pontifical Biblical Commission published a document called "Instruction on the Historical Truth of the Gospels," in 1964. In Part IV, the Commission described the "three stages of Tradition by which the doctrine and life of Jesus have come to us."[90]

Stage One: This, the most ancient part of the Christian Tradition, covers only three years or less, and deals with what Jesus said and did and what the disciples heard and saw. His life, death, and resurrection was the "book" where God inscribed his name and his message. The public life of Jesus, lasting no more than three years, grounds Catholic Tradition.

Stage Two: Their hearts enlightened by the coming of the Holy Spirit, the apostles and other first generation Christians proclaimed Jesus as the Messiah and Son of God.

---

[90] Quoted in the *New Jerome Biblical Commentary*, ibid., above.

Here we see a parallel with the formation of the Old Testament. In the beginning, the proclamation was by word of mouth. But by its end, the Word was put on paper by St. Paul and other Christians whose names we don't know. This part of the Tradition covers approximately thirty years.

It is important to notice the role played by different Christian communities which received and passed on the Gospel. For instance, St. Paul found refuge in a Christian community in Antioch. This mixed Gentile/Jewish community did not ask its Gentile members to accept circumcision or observe Jewish dietary laws. When Paul wrote his epistles to the Galatians and Romans and proclaimed that we are saved through faith in the cross of Christ and not by the prescriptions of the Law, he was reflecting the faith experience of his community. Other Christian communities had a similar impact on the writing of the different books of the New Testament. For this reason, the New Testament offers a variety of perspectives on Jesus and his mission.

Stage Three: This period covers the time after the death of the apostles and lasts approximately sixty years. With the exception of the letters definitely authored by St. Paul,[91] modern biblical scholars conclude that *most* of the New Testament was written during this third stage, including the four Gospels.[92] The New Testament was thus the product of Tradition. It flowed out of the experience and testimony of the second and third Christian generations. One with the risen Christ by the power of the Holy Spirit, they passed on the faith they lived to their children.

---

[91] Bible scholars list I Thessalaonians, Galatians, Corinthians, Romans, Philippians, and Philemon as the books most probably authored by Paul.

[92] Scholars argue whether the writings of St. John belong to the Apostle John, or to the Beloved Disciple, a different person.

Stage Four: Individual books are recognized as inspired writing and are gathered into the New Testament.

We have seen that each book came from an individual church community and reflected its questions and struggles. From the very beginning, then, the Church played a role in the formation of its scriptures. The Church-born process continued. Christians copied each book by hand and sent it on to other church communities, who did the same thing. Each community began to possess small collections of books by St. Paul, the Gospels, and more. But some churches possessed other books which also claimed apostolic origin–like the Gospel of Thomas and the Epistle of Barnabas. This created a controversy. Somebody had to decide which books truly anchored their readers in the Tradition of the Apostles. Somebody had to decide which books were, or were not, the Word of God.

Who made this decision? With the exception of The Book of Revelation, none of the books claims to be the inspired word. So who recognized their divine authority? In the absence of some earth-shaking voice from on high, there was only one authority present to name the inspired books of the New Testament. That authority lived in councils of Catholic bishops, whose decisions were ratified by the Pope in Rome. Historians tell us that this process was not complete until around the year 300. Finally, it was official. The official list of inspired book numbered twenty-seven. Nourished by the New Testament, the life-giving river called Tradition flowed on.

Tradition: Continuity, but also development

The modern Catholic Church does not resemble the small house churches that gathered in Jerusalem, Antioch, and Rome, and it is folly to imagine that she should.

Between then and now, Jerusalem perished, by going from the Semitic to the Greek world, the Church crossed successfully from one cultural world to another, the Roman Empire became Christian, then split and half collapsed, barbarians invaded, Moslems surged and conquered, the Dark Ages became the Medieval world od Christendom, which faded into a world of nations and new empires, with a new world discovered, followed by civil, intellectual, and religious revolutions and wars, followed by the birth of modernity, the rise of materialistic capitalism and two world wars and on and on. In the midst of this, the Church grew, suffered, struggled, thrived, lived through great losses, and adapted to new realities. The history of the Tradition of the Church is the story of *continuity in a framework of development*. It is one of the most amazing stories ever told, one of history's few unbroken threads stretching back for two thousand tumultuous years.

How Tradition moves forward today

The *Catechism* tells us: *"Thanks to the assistance of the Holy Spirit, the understanding of both the realities and the words of the heritage of faith is able to grow in the life of the Church.*[93] This happens in three ways.

First–Like Mary, the Church "ponders these things in her heart." (Lk 2,9) Catholics immerse themselves in the prayerful study and reflection on their spiritual heritage, which is contained in the Bible, in the Liturgy, in the writings of the Church Fathers, in the deliberations of councils, etc.. As St. Gregory the Great said, the sacred Scriptures "grow with the one who reads them."[94]This is the

---

[93] #94

[94] St. Gregory the Great, *Hom. In EZ.* 1, 7, 8: PL 76, 843 D. Quoted by *Catechism* # 94

special responsibility of theologians, under the teaching authority of the Magisterium.

Second–This reflection takes place against the background of challenges presented by current history and culture. Philosophy and modern sciences such as anthropology, sociology, and psychology are used to throw light on difficult questions. The Church begins to apply the lessons of Scripture and Tradition to new problems and new situations.

Third–The Church lives in a kind of reflection/action/reflection dialogue. In the midst of this process, the Magisterium sometimes steps in to offer guidance. Occasionally, this is done by the Pope alone, through an authoritative document such as an encyclical. At other times, a congregation, such as the Congregation for the Doctrine of Faith, issues an instruction under the authority of the Pope. On very rare occasions, the Bishop of Rome and the College of Bishops join together in an ecumenical council.

The difference between (T)radition and (t)raditions

Trying to prove the existence of a great apostasy, Mormons point to such Catholic "innovations" as the Sign of the Cross, statues, relics, feasts, genuflection, and monasticism. These are lumped together with Catholic organization, the Mass and sacraments, and the doctrine of the Immaculate Conception. A Catholic would say that this confused list results from an inability to distinguish between "Tradition" and "traditions," a problem Mormons share with many poorly educated Catholics.

When Catholics talk about Tradition with a capital T, they mean the Great Tradition. At its core is the self-revelation of God in Christ through the Holy Spirit that is proclaimed in the apostolic witness. Secondarily, it means the creeds, doctrine, the liturgy, and essential rules of morality, the Magisterium...all of them steps leading us to a deeper encounter with God and with each other.

This Tradition has to be carefully distinguished from tradition with a small "t." This would include pious practices such as novenas, devotions, customs, and theological interpretations that have appeared at different times and in different places throughout Church history. We could also think of gestures like genuflection, the Sign of the Cross, folding hands at prayer, or kneeling during Mass. Other traditions would be disciplines like celibacy, living in a cloister, or wearing religious garb. All these things can help someone live Tradition with deeper fervor, but they are still part of tradition, and can be changed or even abandoned over time.

A failure to understand this is at the bottom of much inter-Catholic controversy today. Some people attach huge importance to traditions, and their loss causes great stress or even outrage. As a pastor, I have faced emotional outbursts from people, as if I were personally to blame when traditions change or disappear. But as a result, they divide the Body of Christ. In an effort to hang onto traditions, they endanger Tradition.

In Conclusion

The Latter-day Saints look at the Bible through the eyes of a literalist, and teach that God is an exalted human being, the father of two sons who became lesser gods and part of the godhead. None of this appears in the Bible. Catholics ponder the unfolding of the Old and New Testaments and tell us that the story of salvation is the story of a Triune God who gradually reveals himself and his will to a prayerful, listening, sinful, and repentant people. It is a step-by-step progression, like a child growing into an adult. In the face of new questions and new problems, the old truths can be a rock of refuge in the storm. But they can also be expressed in new ways and fashioned into a boat to ride above the most dangerous waves. Ours is a Spirit-filled Church living within the heart of Christ. Guided by the wisdom of its spiritual genetic code, the Church stands confidently at the beginning of a new millennium. Tradition marches on.

Catholic growth points

I remember something I said at the very beginning of this book. The Catholic Church I am describing might not be the Church you are experiencing. Of course. We are like an expanded family whose members live in different places at different levels. I am a senior member of the Church trying to share with others what I have come to know and understand over a lifetime. There were moments when I was scared by what I was discovering. Inside our house of faith are firmly held but different points of view, the educated and the uneducated, the fervent and the ice cold. I could dabble in a little Jung and talk about faith lived by an extravert, by an introvert, by a sensate, by an intuitive, by a thinker, by a feeler, by judgmental people and by perceptive people, these Jungian attributes stirred together to create different visions and versions of the world.

How would I describe Catholic life? In an abstract way we can say it is growth in Christ through the power of the Spirit, in a community whose leaders are also guided by the Spirit. In the concrete it means, we are talking about Catholics who live their faith in the middle of a complicated life with many distractions and temptations, celebrating Mass together, sharing prayer, sharing celebration of the sacraments, pondering the Bible, sharing faith, living that faith in the world of family, work, and play, of for better and for worse.

I put faces on the Catholics I am describing. There are the children who see their faith through the eyes of their parents. When they begin to see it through the eyes of a teenager or young adult searching for a faith of his or her own, some of them will experience a crisis of faith as they make up their minds about what values rule and guide their lives. I think of a scientific genius I knew whose religious understanding remained that of a ten year-old. I think of Catholics who live in great wealth and Catholics who live in great poverty, of Catholics in the big cities and Catholics in the sprawling countryside, and how they understand God's justice, mercy and providence.

I think of someone with a harsh father learning about God the father. I think of beleaguered adults with teenagers, everybody going through their own crisis of faith for one reason or another. I think of other Catholics for whom a twenty minute Mass with a one minute sermon is a good Mass. I think of still other Catholics who consider such a Mass an abomination. I think of pious Catholics who love silent Masses where they can focus on their rosaries. I think of other Catholics who want a lot of music and a thoughtful sermon. I think of Catholics with a good religious background and of Catholics who have no religious training to speak of. I think of students used to great liturgies led by their campus ministers who then come home to sit through a regular liturgy at the parish church. I think of the many Catholics of this era who are busy putting their political ideology ahead of the faith of the Church. For one Catholic, social justice is godless communism. For another Catholic, social justice is the concern we owe our brothers and sisters.

I pray you will experience conversion as your Catholic life goes on. I don't mean I hope you will change your religion. I mean I hope you will take personal responsibility for knowing and loving God as part of a Catholic community. This means the deliberate development of a conscious, growing Catholic life, beginning wherever and whoever you are at this moment in time.

PART FIVE

Touching God,

Touched by God

When we talk about our relationship with God, it is time to talk about the role played by grace. It is time to discuss things like worship, sacraments, sacrament meetings, and the Mass. We need to ask, What is the role of the temple in Mormon worship? What do Catholics mean by the Mass? What is the difference between the Mormon way of prayer and the Catholic way of prayer? Come Holy Spirit, God's Love, God's Light, and teach us what we need to know

16

Grace, Freedom, and Works

The Encyclopedia of Mormonism sees a close resemblance between the Catholic teaching on grace, with its teaching on the importance of works, and the LDS teaching, which also stresses works. Maybe. The Saints stress external actions called ordinances and Catholics stress external actions called the Seven Sacraments. Both see justification as a delicate balance between God's grace and the free human will. Both say that we can cooperate with grace and grow toward deeper holiness in a process that lasts a lifetime. But if there is agreement on these points, there is, as we will see, even wider disagreement.

FROM A MORMON PERSPECTIVE

The LDS starting point: The purpose of life

As one LDS author put it, "Our one great objective is really and truly to become like God in Heaven–*as perfect as God is himself.* If we fail in this purpose, we fail in life."[95](My emphasis) A small handout used by the Mormon missionaries outlines the Latter-day Saint story of salvation. It tells us that Heavenly Father's spirit children come to earth to fulfill three purposes: 1) To gain a mortal body 2) To prove themselves.3) To attain godhood.

And so life is a time of testing, a challenge to climb to the top of the highest possible hill on the path toward divinity. As spirit children standing before Heavenly Father at that

---

[95] Mark E. Petersen, *One Lord–One Faith!* (Deseret Book, 1963) p. 194

great meeting in pre-existence, we knew the risks and accepted the challenge. Those who are successful will go on to celestial glory and final exaltation as gods or eternal companions. The less successful will find lesser glories, and those who are called the "Sons of Perdition" will be banished into eternal darkness.

Mormons who live by this purpose are wonderful, godly people. I have the example of my own relatives as living proof. Even though I cannot accept Joseph Smith as God's true prophet, the sheer goodness of so many Mormons shows that they are listening to the voice of the Holy Spirit.

We are bound by Law. God himself is bound by the laws of justice and mercy

According to Joseph Smith, "Everything associated with our existence is governed by laws, which are unchanging and everlasting."[96] All reality has to obey irrevocable Eternal Laws whose existence is separate and perhaps even superior to the being of Heavenly Father himself. Among these laws are the *law of justice* and the *law of mercy*. Heavenly Father did not create those laws. They existed before him, from all eternity. He has to follow these two opposite principles, the one demanding punishment, the other offering forgiveness. This became important when we talked about the "fall" of Adam and Eve.

God's plan *depended* on the Fall of Adam and Eve

As we have already seen, the Fall "was not an accident, not an obstruction to God's plan, and not a wrong turn in the course of humanity."[97] As the *Encyclopedia of Mormonism*

---

[96] Von Harrison, Op. Cit., p. 20
[97] Ibid., #485 [113] Ibid.

puts it: "The Fall was a *necessary step* in the eternal progress of mankind and introduced the conditions that made the mission of Jesus Christ absolutely necessary for salvation."[113] (My emphasis) Following the Law of Justice, Adam's Fall brought about *pre-planned* consequences: 1) The expulsion of Adam and Eve from Paradise. 2) A fallen state characterized by weakness and unworthiness. 3) "Temporal death," which meant Adam and Eve and their posterity had to undergo the separation of the spirit body and the physical body. 4) "Spiritual death," which meant that they were shut out of God's presence.

Then it was time for the Law of Mercy. Mercy was met at the great council held between the Father and his spirit children before earthly life began. God the Father asked someone to die an atoning bloody death on the cross. As we saw in an earlier chapter, Jehovah/Jesus, his firstborn son, volunteered to make the ultimate sacrifice and save humanity from consequences of the Fall. Mormons teach that the merits of Christ's Atonement were applied retroactively and paid the price of Adam's guilt. Because he was no longer guilty, Adam's children inherited no sinful guilt. Every newborn child is completely innocent. But as soon as he reaches the age of eight and becomes capable of free choice, he begins a sinful life and needs Christ's Atonement for his personal sins. Again, the Law of Justice goes into force.

For the LDS, evil seems to be as eternal as God

We touched this in our chapter on the Holy Spirit. In LDS thinking, evil is somehow as eternal as God. As Joseph Fielding Smith, Jr., put it, "All spirits, whether they be good or evil, are eternal."[98] From eternity, good and evil exist

---

[98]*Religious Truths Defined*, op. cit., p. 67

together in a necessary relationship. Without evil and the freedom to accept or reject it, Heavenly Father himself would not have become god. Mormons call this "the law of opposition." Without the temptations of evil spirits, man's probation on earth, which depends on free choices (or agency, to use a favorite LDS term), salvation could not happen.

We already saw that Satan played an essential role in the Fall. The conclusion seems obvious. Christians say, "outside of Christ there is no salvation." Mormons seem to add, "outside of Satan, there is no salvation."

We have to prove our mettle. McConkie writes, "Opposites *mustexist*–good and evil...there must be an opposition, one *force* pulling one way and *another* pulling the other."[99] (My emphasis) This sounds like the teaching of the Zoroastrians, one of the sources of Gnosticism which endangered the ancient Church. It also sounds a bit like Manicheanism, which affected St. Augustine and led to Protestant pessimism.

Against all this background, the LDS teaching on grace

Let us make a quick summary. The merits of Christ's Atonement canceled Adam's guilt and any guilt he could have passed on to his children. But when we are old enough to use our agency, we must face the law of opposites and choose the good over evil, without any memory of our life in pre-existence to guide us. We inevitably cave in to Satan and the evil world and become sinners. This leads up to the Mormon teaching on grace.

---

[99] P. 26, under "Agency"

Unmerited grace, a free gift from God

Mormons teach that "mercy is never fully 'earned' by its recipients."[100] The *LDS Reference Encyclopedia* describes grace as a gift from God won through the atonement of Christ.[101] The *Encyclopedia* expresses the work of grace in a few concise statements: 1) By grace man is given the gift of immortality (Resurrection). Immortality is a totally unearned gift to all human beings. 2) All the other fruits of grace depend on our works, but they are larger than anything we can attain by our own power.

The question of grace and works

Resurrection, freely given to everyone through Christ's atonement, is only the first step. McConkie tells us that even those who gain resurrection and immortality "may find themselves damned in eternity."[102] Further growth depends on our use of free agency and our obedience to the laws God has given us. Further growth depends on faith and repentance. But other works are also necessary: Baptism, the laying on of hands to receive the gift of the Holy Ghost, observance of the Word of Wisdom, and the payment of tithing, to name the most obvious.

For further growth, a Saint must be willing to make the journey through the *"strait and narrow path which leads to eternal life"* He strives to fulfill the "law of justification." McConkie tells us that this includes: "'All covenants, contracts, bonds, obligations, oaths, vows, performances, connections, associations, or expectations" (D&C 132:7), in which men must abide to be saved and exalted, must be entered into and performed in righteousness so that the

---

[100] *Encyclopedia of Mormonism*, #776
[101] Op. cit., pp 158-164, under "Grace."
[102] Ibid.

holy spirit can justify the candidate for salvation."[103] A good LDS is active in the priesthood or women's auxiliary, and continues his or her efforts to repent and obey the commandments. Most important are the endowments received in the temple and marriage for time and eternity.

A Catholic could sympathize with much of this, but he would have to ask: Does a person perform acts leading to salvation by his own strength, or only with the help of God's Holy Spirit? Mormons seem to emphasize personal power and responsibility first, with grace as a final backup. The *Doctrine and Covenants* echoes Pelagius, saying that "men should do many things of their own free will...for the power is in them, wherein *they are agents unto themselves*." (D&C 58:27-28, my emphasis) In other words, we can begin our march toward salvation without the help of the Holy Spirit. But at some point, all people need help when they run into the inevitable brick wall. Mormons say that the graces God gives are given, "*After* all we can do' (2 Ne. 25:23)–that is, *in addition* to our best efforts." (My emphasis) [104]

In appreciation

As I studied the LDS sense of grace, I came across this beautiful passage:

Righteousness begins in the heart–the "broken heart." *It begins when individuals see themselves where they really are: in a fallen state, as* "unworthy creatures who are unable to elves out of their own sins. As they confront the monumental gulf between "the greatness of God and their own nothingness," their hearts break....Righteous

[103] Op. Cit., p. 408, under "Justification."
[104] Ibid.

souls then seek to become right with the Lord, by asking sincerely for forgiveness. As the Lord blesses such with his grace, they desire to respond with even greater faithfulness, love, and obedience. [105]

Beautiful as these words are, they reveal the LDS sense that we go as far as we can before finally turning with broken hearts to God.

This said, we gratefully note that LDS teaching on grace moves away from the pessimism of classic Protestantism, which views our race as totally fallen, worthy only of hell, and utterly incapable of good works of any kind. Even though the Saints view the holy spirit only as an impersonal force, they do see the spirit as universally present. I have witnessed this keen awareness of the spirit in my LDS friends and relatives, who see their pursuit of holiness as a lifelong endeavor.

FROM A CATHOLIC PERSPECTIVE

The main thing we need to learn from this discussion

For Mormons, we begin the work of salvation on our own, and only turn to God when our weaknesses turn into a brick wall. For Catholics, there are some realities that are naturally good. But without grace, we cannot make the smallest step toward salvation. *In Catholic teaching, grace is not "something" that God gives us from afar. Grace is God himself, God coming to us as creative gift, God living within us as the Breath of Love and Life. "Grace is God in Graciousness."*[106]

---

[105] #1236
[106] Dreyer, Elizabeth, *Manifestations of Grace, (Glazier, Wilmington, Del., 1990*, P. 163

If the reader can fix this one point in mind, he could set the rest of this discussion aside.

The problem of evil

Modern Catholics emphasize that we *experience* "God in graciousness" against the dark background of evil in the world and in our lives. Always, there are rumors of war. Children do die of sickness and hunger. Marriages and priestly vows do end in broken promises. When we are honest, we have to admit our moral weakness despite our best intentions and we have to confess the personal sins which we inflict on others. Just outside the door lurks the spirit of lust, greed, ambition, or violence.

But, in the midst of a world gone cold, there is also the experience of warmth and life spelled out in the ordinary lives of ordinary people. Hate is healed by mercy, revenge, by forgiveness, selfishness by unexpected generosity. This is done only with the support of grace. In the end, a Catholic will point to the Holy Spirit. It is the Spirit who brings God's love into our hearts and into the world. Within us by the power of the Spirit, he *is* God's grace poured into our hearts and present in all of human history. Within ourselves, maybe before we can even name the experience, the Spirit lifts us up on the road to salvation.

The Catholic understanding of the role of moral law

In LDS thought, Law seems to have an existence of its own, separate from the existence of God. But in Catholic thought, God is the source of all reality. It follows, therefore, that God is the source of moral law and obligation in our world. In the Old Testament, law flows from the covenant between God and his people at Mt. Sinai. The various laws appearing in the Torah express the relationship between

God and Israel. Yahweh has committed himself to the people, and the people have committed themselves to their God. Laws are not abstract, pre-existing realities, but the expression of the intimacy between God and an obedient people.

In the New Testament, Jesus gave us two commandments which flow from our relationship with God in the Holy Spirit. We must love God, and we love God by loving our neighbor as ourselves. Augustine summarized the New Law of Christ in a few brilliant strokes: "Love God and do what you will." [107]

In Romans, St. Paul stressed that we are not saved by some eternal law imposing itself upon us from without. For St. Paul, Law is the result of an intimate communion "between the heart of a loving God and the heart of the believing human person."[124] It is the living Spirit of God who moves us onto the spiritual path, and the Spirit who writes the New Law of Christ within our deepest selves. This Law of the Spirit is the living presence of God's very Self dwelling within us.

Modern Catholic theologians emphasize that there is no such thing as a distant God who reaches out to us through some impersonal power. God is totally present wherever God acts. Grace is God's gift of himself to us in love, healing, and forgiveness. God offers himself in grace to "every person at every period of history."[108]Catholics would agree with Mormons that the gift of freedom is crucial. But it is not a choice between two already existing realities: Good and evil. In freedom, we choose the good, God's love. It is only when God's love is rejected that evil comes into existence. From this point of view, history is a

[107] Timothy E. O'Connell, *Principles for a Catholic Morality*, (Seabury Press, Minneapolis, 1978) p. 1340-1 [124] Ibid.
[108] Haight, p. 150

dialogue in which God speaks to us with love. We find God's gift of himself in our lives and in our experience, and we freely respond to his call.

Following the Vatican II *Constitution on the Church*, theologians speak of a universal revelation in which all men and women are given a glimpse of the graceful presence of God in the world in which they live, even if they do not know how to call God by name. Because of universal revelation, there is universal grace. Anyone who responds can come to God's kingdom, and the world has a destiny whose possibilities we are only beginning to discover.

What the gracious God accomplishes in us

—Forgiveness

We stand broken before the goodness of God. There is a great barrier in our hearts which blocks us from receiving the fullness of life. For this reason, Christ and his grace are deeply connected to forgiveness. He came to call sinners and taught us to say "Forgive us our trespasses." It is basic to the Gospel to say that Mercy forgives. All the great theologies of grace stress this theme.

—Healing

Why, St. Paul asks, do I do what I don't want to do, and don't do what I want to do? We all suffer the deadly wound of pride, selfishness and spiritual laziness. Our freedom is chained by this wound; we are unable to give ourselves to God or each other. Unless this wound is healed, we cannot even begin the journey to holiness. The God who loves us first comes into our lives to cure this sickness and give us a strength to reach beyond our strength from the beginning to the end of the journey.

—A share in God's own life

In the language of St. Thomas Aquinas, through Christ in the Spirit, God gives us a share in his own nature. Is this just a metaphor? Those who have experienced the presence of God in grace describe "being elevated by contact and union with God through his love."[109] Quoting the Vatican Council, the *Catechism* tells us:

> *Of all visible creatures only man is "able to know and love his creator." He is "the only creature on earth that God has willed for his own sake," and he alone is called to share, by knowledge and love, in God's own life.*[110]

The New Testament uses images like "rebirth," "new being," or "sons of God." These expressions describe a life different from a life untouched by God's presence in grace.

—Freedom and responsibility

To sin is to experience what it means to be hemmed in. Over and over again, this biblical image is used to describe the experience of sin. Our sin traps us...we cannot say yes or no... the world frightens and overpowers us. But, as one psalm after another proclaims, "God intervened and I was free." From the Book of Exodus to the story of Christ's death and resurrection, the theme is the discovery of freedom. It takes the gracious presence of a loving God to bring such freedom into our hearts and lives.

With the gift of freedom comes the gift of responsibility. The freedom we receive is the freedom of a clear running stream flowing within boundaries. If freedom crosses those

---

[109] Ibid., p. 153
[110] CCC #356

boundaries, it is like a river in flood that has broken its banks only to bring destruction and death. In our sinfulness, we refuse to live within the boundaries of love and use everything and everyone for ourselves. We are so self-centered that it is impossible for us to reach toward real love and real life. Our habits bind us, our inner weakness and turmoil paralyze us. In Grace, God's favor, kindness, mercy and love sets us free despite our stubborn sinfulness. One with Christ, we begin to live our life in a new way.

—Grace, freedom, and law

God-come-in-grace does not destroy our freedom. God sets us free to reach to new horizons, not with mere human strength, but with his own. God gives us the power to delight in the good, to rejoice in the true, to revel in the beautiful. In response to the Mormon teaching that all things are bound by law, a Catholic would agree with St. Paul that a person touched by God's grace is free from every law. Laws are external forces, but the Christian in the Spirit has begun to live with God's own inner law, which is the law of love.

—Freedom from death

Because of sin, death becomes a terrifying fall into a dark abyss. Through the death and resurrection of Christ, death loses its sting. "To the extent that one is grasped by God's grace and surrenders to it, in the same measure can death be met with peace."[111] It is no longer an experience of un-nameable horror, but the door through which we go with God into the face to face experience of God. I was present when my brother died of cancer. His eyes opened wide at a

---

[111] Haight, p. 153

Presence. He didn't die. He left. Now, I am not so afraid of death.

—Freedom for God and his will

Things have changed at warp speed through the last half of my lifetime. No age in history has emphasized freedom like our modern age. We are free from rules, from limits, from authority. There is this huge emphasis on self-defined individual rights. It seems to be taken for granted that everything and everybody must give way to one individual taking a stand in principle for something we weren't even thinking about thirty years ago. I think of the current transgender revolution. Ten years ago, there were only four clinics that helped people undergo surgery to "confirm" their gender choice. Now there are thousands, with many catering especially to children.

But when does a claim to individual rights go past responsibility to my true self and the common good? When is my choice for some right actually a kind of pathology? This is not an unreasonable question. Think again about a river outside its banks. Freedom that has no limits becomes chaos.

We forget that real freedom involves not only liberation *from*, but also liberation *for*. In this freedom, we make ourselves one with God who is our source, the One who sustains us in every millisecond of our lives. To imagine that freedom means freedom from God and his purposes would be nonsense. We would be like words that choose to fall off the page that holds them in place. Real freedom involves surrendering ourselves to God's purpose in our lives.

The Church is in the middle of a difficult moment that is costing her dearly, especially among our youth who buy into the idea of unbound freedom proclaimed in modern culture. When the Church opposes or questions or wonders, she is called intolerant. In my mind, what we are looking for is the best point of view from which to ponder the challenges we face. The Church thinks and acts within ancient intellectual structures that helped found Western Civilization. It is not so easy to simply set them aside. I have my own strong opinions, and I pray for grace and patience. One question looms large that should be asked by everyone standing up for the infallibility of his choice: What if I am wrong?

—Liberation for the world and its history

This part of the theology of grace is being written today. We understand that grace is not simply a matter of our individual salvation. God-come-as-grace sets us free so that we can serve the world and its history. We are not hoping that the world and its troubled history will come quickly to an end. Wiser now because of the experiences of the last century, we realize that history might only be at its turning point. As we noted in our previous chapter, this was surely the vision of Saint Pope John Paul when we entered the twenty-first century. He divided Christian history into three parts, and placed us at the beginning of the third climactic era.

In every era, powerful men try to construct a worldly paradise by their own wisdom and strength. The result is often war and great suffering. This colossal pretense continues. Christians have come to see that God calls us to unite with Christ in the search of real freedom and real community. Without grace, which is another word for the Spirit of Christ alive in our lives, there isn't even a beginning.

Catholic growth points

Protestants follow a gloomy teaching of St. Augustine to the letter, and believe that we cannot do a single good thing without the grace of God. In contrast, Catholics teach that there is natural good in this world. But when it comes to salvation, we get nowhere without grace and the urging of the Spirit. So, ponder the reality of what Catholics call "actual grace," in which God moves us toward prudence, justice, fortitude, kindness, forgiveness, goodness, and justice. When these virtues operate in our lives, Grace is at work. Then, ponder Sanctifying Grace, a new nature that makes us alive in Christ, sustained by faith, hope, and love.

17

Ways of Prayer

There is this old Latin expression: Lex orandi, lex credendi—The way you pray expresses the way you believe. Catholics and Latter-day Saints come to prayer guided by their presuppositions about God, the meaning of Jesus, our human nature, and our eternal destiny. These beliefs will direct each individual in their prayer.

FROM AN LDS PERSPECTIVE

I wish I had an LDS friend who would write a chapter on the role of prayer in his life. As I begin this chapter, I feel quite inadequate. My kind and gracious LDS relatives strike me as people who are nourished by prayer. But even though I am sure that good Saints find prayer to be a peaceful and rewarding experience, LDS writers have little to say about the subject. For instance, in his book *Religious Truths Defined*, President Joseph Fielding Smith covers the breadth of LDS belief, but prayer is given a bare two pages. The Encyclopedia of Mormonism article on prayer is equally brief. When LDS spokesmen do speak of prayer, they often repeat word for word the same handful of thoughts based on the Doctrine and Covenants.

The grounding beliefs

All prayer is grounded in fundamental beliefs. For the LDS, Heavenly Father is a literal parent who lives far away, contacting us in a way one LDS president compared to a transatlantic telegraph message. Our long distance relationship with Heavenly Father resembles the relationship between an Old Testament patriarch and his son or daughter. The Father demands in love the absolute obedience of his child. If a child obeys, his reward is certain. If he disobeys, his punishment is equally certain. The Father wants self-reliant children who develop the inner resources to become gods or high priestesses in their own right. As one writer put it,

> We were "placed upon this earth to walk alone through many experiences.... Heavenly Father will not go through these experiences for us. But he is available to guide us and strengthen us as we walk through these growth experiences. We should stay close to him for guidance and advice."[112] (My emphasis)

If you pray, follow the correct pattern

Even though they mention other forms of prayer, Latter-day Saints seem to emphasize what Catholics call prayers of petition. Their prayers have to follow a definite required form if they hope to be heard by their god in his mansion beside the great star Kolob, whose location is unknown to any astronomer. In *Mormon Doctrine*, Apostle Bruce McConkie tells his reader that a Mormon must pray "in faith according to an *approved pattern* so that actual blessings may be gained from the deity."[113]

---

[112] James B. Cox, *How to Qualify for the Celestial Kingdom Today*, (Ensign Publishing, Riverton, Utah, 1984), p. 96

[113] Op. cit., p. 583, under "Prayer."

When a Saint prays according to the proper procedure, he kneels and crosses his arms.[114] His prayer is addressed to the Father in the name of Jesus Christ. As we have noted several times, Latter-day Saints *never* pray to Jesus or the Holy Ghost. They use a very specific language of prayer, such as the pronouns thee and thine instead of you and yours. Their prayer may include expressions of praise, thanksgiving, and adoration, but their chief purpose is to ask Heavenly Father for advice and blessings. They are admonished not to repeat the name of God or Jesus Christ too often in the course of prayer. Every proper prayer ends with the word Amen.

McConkie writes that prayers are divided into public and private prayers. He lays great stress on family prayer in the morning and before the evening meal. Both public and private prayers should be short and should be spoken directly from the heart. Quoting President Francis M. Lyman, he stresses that *"Prayers should be offered under the direction and inspiration of the Almighty. Every elder in Israel should learn to subject himself to the Spirit of the Lord in all his prayers."*[132]

The tough love school of preparation for godhood

One LDS author seems to say that, if he is confident that we are making good progress on the right path, Heavenly Father will choose to let us walk alone. After all, God expects us to use our agency and to strive by our own power. If we do not become skilled at the use of our own power, we will not become gods. But Heavenly Father will intervene if he feels we need his help. The best thing we can do is "check with heaven in all things as we perform to the

[114] Folding the arms seems to date to the 1940's, but Mormon writers are unable to say why this pattern appeared. [132] Ibid. P. 581-3

best of our abilities." [115] This will prepare us to receive needed revelation through the Holy Ghost.

Revelation: an answer to prayer

Non-Mormons often fail to appreciate the LDS confidence that they are constantly guided by revelation, even on mundane things. But in order to receive needed revelation, a Saint must meet certain criteria. He must rise to a level of faith that knows no doubts...he must love God and all men...and he must qualify for the companionship of the Holy Ghost by prayer, righteous living, and study of the gospel. A Mormon is told, "Use the above as a checklist to see if you are prepared to receive revelation. If not, then you must prepare yourself so that you may enjoy that gift." [116]

Hearing an answer to prayer

And so a faithful Saint who has made the necessary spiritual preparation is confident that God will bless his prayer with a revelation. When they pray about a decision, Mormons ask for a confirmation (D&C 9:8-9). This is a revelation which is recognized as a "burning in the bosom." In other words, a testimony. President Marion G. Romney once told the faithful:

> Study your problems, and prayerfully make a decision. Then take that decision and say to the Lord, in simple, honest supplication, "Father, I want to make the right decision. I want to do the right thing. This is what I think I should do; let me know if it is the right course." Doing this, you can get the burning in your bosom, if your decision is right. If you do not

---

[115] James B. Cox, op. cit., p. 96
[116] Quoted by Cox, pp. 98-99

get the burning, then change your decision and submit a new one.[117](My emphasis)

Devout LDS live in the awareness of the holy spirit, that impersonal energy between them and God. They also believe they have been given the companionship of the Holy Ghost, the third and lowest figure in the godhead. Because of this, they serenely believe they have a perfect knowledge of the difference between good and evil. According to the Doctrine and Covenants, they will receive the answer to pray in their mind and in their heart. The revelation will appear as a warm sensation within the breast...a "flow of intelligence" in their minds leading to the answer to prayer. The revelation thus received will enlighten the understanding and enlarge the soul.[118] But if a decision brought to prayer is wrong, then none of this will happen. A person will receive what the Doctrine and Covenants calls "a stupor of thought," which D&C 9:9 says will cause a person to become disinterested in the decision he brought to the Lord.

But what if there is no answer, no revelation? One author suggests that "only yearning prayer gets through" to God. What is yearning prayer? We yearn when we mean and care intensely, and at the core, are as anxious to listen as to ask.[119] Another author suggests:

— We should check to see if our request is appropriate.
— We should evaluate whether our faith is sufficient to expect an answer.

---

[117] Marion C. Romney, "How to Improve My Communications With the Lord," *Improvement Era*, April, 1966, p. 275.

[118] Cox, p. 102

[119] Truman G. Madsen, *Christ and the Inner Life*, (Bookcraft, Salt Lake City, 1978) p. 15

— Do we feel good about ourselves, Heavenly Father, and others?

— Have we followed the formula of prayer–made a decision, sought for help, then done all we could?

— If the time is short and we have done all things to receive revelation, then Heavenly Father is allowing us to act on our own.[120]

In appreciation

I can express my appreciation best by calling attention to the good Latter-day Saints in my life, beginning with my brother. He takes deeply to heart the belief that his faith is one of "prophecy and revelation," to quote his own words. A conversation with a devout Mormon is to hear repeated expressions of trust in the power of the holy spirit. Latter-day Saints, led by prayer, are honest and self-sacrificing people who are concerned with the troubles and struggles of others in this world. Non-Mormons are challenged by such an example to ponder their own relationship with God and their own life of prayer.

FROM A CATHOLIC PERSPECTIVE

For me, prayer is a surge of the heart; it is a simple look turned toward God, it is a cry of recognition and of love, embracing both trial and joy.–St. Therese of Lisieux

Basic beliefs grounding the Catholic understanding of prayer

---

[120] Cox, op. cit., p. 103

Catholic books on prayer would fill a large library, because the prayer of a Catholic is a profound and dynamic experience that can be explored from many directions.

First, guided by Catholic teaching on grace, Catholics understand that they cannot even begin to pray without the sustaining, life-giving, personal presence of the Holy Spirit.

Second, Catholics emphasize that we are *not* the ones who begin the conversation. Always, God speaks to us first. In a sermon on the story of the woman at the well in the Gospel of St. John, Augustine said,

> *It is Christ who first seeks us and asks us for a drink. Jesus thirsts; his asking arises from the depths of God's desire for us. Whether we realize it or not, prayer is the encounter of God's thirst with ours. God thirsts that we may thirst for him.*[121]

The Samaritan woman was startled, even alarmed, when Jesus approached her, because of the barrier between Jews and Samaritans. But Jesus broke that barrier. And God breaks the barriers that keep us from knowing and loving him, if only we will hear him and open our hearts. .

Third, Catholic prayer assumes the intimate presence of the Trinity dwelling within our deepest core. Catholics believe that the Triune God is totally present wherever God acts. And so, when we pray, we are lifted by the Spirit. When we pray, Jesus living within us through the power of the Spirit, intercedes for us. When we pray, the Father, as the source of all that is, pours his life and love into our hearts.

Fourth, prayer is not just about asking for things. In the highest form of prayer, a Catholic sits still in God's loving embrace. Because the Holy Spirit abides within us, the

---

[121]*Sermo* 56, 6, 9 PL 38, 381

living God is closer to us than the beat of our own hearts. "Prayer is the living relationship of the children of God with their Father... with his Son Jesus Christ... and with the Holy Spirit."[122] I will always remember an old mountain mystic brought to town by Health and Welfare after her husband the gold-miner died of a heart attack. I visited her in her tiny room. She was in bed, watching me through thick eyeglasses. "Mrs. Sloan," I asked, "Do you pray?" She chuckled. "Oh, Father, God is just folks." I suddenly realized I was in the presence of a spiritual master. "What do you do?" I finally asked. "I look at him and he looks at me."

In the Catholic Catechism (#2558-2758)

In its section on Christian prayer, the Catechism offers a profound summary of the role prayer plays in Catholic life. The Catechism describes prayer as God's gift, a covenant, and communion.

Prayer is a gift. As we just said, we don't begin the relationship. Christ comes looking for us, bearing the gift of his love. We have only to hold out our hands and respond with love of our own. But even this response is a gift from God in the Spirit, welling up from within the deepest depths of our hearts, carried on the Breath. We are like swimmers floating on a crystal lagoon. We propel ourselves forward, but only because the water supports us.

Prayer is a covenant. It is a meeting with God in the deepest corners of the heart. It is the receiving and offering of life. The heart is our hidden center and from that place of truest freedom our lives flow outward into the world. It is in the heart that we are touched by the Spirit, filled with

---

[122] St. Gregory of Naziansus, *Oratio*, 16, 9: PG 35, 945

Christ, and receive life from the Father. It is from the heart that we respond and try to live as God's children.

Prayer is communion between the children of God with their Father, with his Son Jesus Christ, and with the Holy Spirit. Through his baptism, a Catholic is one with Christ. As his prayer life deepens, he enters the depths of the Trinity. God is the reality that surrounds him and the life that fills him. This oneness with God extends throughout the whole church whenever it is at prayer, especially in the Eucharist.

Is there a divine command telling us about our language and posture during prayer?

As far as individual prayer is concerned, there are no specific instructions. In the beginning, Christians prayed standing, with their arms held out. We see this posture of prayer today, in particular when the priest is praying at Mass. For some Catholics, kneeling is the only way to pray. But others pray while they walk or work. There is no specific language of prayer, such as the obligatory use of "thee" or "thou." Personal prayer is from the heart, and each Catholic uses his or her own heart language when addressing God.

We are all called to prayer

As our lives unfold, God gradually reveals himself. We begin to understand who we are and how God is present as Father, Son, and Holy Spirit. Prayer rises from this experience of mutual discovery. Itprompts the need for conversion in our lives, and begins the struggle to convert an unjust society. The dramatic unfolding exchange between God and the human race captures the story of the history of salvation.

Prayer begins at creation

From the Catholic viewpoint, prayer begins with creation. The arching heavens and the living earth are the place where God speaks to us first in wisdom and power. In the Genesis story of God's covenant with Noah, we find the sign of covenant in the rainbow in the sky. Our response, rising up in the Spirit, is a prayer of praise and thanksgiving.

Prayer in the Old Testament

The Old Testament is a journal of God's speaking and the human response. It begins with the call of Abraham, who watched a blazing torch move between sacrificial offerings, and then made covenant with God. It continues through Moses, David, and the prophets. So much did the Jews become people of prayer that an entire book–the Book of Psalms–is filled with their words of praise, gratitude, sorrow, and hope.

The prayer of Jesus

In the fullness of time, Jesus came. The *Catechism* tells us that, in the Jewish style, he learned to his first words of prayer from his mother. As a Jew, he prayed "in the words and rhythms of the prayer of his people, in the synagogue at Nazareth and the Temple in Jerusalem."[123] But his prayer burst forth from a deeper source. Through his divine nature, Christ is the living Word flowing from the Father's boundless heart. From all eternity, *Love speaking* thunders forth an infinite cry of love. From all eternity, *Love Spoken* shouts back its own ecstatic word of love. From all eternity, Love Speaking and Love Responding become *Love Shared*.

---

[123] #2599

They are bound together into one divine life by the Creative Spirit they give and receive together. The give and response of prayer is at the very heart of the Trinity.

Again and again, the gospels show Jesus at prayer: before his baptism and transfiguration...before his election of the Twelve and their mission...and before his passion and death. His prayers were often made in solitude. They confessed and blessed the Father, and surrendered to his will. They expressed thanksgiving and petition, trust and acceptance.

Jesus taught us how to pray. He insisted on conversion and purity of heart... reconciliation with one's brother...forgiveness from the depth of the heart...prayer for enemies and persecutors... prayer directed to the Father. Jesus told us to ask the Father in his name, because he is the way, the truth, and the life, our only mediator.

Prayer within the Church

In a beautiful passage, the *Catechism* repeats its basic teaching about prayer, Christ, and the Holy Spirit:

> *The Holy Spirit is the living water "welling up to eternal life" in the heart that prays. It is he who teaches us to accept it at its source: Christ. Indeed in the Christian life there are several wellsprings where Christ awaits us to enable us to drink of the Holy Spirit.* [124]

Enlightened by the Holy Spirit, Catholic prayer flows from Scripture, the Liturgy of the Church, the virtues of faith, hope, and love, and the desire of ordinary people to be the faithful sons and daughters of God. Let me expand

---

[124] #2652

this thought. The *Catechism* encourages its readers to let their prayer flow from the regular reading of the Bible. The ancient Benedictine prayer form called "Lectio Divina" is enjoying a new popularity. Based on Scripture, it brings a person to silence, resting in the heart of God. The Mass, as we will see, is the great prayer of the Church. Our prayer is also nourished by the seasons of the liturgical year and the observation of great feasts like Christmas, Easter, and Pentecost.

The Holy Spirit moves us to prayer. We enter prayer through faith in the presence of the Lord. We pray in hope, seeking and discovering God in the events of each day. The *Catechism* tells us that prayer is the life of the Christian heart. Quoting St. Gregory of Nazianzus, "We must remember God more often than we draw breath." There is within the Church a rhythm of prayer which nourishes continual prayer: Daily prayers in the morning and evening, grace before and after meals, the Liturgy of the Hours recited by priests, religious, and many lay people, the Rosary and, of course, Mass on Sundays.

Most books on prayer list traditional expressions of prayer: Blessing and adoration, prayers of petition, prayers of intercession, prayers of thanksgiving, and prayers of praise. Searching back into the ancient Catholic Tradition, we find three major expressions of prayer: vocal, meditative, and contemplative. They have one thing in common—they flow from the heart.

—Vocal prayer

The Jews expressed their prayers vocally. Jesus prayed aloud the great psalms of his people, and taught us to say the Our Father. When we pray aloud from the depths of our heart, our whole being is expressed in prayer. Men and women in religious orders pray the Divine Office together.

Other Catholics, in other places, do the same. In the Mass, the priest prays aloud, and the people join him, beseeching the Lord.

—Meditation

When I was a seminarian, I learned to meditate and I have lived long enough to see many ordinary Catholics practice this great prayer tradition. We use the Scriptures, especially the gospels, icons, the Rosary, and spiritual books. When we meditate, we let the message challenge us as we live our lives. As we ponder, we feel movement within our hearts. Sometimes it is the peaceful feeling so sought by the Latter-day Saints. At other times it is a movement toward repentance, or a desire to make a difference. All this is done in the light of the Holy Spirit and the living presence of Jesus Christ. We use thought, our imagination, our emotions, and our idealism. Meditation prayer is a journey. We grow closer to Christ and learn to live with his mind and heart.

—Contemplative prayer

For Catholics, this is the deepest form of prayer. St. Teresa of Avila tells us, *"Contemplative prayer in my opinion is nothing else than a close sharing between friends; it means taking time frequently to be alone with him who we know loves us."* The heart is the place for this encounter, and it can happen any time. We focus our hearts and place ourselves under the guidance of the Holy Spirit who has already called us to this moment. *"We let our masks fall and turn our hearts back to the Lord who loves us, to hand ourselves over to him as an offering to be purified and transformed."*[125]

[125] #2711

Through contemplative prayer, we are admitted ever more deeply into the life of the Trinity. Carried in the Spirit, we surrender ourselves to the embrace of the Father and to deeper union with Jesus Christ. As a result of this communion, we are confirmed by the Spirit to the image of God.

Contemplative prayer is simple and yet profoundly intense. We are deeply grounded in love. Our gaze is fixed on Jesus. "God is just folks," that old mountain mystic once told me when I was a young priest. "I look at him and he looks at me." The searching gaze of Jesus purifies the heart and helps us see the world in a different way. We share in the "yes" of Jesus and the "Let it be done to me according to your word" of Mary.

Contemplative prayer is a prayer of silence, beyond words or expressed in a simple word or phrase. Divine heart touches and embraces human heart. We are one with Christ in the mystery of his death and resurrection. Alive as never before from that encounter, we return to the world with new light and new energy.

Catholic growth points

What is the role of prayer in my own life? Wonderful books and CDs on prayer exist in an overflowing abundance. Can I find them in my home? Did my children learn their first words of prayer from me? Have they seen me at prayer? Have I encouraged them at their own prayers? Have I found time in the middle of my busy schedule for prayer and made it a personal responsibility? If prayer become difficult or distracted, do I give up, or do I try to deepen my prayer journey?

18

Ordinances, Sacraments, Sacrament Meeting, and the Mass

Here, for once, Mormons do not confuse us by using the same word with a different meaning. They talk about "ordinances." Catholics talk about sacraments. This chapter talks about the ways Mormons and Catholics meet God.

Mormon Ordinances and Catholic Sacraments

Two classical explanations of Mormonism, *A Marvelous Work and a Wonder,* and *Religious Truth Defined,* do not mention "sacraments" in their index. The much more detailed and always blunt *Mormon Doctrine,* by Bruce McConkie, mutters:

> *In the Apostate (ie Catholic and Protestant) church, the sacraments are said to be certain religious ceremonies or rites...in the true church, the rites and ceremonies are not classified as sacraments.* (p. 662)

Mormon Ordinances

Mormon Doctrine gives us a long list of "ordinances:" Baptism, baptism for the dead, baptism of fire, blessing of children, celestial marriage, commandments, consecration of oil, dedication of graves, endowments, gifts of the Holy Ghost, blessings, prayer, sabbath, sacrament, sacrifices, temple ordinances, vicarious ordinances, washing of feet. (p. 548)

I have underlined the ordinances on the list considered necessary for salvation or for further progress toward godhood. Others do not seem to involve rites or ceremonies at all, and some might be listed by Catholics as "Sacramentals." But as we ponder the ordinances, we see echoes, some faint and some strong, of the Catholic seven sacraments. For instance:

— *Baptism* Mormons baptize by immersion and by the power of the Aaronic, or lesser priesthood. Mormons distinguish baptism by water from *Baptism in the Spirit*, which can only be done by a member of the Melchizedek, or higher priesthood.

— *Gift of the Holy Ghost by the laying on of hands* This occurs after baptism, and is considered one of the "basic ordinances" of the gospel.

— *Sacrament* Performed each Sunday by young members of the Aaronic Priesthood. It involves the blessing and distribution of bread and water.

— *Ordination* This involves the laying on of hands by one who has the required priestly authority, in either the Aaronic or Melchizedek priesthoods.

— *Temple Ordinances* One of the key steps to godhood. Included are "the endowment ceremony" and "celestial marriage," and if necessary, "the sealing of children." These ordinances can be performed only in the temple, where they can also be performed by proxy for the dead. Such proxy performances of these crucial ordinances will enable deceased relatives to enter with their family into highest glory.

— *Endowments* Explained at much greater length in the chapter "What Happens in the Temple?" This secret ritual involves anointing and washings, instructions concerning the great Plan, and other mysterious rites and symbols known only to the initiated. A crucial step on the way to godhood.

— *Celestial marriage* Also performed only in the temple. Through this ceremony, a man and woman exchange vows and are "sealed" as husband and wife for eternity. Another necessary step for godhood.

Catholic Sacraments

The traditional *Baltimore Catechism* speaks about "the seven sacraments," and defines a sacrament as "an outward sign instituted by Christ to give grace." This definition risks turning a sacrament to a thing, a kind of instrument under the control of the Church which, when administered by the proper authority under the proper circumstances, gives a mysterious something called grace. My Third Grade version of the *Catechism* had the famous picture of a lake filled with grace, and seven faucets distributing that grace into deserving hearts.

Modern theologians take a different approach. First, as we have already seen, the term "sacrament" describes *a general way of viewing life*. The word comes from the Greek word "sum-ballo." *Ballo* means "to throw," hence the English word "ball." When *sum* is added, the term means "to throw together." Within this, there is the notion of an encounter. Next, we look at the way modern theologians describe grace, which is not a thing, but the sanctifying presence of the Spirit, the life of Jesus brought into our lives through the power of the Spirit. And so, a sacrament is the *Spirit-filled encounter between myself and Christ*.

When I teach converts, I like to call a sacrament a "bridge experience." I start with nature, which is full of bridges that can bring our hearts together with the heart of God. I wrote this a long time ago:

> We discover that reality can be experienced at a number of different levels. For instance, we are watching a sunset. To the scientist by our side, the sunset is a sign of abundant dust in the atmosphere. To a pair of lovers standing apart by themselves, it is a sign of the goodness and joy of life. And to someone filled with faith, the astonishing light, the silence, the wind in his face, these are bridges that bring him into the presence and peace of God. He is closer to him than his own heart.

As I have said in other places in this book, for those who live in faith with open hearts, the whole universe, nature, history, events, objects, people, rituals, and words can be, at the deepest level, "signs" which bring us into the presence of the living God.

A moment of recognition

"Sacrament" is like the famous painting in the ceiling of the Sistine Chapel in Rome, where God the creator reaches out, touching the fingertip of Adam, who reaches back to touch the hand of God. We use "encounter" instead of "meeting" because a sacrament involves that moment of recognition when glances meet and a person becomes aware of the mystery of the other person. As Joseph Marto said in *Doors to the Sacred*, the experience of sacrament "opens up the possibility of falling in love with God." (p. 141)

The Seven Sacraments

In our own lives we can experience the seven ways in which Christ reached out to the people of Israel, introducing others to new life, sending down the Spirit, healing the sick, forgiving sins, ministering to their needs, blessing their marriages with his presence, and sacrificing himself on the cross. The Church invites us into these moments through the sacraments. There, we encounter God as the creator, the Spirit who sets the heart afire, and our living Daily Bread. (Baptism, Confirmation, Eucharist). Under the hand of the Church we meet the God who pardons, the God who blesses marriage promises, the God who gives us his shepherds, and the God who heals. (Reconciliation, Matrimony, Holy Orders, Anointing).

The Church is a sacrament

Going further, as the Body of Christ, the Church herself is a sacrament. For two thousand years, hundreds of millions of Catholics have born their testimony. Within the Church and in the midst of brothers and sisters, we know and experience the living Jesus Christ. When the Church preaches the message of Jesus, her children know in faith that the Word of God has been spoken. When people celebrate Eucharist together, the Spirit sings and Christ is in their midst. When the Church speaks the healing words of Absolution, a sinner feels the salve of Christ's forgiveness. When the Church offers her sons and daughters the Host in Communion, they walk away with a sense of Christ Who Comes. When the Church reaches out to the sick and the poor, her hands become Christ's hands of healing.

Christ is the greatest of all sacraments

Following the reality of sacrament to its conclusion, we can say that Christ is the primordial Sacrament. When the Son became one with our flesh in the womb of Mary, humanity discovered a living bond with the God of the Universe. When Jesus preached and healed, the wisdom and mercy of God were on our streets. When Jesus sagged in death on the hill of sacrifice, God's life spilled onto the ground and over the world. During the Liturgical Year, we walk with Christ on this journey. When we celebrate the great feasts of Christmas, Easter, and Pentecost, our faith-filled remembering makes us one with those disciples who followed Christ to bitterness and glory. It is a long pilgrimage of sacrament, and those who walk that way year after year are gradually drawn into the very heart of God.

The Mormon "Sacrament of the Lord's Supper," and the Catholic Mass

For Mormons, the "Sacrament Meeting"

After dismissing the Catholic Mass as a "meaningless ceremony," Joseph Fielding Smith Jr. explains the role the sacrament meeting plays in Mormon worship.

> *The prime purpose of the sacrament, was revealed to be a* commemoration *of the atoning sacrifice of Jesus Christ....The sacrament meeting is a time for reflecting on the mission of the redeemer and renewing our covenants to keep his commandments.* (*Religious Truths Defined,* p 135)

The "commemoration" theme is typical of some Protestant churches, which assume that Jesus' death is gone into the past. And for those who wonder what covenants a Mormon renews at this time, I summarize an article in which Smith says:

> We sanctify ourselves in partaking of it (the sacrament) before our Heavenly Father, and in the name of Jesus Christ...We eat in remembrance of his body and his blood...we are willing to take upon ourselves the name of the Son, and not be ashamed of him...We will always remember him, love and honor him...(and) we will keep his commandments, which he has given us.
> (*Church History and Modern Revelation*, p. 135)

As I quote this passage, I think again of the question, are Mormons Christian? I remarked on their deep love for Jesus, even though they express this love with an understanding of Jesus that is different from the faith of Catholic Christians.

The sacrament meeting takes place in the midst of an ordinary Sunday service. The "sacrament" is in the hands of boys who are members of the Aaronic Priesthood. Two young Aaronic priests, between sixteen and nineteen years of age, prepare and bless bread and water. The bread is plain white bread cut into squares. Wine was once used, but after a special revelation, Mormons now use water. Mormons believe that the formula of blessing was revealed to Joseph Smith, and so the young men take care to repeat it word for word. Two deacons, younger boys from twelve to fourteen, then carry the sacrament to the congregation.

For Catholics: the Mass

Some questioners search through the Bible, looking for the word "Mass." Failing to find the specific word, they call this most central moment of Catholic life a misleading fabrication. But a deeper examination shows that the Mass has deep biblical roots. The ceremony is complicated because, for historical reasons, it is two religious ceremonies joined into one.

First of all, we ponder the meaning of the word "liturgy." It means the public prayer of the Church. Examples of liturgy would by the Divine Office, the ceremonies in which sacraments are celebrated, and the Mass. There is a saying in the Church: "The way we worship is the way we believe." That is why the bishops of the Council of Nicea, confronted by the Arian heresy which denied the divinity of Christ, studied the worship of the ancient Church. There they discovered the worship of Jesus Christ, divine Son of God. It was clear that a belief in the divinity of Jesus was rooted from the very beginning in the public prayer of the church.

The Mass is about God's people united with Jesus Christ. Most of the prayers of the Mass are directed to God the Father. Catholics are one with Christ in these prayers, their voice carried on the breath of the Holy Spirit. The Mass is divided into two parts, the Liturgy of the Word and the Eucharist. In the Liturgy of the Word, Catholics believe that Christ is present in the Words read in Scripture, and in the sermon. In the Liturgy of the Eucharist, the living Christ is present in the bread and in the wine.

The Liturgy of the Word

When the people of Judah were carried away into exile by Babylon, in 587 B.C., they took their holy books with them. In captivity, male Jews would gather together to read from the Law and the Prophets and some of the writings like the Psalms. They would sing, read, pray, and remember. This gathering was called "synagogue." When they returned from exile, synagogue became a Jewish institution located in every village. Jesus attended synagogue, and we see St. Paul and the earliest Christians continuing to gather there. Eventually, the leaders of the synagogues expelled the followers of Jesus, who took the synagogue service with them, making it part of their worship as Christians.

The Liturgy of the Word includes an opening greeting by the priest, hymns, a prayer in the name of the community, readings from both the Old and New Testaments, a reading from one of the Gospels, a sermon, common petitions, and a hymn. A similar format appears in most Protestant services. The prayers and readings vary from day to day and from season to season. In general, the Liturgy of the Word takes us on a journey through the Scriptures. Its readings anticipate and celebrate three great feasts: Christmas, Easter, and Pentecost. The readings follow a three year cycle and form the core of Catholic spiritual life.

The Liturgy of the Eucharist

This part of the Mass goes much deeper into the Jewish tradition. We glimpse it in the Book of Exodus, the story of Israel's escape from slavery in Egypt. The Liturgy of the Eucharist is based on the Jewish ritual meal celebrating that escape, called the "Passover." Scholars also see traces in the "fellowship meals" celebrated by religious groups during Jesus' day. And so, on the night before he died, Jesus and his disciples celebrated a meal. The meal followed a certain form: a) The sharing of food, and b) the telling of the story of God's salvation through scripture and the spoken word.

To understand, we need to ponder the role of *remembering* in the Jewish mind. In their Passover celebration, Jews remembered their escape from slavery in Egypt. During the ritual of the Passover Meal, they told the story together. In their remembering, they believed that they were doing something far more profound than simply recalling the way Moses led his people out of slavery. It allowed them to become part of the Exodus itself. When they remembered, they were *one* with Moses and the enslaved people, led by God on their exodus journey toward freedom. As someone put it:

> *This ritual meal was...a complex symbol which Jews could enter and encounter the God of their fathers. It was a door to the sacred through which they could pass from every day profane existence into the sacred space and time of the Exodus.* (Doors to the Sacred, p. 238)

Jesus was celebrating this meal with his disciples on the night before he died. But in the middle of the meal, he gave it a new meaning. When he broke a piece of unleavened bread representing the Messiah to come, he said, *"Take and eat, this is my body."* At the end of the meal, he took the cup representing the cup Jews hoped to share with the Messiah, and said, *"Take and drink, this is my blood of the new and eternal covenant."* And then he said, *"Do this in memory of me."*

Like the Jews, Catholics *remember*. The Mass is a time when we remember the story of Jesus' passion, death, and resurrection. We don't see Jesus' death as something lost in the past, but as *a moment in God's time, a moment that never ends, a sacred moment that becomes our moment.*

And so we believe that the Mass is a door that brings us into the very center of the story of salvation. Like the Jews, we believe that, when we remember, we are standing before the cross with Mary and John. Our eyes are on the dying Jesus as he takes our hearts and makes them his own. Our eyes are on the risen Jesus as he gives us new life. We believe that, when we receive Communion, Christ draws us into his sacrifice, and into the new life of his Resurrection.

The Real Presence

Let me ponder for a moment the Catholic belief that Jesus is truly present in the host and in the cup. We go back to the notion of sacrament. God touches us through earthly realities. I encounter Christ in a sunset, in the smile of a child, in the Word of God, and in the Host and cup of wine I hold up before the people after the moment of Consecration.

Is Christ really present in the cup and in the bread? A theologian put it into an interesting perspective when he asked: "Have you ever heard of the *unreal* presence of Christ?" In the Last Supper, Jesus took a piece of bread and wine in a cup, and identified himself with them. "This is my body...this is my blood," he said. Theologians give explanations like Transubstantiation and Transignification, which involve a journey into philosophy and a lot of deep thought. But in my old age, I like to understand it this way: *Jesus is risen.* He is no longer that person of flesh and blood who sat at the table of the Last Supper. He is a resurrected being alive now within the reality of God. This means he is not bound by the laws of space and time. The Mass, searching for words, uses the term "spiritual." A bit of bread and some drops of wine become symbols or bridges that lead us to his living presence. A person who receives Communion invites the living Jesus into his heart, and he abides there. This is what I think about when I receive Communion. I am one with Jesus in his sacrifice on the Cross. Risen, he lives within my deepest being. That is all I need to know.

In summary

And so, when Catholics gather to keep faith with this commandment of Jesus, they gather a) To hear the words of Scripture, which are the Word of God addressed to us in the midst of the joys and sorrows of our lives. The sermon is part of that Word. b) When the priest begins the Eucharistic Prayer, we stand with Mary and John before the cross. When we come forward for Communion, we share food that has become the body and blood of Christ, and so we *enter into* his sacrifice. At the deepest levels of reality, the bread and the wine have become the living signs of his real presence in the moment of his sacrifice. The reception of communion becomes a way to be one with the Risen Jesus, to say yes to his covenant with us, and to be a renewed part of Christ's Body. At the end of the Eucharistic ceremony, after Communion and a final prayer, the people are formally dismissed, invited to carry the Christ whose love they have just experienced into the corners of the world.

Catholic Growth Points

---Beginning with nature, have I learned to see the world in a sacramental way, so that life is full of "bridge experiences" where God's world and my world come together? Do I teach my family to see the world in the same way?

---Like St. Ignatius of Loyola, have I considered making frequent "examinations of *consciousness*," naming the times in the day when Christ has become present to me through persons, events, my reading, and other discoveries?

---Have I taken time to ponder more deeply the meaning of the Mass? Do I listen closely to the readings, heart searching for the Word of God?

---Have I learned to *re-member* my oneness with Christ? To unite myself with Christ's love on the cross, to open my heart to the meaning of his resurrection? Do I put other choices (such as taking a child to a soccer game) in front of my call from God to be together with my family, one with His Son at Mass?

---Do I remember and celebrate key sacramental moments in my children's lives? Help them celebrate their baptismal date? Treasure the memory of their First Communion?

---Do I give them the good example of my own frequent confessions and Communion?

19

What Happens in the Temple

Few things within Mormonism are as fascinating as their temples. When I was a child, there were only a few temples, all of them in the western part of the United States. But today, the number of temples is growing at an exponential pace all over the world. There was one temple in the Boise area, where I live, then an even more splendid temple only a few miles away, and now there are four temples within the state.

In recent years, Latter-day Saints have made a great effort to build temples within reach of all the faithful, and by now these impressive buildings are scattered throughout the world, with more coming. Non-Mormons are fascinated by the temples and there are all kinds of stories about the secret rites happening there. Most of these stories are not true.

The first thing we need to know is this: *A Mormon temple is not a place of worship.* Instead, it is a place for the rituals leading to godhood, a place for enabling the deceased to join their LDS families in eternity. A temple is used for baptism for the dead, for the reception of "endowments," and to seal marriages for time and eternity. But exactly what happens in these rituals is a secret.

As I proceed, I realize that the temple and its rituals are very sacred to the LDS, and so I will treat the subject with respect. We will talk about baptism for the dead, the endowment ceremony, and celestial marriage. If you want to see the story in detail, there are sources on the Internet.

"Temple Work," or Baptism and Vicarious Endowments for the Dead

> *The Prophet Joseph Smith taught that the greatest responsibility we have in this world is to identify our ancestors and go to the temple on their behalf.* (Gospel Principles, p. 249)

As we have seen, Mormons believe that baptism and the reception of endowments and marriage in the temple are absolutely essential in order to reach exaltation. But what about those who die without taking these crucial steps? Will they be separated forever from family members who have joined the LDS Church and go on to the celestial kingdom? What about the millions of people who died before the founding of the Mormon Church? Is there no hope for them? Will they be trapped forever in a lesser glory?

Mormons teach that God has revealed a way past this dilemma. When I was a youth, my LDS cousins used to talk about "temple work." I now understand that they would go to the temple and, in a huge baptismal pool, be baptized as proxies for the dead. This still happens today. In another part of the temple, adult Mormons can receive "endowments" in the name of a deceased person. When this happens, missionaries from spirit paradise will then cross the boundary into spirit prison and give the owner of that name the good news. The dead person will have a chance to freely accept or reject this final chance for salvation. Those who accept will go on to celestial glory.

Proxy baptism for the dead and the reception of endowments explains the tremendous LDS preoccupation with genealogy. A great cavern has been carved into a granite mountain near Salt Lake City to store the names of millions upon millions of people gleaned through monumental effort. Every Saint is asked to spend countless hours tracking down the names of deceased family members, reaching as far back into the past as possible. This is a joyous task. Latter-day Saints look forward to the day when they will be reunited with those distant relatives, so that they can return together to their Heavenly Father.

Endowments:
The Most Sacred Experience in the Life of a Saint

> *A little handbook for new Mormons, called* Welcome to the Kingdom, *tells us that* endowments *are special instructions, blessings and covenants received only in the temple. Done in absolute secrecy, the endowment opens the door to a Mormon's further progress on the path to becoming a god. It leaves a mark not forgotten."126*

Bound by an oath to secrecy, LDS sources give only the vaguest description of an endowment ceremony. *Welcome to the Kingdom* gives a new convert this sketch of what happens in a temple:

> *The endowment instruction includes an overview of the creation and its purpose, the condition of Adam and Eve in the Garden of Eden, the consequences of their disobedience, and the plan of redemption by the Son of God....Finally, the restoration of the gospel with its priestly power...(and) The "absolute"...condition of...purity and devotion to the*

---

126 Op. Cit., p. 70

right...and a strict compliance with Gospel requirements is explained." [127]

Those who have not experienced the endowment ceremony are told there are things they will not understand until they have shared in it. This secret knowledge existing within the LDS Church demonstrates a point made in the chapter, "Are Mormons Christian?" where I contend that Latter-day Saints are modern examples of the ancient Gnostic tradition. But even though the Saints are silent on the temple ceremonies, former Mormons have described the endowment ceremony in detail. With some reluctance, I will use information from *What's Going on Here?*, a small pamphlet by Bob Witte and Gordon H. Fraser, former Saints who are now born-again Christians.

Ritual Washings and Anointing. The Garments

A small crowd of people who are "going through the temple" arrive at the entrance, a small suitcase in one hand and a "temple recommend" in the other. After a soul-searching interview with their bishop, they have received their recommend as a proof of their good standing in the church, and they cannot enter the temple without it. Entering first are a young couple who will receive the endowments and be married in the temple. Others are friends and family members accompanying the couple. Still others have come as proxies for deceased relatives. Others are undergoing the endowment ceremony again to renew their religious fervor. My brother did this often.

In the suitcase are the clothes they will wear for the ceremony. Men and women go to separate dressing rooms where they will eventually dress in their garments, which

[127] Ibid.

they will wear for the rest of their lives as a sign of covenants made on that day. The garment resembles long underwear with short sleeves and legs cut off above the knee. Female garments have been abbreviated to some extent to accommodate modern fashion. Four special symbols are embroidered on this garment. Each person now receives a new name, to be kept secret. The name is usually taken from the Bible, and everyone undergoing the Endowment on that day receives the same name.

After a special anointing by temple workers of the same sex, the candidates return to the dressing room and put on their temple clothing over their garments. Men wear white shirts, white trousers, white belts, white socks, white tie, and white moccasins. Women put on a white slip, white dress, white hose, and white moccasins. When they die, they will be buried in these garments. When I attended the funeral of a cousin who died in an automobile accident, he was dressed in those garments. Those who enter the temple also carry other special clothing they will put on later in the ceremony.

The Drama

We are describing the ceremony as it takes place in a full-sized temple, like the temple in Salt Lake City. Many of the new temples are much smaller, with only four rooms. One room will obviously have to serve several purposes.

The endowments are a series of instructions about the Mormon story of salvation that takes place in a series of rooms. In the first room, which resembles a small theater, temple candidates will receive preliminary instructions. As they go through the other rooms, they will witness a sort of "play" that dramatizes the unfolding of the Mormon story. In the early days of the church, the play was performed by live actors, a practice that still continues in the Salt Lake

Temple. The play was replaced by a multi-media presentation called a "diorama," and today, by a video.

The next room is the *Creation Room*, where Elohim (God the Father), Jehovah (Jesus, the literal son of the Father and the God of the Old Testament), and Michael (another of the Heavenly Father's spirit-children who led the war against Satan, and helped organize the earth) discuss the Great Plan of salvation. Elohim puts Michael into a deep sleep and he awakens as Adam, with no knowledge of his pre-existent state, or of the Plan. Eve is formed from his rib, and is also unaware of her pre-existence as Michael's spirit-sister. They are immortal beings who cannot die.

The candidates move on to a beautifully decorated room representing the *Garden of Eden*, where another video continues the instructions, again in the form of a kind of play. Elohim leaves Adam and Eve in the Garden with a commandment about the Tree of Knowledge. Lucifer appears and tries to ruin Heavenly Father's Plan. He tempts Eve, and she eats the forbidden fruit and falls into the mortal state. Adam, seeing that Eve has fallen, also eats the forbidden fruit so that he can join her in mortality.

Elohim and his eldest son appear, catch Adam and Eve in their disobedience, and drive Lucifer out of the Garden. Then Elohim imposes *The Law of Obedience* on Adam and Eve. She must obey her husband and, if Adam promises to obey God's law, Elohim will provide a savior who will lead them back into his presence. Then Adam and Eve are driven out into the dreary world.

In the next room, the play continues. The candidates find themselves in a room full of conflict and tumult, representing the *lonely and dreary world*, or the world in which we now live. Lucifer is the god of this world, and his disciples, representing false religion, try to seduce Adam. Peter, James and John appear and help refute Lucifer and his disciples. The three apostles identify themselves as the true messengers of the Heavenly Father by giving secret signs of the Priesthood that were given to Adam while he was in the Garden of Eden. Adam recognizes the signs and acknowledges his visitors as true messengers of the Father.

Laws

At this point, a couple representing the men and women receiving their Endowment comes to an altar and receives the *Law of the Gospel*, which demands respect for the Lord's Anointed (those who hold the priesthood, especially high church authorities), along with clean speech and sober living. All rise and make the secret signs just demonstrated by the apostles, and swear to keep the *Law of the Gospel*. Peter instructs them how to put on the sacred temple garments they are carrying, which include a white robe, a white cap, a green apron, and a white cloth belt called a girdle. All the women present are put under covenant to obey the law of their husbands, who are the priesthood holders in their family.

Another couple comes forward to represent the rest in accepting the *Law of Sacrifice*. All rise, make the same secret sign, and swear to "keep the law of sacrifice as contained in the Old and New Testaments."

Tokens and covenants

At this time the actor representing Elohim tells the candidates that they are going to receive the *First and Second Tokens of the Aaronic Priesthood*, with their "accompanying names, signs, and penalties." They vow never to reveal theses secret tokens, even in the face of death. The *First and Second Tokens of the Aaronic Priesthood* are secret handshakes. The women receive their secret name, but not the name of their husbands. He receives both names. Everyone swears that they would rather die than reveal the secret name that has been given them, or the "two Tokens of the Aaronic priesthood."

The group now moves to the *Terrestrial World*, whose most noteworthy decoration is a great veil representing the passage between earth and the house of the Father. There, the participants receive the *Law of Chastity*. First the women and then the men stand, make the sacred gesture, and covenant to keep marital fidelity.

They are now ready to receive the *Tokens of the Melchizedek Priesthood*. The first is called the "Sign of the Nail," and the second is called the "Patriarchal Grip" or the "Sure Sign of the Nail." The first turns out to be a sort of handshake accompanied by a kind of embrace, and the second is a special handshake along with the threefold repetition of a secret phrase.

Between the reception of the two tokens, a couple again approaches the altar to represent the others in covenanting to keep the *Law of Consecration*, by which they consecrate themselves, their time, talents, and all blessings "for the building up of the Kingdom of God on earth and for the establishment of Zion."

A prayer circle, a veil, and the four marks of the priesthood

Without revealing any of the details, my brother told me ant this is his favorite part of the temple ceremony. A speaker tands before the veil, which is decorated with secret symbols, and summarizes the instructions, ordinances, and covenants the group has received. He also reviews the tokens, with their key words and signs. He reminds them that these things are not to be discussed outside the sacred walls of the temple. After forming a prayer circle to "form the true order of prayer," an actor representing Peter turns to the veil with its four mysterious marks and tells them that they are the four marks of the Holy Priesthood, corresponding to the marks found on the garments they will wear for the rest of their lives. He explains the four marks. There are also holes in the veil, and someone representing Heavenly Father puts his hand through the hole and tests the candidates about the knowledge of the sacred signs. This figure then ushers the men into the next room. Each man then ushers in his wife or fiance', using the secret name they have learned.

Marriage for Time and Eternity

The room behind the veil is called the *Celestial Room*. It is decorated in white and gold, and is a place of brilliant light. A man and a woman dressed in white represent Heavenly Father and his High Priestess (or Eternal Companion). Those who wish can stay for a while in this place of peace.

The young couples who will be married for time and eternity go to a small, beautifully decorated room with a white altar in the middle. This is called the *Bridal Room*. The young man and young woman kneel on opposite sides of an altar and grasp right hands in the Patriarchal Grip. The man swears to receive the woman for all time and eternity as his wife, keeping all laws and ordinances pertaining to marriage. Then the woman does the same. The general authority who is present pronounces their marriage blessed and sealed for time and eternity. The couple kisses and the surprisingly brief marriage ceremony is over.

Other Rooms

Three other important rooms are present in a temple. Two of the rooms are for sealing for time and eternity. In the first room, parents are sealed to their children. In the second room, parents are sealed to children who have died, and men are sealed to deceased wives. My brother entered this room and was sealed to his first wife. He assumes that he will have two wives when he enters the Celestial Kingdom. Another room is called the *Holy of Holies*, visited only by the prophet of the church.

What does all this mean?

Outsiders frequently mock the sacred ceremonies of others, unaware that such attitudes merely confess a large deal of ignorance. As a Catholic, I have smarted under the blind contempt some non-Catholics have for the Mass. And so I have tried to discuss the temple and its endowments with respect.

Anthropologists of religion say that every religion contains rites and ceremonies that bring the believer into the heart of what they view as the meaning of life. In such a place, people often experience an encounter with the divine. As a Catholic, the Mass brings me to God and his New Covenant made in love...to a renewed sense of oneness with Jesus in his passion, death and resurrection...to a renewed awareness of the Holy Spirit...and to a new awareness that I am part of the Church in its long pilgrimage march.

The LDS temple and its rituals also bring faithful Saints into a discovery of the Holy, with the literal Heavenly Father beckoning them to continue the journey toward godhood in the company of their family. For Latter-day Saints, it is a *rite of passage*, the greatest of all steps into immortality. By maintaining strict secrecy, a Mormon has the satisfaction of being a special person with access to a superior knowledge unattainable by lesser hearts.

Non-LDS ask where the Endowment Ceremony comes from. In an argument that reminds us again of Gnosticism, Latter-day Saint apologists maintain that the secret rite was revealed to Adam himself and practiced by Solomon in his temple. There is no historical proof for this. The LDS admit that no traces are found in the Bible, but they say that this is because the ceremony was secret and because apostates tried to destroy the priesthood which established the ceremony. Again, this is one of the tactics used by the Gnostics.

Whatever the source of its ceremonies, the temple catches a Saint up in the Plan. He is on his way to godhood.

Catholic Growth Points

When a Mormon wants to root himself in the deepest elements of his religion, he goes to a temple. For Catholics, the deepest reality is to share in the passion, death, and resurrection of Jesus, and to go forth with his mission. We do this every time we celebrate the Mass together. An especially deep and poignant time for this experience is the celebration of Holy Thursday, Good Friday, Holy Saturday, and Easter.

PART SIX

Authority

Some Catholic and LDS high school students were involved in an argument over religion. The Catholic students began to quote the Bible. The LDS students responded that a biblical argument is unsound, because the Bible is flawed and no longer speaks the truth.

In order for Mormons to justify the existence of their church, they have to claim that a catastrophe destroyed the Church Jesus founded. Echoing some Protestant churches, they say it fell into something they call "the Great Apostasy," in which the Church after the apostles strayed completely from its mission. Along the way, corrupt priests removed "plain and precious things" from the original Bible. This created the need for a restored church, a living prophet, and modern revelation like the Book of Mormon, *the* Doctrine and Covenants, *and the* Pearl of Great Price.

This section will begin by discussing the priesthood, whose authority anchors both the Mormon and the Catholic Church. We will then address Mormon arguments that question the authority of the Bible, and finally, we will address the red-hot issue: Was there a Great Apostasy that destroyed the true church founded by Jesus himself?

20

The Authority of the Priesthood

Both the Mormon and Catholic churches are centered around a priesthood. Once again, they are talking about different realities. Mormons trace their priesthood to Adam and backward into infinity, Catholics trace their priesthood back to Jesus Christ.

Priesthood from a Mormon perspective

Latter-day Saints say that they respect the work of non-Mormon priests and ministers, but such people labor in vain because they do not have the *legal power* to act in God's name. The Saints insist that such power and authority belong only to Mormon males ordained to the Melchizedek Priesthood.[128]

The Melchizedek Priesthood: A brief history

There is no mention of the Melchizedek Priesthood in the *Book of Mormon*. But there were priests and high priests, appointed by the king. When Christ finally appeared among the Nephites and Lamanites and began to organize the authority structure of his church in America, he said nothing about a priesthood. Instead, he called and ordained twelve men as apostles, and authorized them only to baptize and give the Holy Ghost.

---

[128] Quoted by R.L. Millet, *Magnifying Priesthood Power*, Horizon, Provo, Utah, 1974, p. 11

Joseph Smith said that, in 1829, on an unknown day in an unknown place, he and his disciple Oliver Cowdery were ordained to the Melchizedek Priesthood by the apostles Peter, James, and John. This gave them the legal authority to act in God's name. Again, we think about Gnosticism. In 1831, Smith began to ordain other disciples to this priesthood, and it exists today as the central structure within the Mormon Church.

According to the *Encyclopedia of Mormonism*, the Melchizedek Priesthood is "an eternal priesthood." (#884) David O. McKay, a deceased LDS president, told his people, "Priesthood is inherent in the Godhead." This means that the Heavenly Father of the Mormons could not have become a god if he was not a Melchizedek priest, like his father and his father's fathers before him. His priestly powers had been passed down in an endless line stretching backward forever.

Like any modern male Latter-day Saint, Heavenly Father received his priesthood while he lived in a mortal state. Called by revelation and prophecy to receive the priesthood, he made his oath and covenant and was ordained by someone holding priestly authority. He then "magnified his calling" as all priesthood holders are asked to do, and his growth in the Melchizedek Priesthood played a key role in his achievement of exaltation and the status of a god.

The priesthood arrives on earth

Adam, who was Michael the Archangel in pre-existence, "Received the holy priesthood, with all its power, authority, and keys."[129] In his turn, Abraham was ordained by Melchizedek himself. This story is told briefly in the *Book of*

---

[129] *Encyclopedia of Mormonism*, #884

Abraham 1:25, which is part of *The Pearl of Great Price*.[130] The *Doctrine and Covenants* (84:6) teaches that Moses received the Melchizedek Priesthood from his pagan father-in-law Jethro, and held the Melchizedek Priesthood until his death.[131] Because of the rebellious attitude of the Jewish people, the LDS say Moses was "translated" at his death, and the keys of the priesthood went with him.[132] The Jews were left with an "appendage" of the great priesthood, the Aaronic Priesthood, which had only limited authority. From then on, the Melchizedek Priesthood was given by God to different prophets, but it no longer belonged to the people and the true church no longer existed on earth.

Although the ceremony is not mentioned in the gospels, Mormons teach that Jesus Christ ordained Peter, James, and John to the Melchizedek Priesthood when they were on the Mountain of Transfiguration When Jesus told Peter, "You are Peter and upon this rock I will build my church," (Matt. 16:17-18) he was referring to the priesthood and the power of the keys. After Jesus' ascension into heaven, the apostles continued to direct the church in his name and conferred the priesthood on those who were worthy. But when the church fell away in apostasy, the priesthood was taken from earth. Without the priesthood, the true church ceased to exist.

What is the Melchizedek Priesthood?

The priesthood is *the power to do what the Mormon god does.*

---

[130] Part of the *Pearl of Great Price*

[131] Mormons ignore the fact that Jethro was a pagan and not a Jew

[132] *Encyclopedia of Mormonism*, #884

President George Q. Cannon told his followers that the Melchizedek Priesthood "is... *the power and authority by which our Father and God* sits upon his throne and *wields the power he does.*"[133] (My emphasis) BYU professor Robert L. Millet described the priesthood as

a part of God's own power....the power by which the Gods manage and direct their innumerable creations...the governing force by which worlds are brought into being, peopled, redeemed, exalted and glorified.[134]

The Saints teach that Heavenly Father shares the power of his priesthood with his sons on earth.[135] Ordination to the Melchizedek Priesthood invites the humblest Mormon male to play a role in the government of god. He can "speak the will of God as if the angels were here to speak it themselves."[136] He literally represents Heavenly Father [156] when he performs his priestly ordinances and fulfills his assigned office within the church authority structure, or when he fulfills the responsibilities of priesthood within his own family.

The priesthood is *the key to godhood.*

Even more awesome, participation in the power of the priesthood is the key to godhood. Millet, quoting President Joseph Fielding Smith, tells us "There is no exaltation in the Celestial Kingdom without the Higher Priesthood." When a Melchizedek Priesthood bearer performs the priestly ordinances (baptism, confirmation, washing, anointing,

---

[133] *Journal of Discourses*, 25:245

[134] Millet, op. cit., p. 12

[135] President John Taylor, *Morning Star, 9:323*

[136] Conference Reports, October, 1901, p. 2., quoted by Millet, p. 12 [156] Ibid., p. 13

sealing), he "gains experience in the operations of God's power" and proves himself worthy of greater endowments "of light and power."[137] This brings me back to those family reunions I attended when I was a boy. My family held Grandpa in great reverence, not simply because he was Grandpa, but because he was the priesthood bearer whose blessing helped wife, sons, daughters, and grand-children grow toward exaltation and godhood.

The President of the church and the power of the keys

Those faithful Saints ordained to the Melchizedec priesthood have the power to act in God's name, but they cannot act if they have not received their portion of the power of the keys. This legal authority must be delegated by the president of the church, who holds the fulness of that power. And so, when a man is chosen for a leadership or administrative position, he is delegated the keys that authorize him to act at his level of responsibility. This gives the president/prophet control over every priesthood holder in the church, and avoids the multiple splits seen in the Protestant churches.

The mission of the priesthood

Elder Mark E. Petersen tells us that without the power and authority of the priesthood there would be no salvation, "For it is through the Church that the Lord saves his faithful people, and it is through the priesthood...that the Church fulfills its destiny."[138]

The Aaronic and Melchizedek priestly orders work together to preach the Mormon gospel, convert and baptize

---

[137] Ibid.
[138] "The Duties of the Melchizedek Priesthood," in *Priesthood*, op. Cit., p 48

believers, bestow the gift of the Holy Ghost, administer the sacrament of the Lord's supper, watch over and preserve the church from error, visit the house of each member, and exhort them to watch over their families.[139]*Mormon Doctrine* gives us an alphabetical list of the works that are performed by priests possessing the proper power and authority:

> *Baptism, Baptism for the dead, Baptism of fire, blessing of children, Celestial Marriage, consecration of oil, dedication of graves, endowments, gift of the Holy Ghost, laying on of hands, ordinations, patriarchal blessings, sacrament, temple ordinances, vicarious ordinances, washing of feet."* [140]

Supporting the authority of the priesthood

The Saints emphasize the solemn duty of each member to "support" priesthood bearers. Young girls are taught to reverence the all-male Melchizedek Priesthood and learn how they can help "sustain" priesthood members in their tasks. It is considered wrong and shameful to criticize priesthood leaders. President George Q. Cannon warned his followers, "Whoever arrays himself in any manner against the authority which God has placed in His Church for its government, no matter who it is–unless he repents, *God will withdraw His Spirit and Power from him."*[162]

In appreciation: conclusions from this study

As I said in the introduction, it would be difficult to understate the importance of the Melchizedek Priesthood in LDS life. The priesthood gives Latter-day Saints a spiritual mystique, a hope in the possibility of godhood. Since any worthy male can be called and ordained to the different

---

[139] Ibid. P. 54-55

[140]*Op. Cit.*, p. 548, under "Ordinances."

levels of the priesthood, it provides the church with a broad base. Even though the church lays great stress on personal revelation, the First Presidency with its power of the keys maintains control over the organization. The Mormon authority structure is a pyramid, a tight-knit, clearly focused religious organization filled with great energy down to the local level.

Because every saint is responsible to the authority of a higher saint, it is hard for anyone to question the system. Local leaders maintain tight authority, quickly dismissing dissidents from the Church. And so the LDS do not fracture into splinters in the manner of many "Spirit-led" Protestant churches. The authority of the First Presidency delegated to stake presidents and bishops governs every activity of the church. Because of this, officially announced LDS goals, such as the obligation to store food, are quickly accomplished.

I have seen some real holiness among LDS people. It is impressive to note the effort priesthood holders make to magnify their calling by prayer, study, and priestly activity–always strengthened by the support and guidance of the mandatory priesthood quorums, who follow a mandatory agenda from above. A father who takes his priesthood responsibilities seriously will play a powerful role in the spiritual growth of his family. A mother who supports and sustains her husband enjoys a satisfactory place in the scheme of things. Her Relief Society will help her in her personal and spiritual development, but she will also be guided by her husband. My grandmother once noted that she was obliged to obey my grandfather because her very salvation was at stake.

Priesthood within the Catholic Church

The Catholic priesthood, rooted in the Trinity and in the life and death of Jesus Christ

If human life has a purpose, it is because it springs forth from the life of the Trinity and reflects the communion that forms the reality of God himself. But at some distant, tragic moment, men and women abused their freedom, stifled the Spirit, rejected Love, lost community, and fell into the oppression of sin. As history continued to unfold, the human race sank deeper and deeper into lonely darkness. Only God could heal its lost and wounded heart.

True to himself, God the Father, who is Love, sent his Son, who is the Heart of his Love, to be his Word of compassionate love for us, our savior and redeemer. *"It was for this purpose that God sent his Son, whom he appointed heir of all things."*[141] Sent from the Father, Jesus Christ, the Word made flesh by the Breath of the Spirit, became one of us. As Hebrews put it, *he became the High Priest who would offer his own body and blood for our salvation.* (Heb 1, 2) Christ died once and for all for our redemption, but his work goes on. This is the work of the Catholic priesthood.

A brief history of the Catholic priesthood[142]

For most of its history, the Catholic Church has explained priesthood in "sacral" terms: a language it shares in common with Judaism. In this perspective, the priest is *the sacred person who mediates between human beings and God*

---

[141] *Lumen Gentium* #13

[142] My comments are based on three excellent books on the Catholic Priesthood: Avery Dulles, S.J., *The Priestly Office*; Kenan B. Osborne, O.F.M., *Priesthood*; Robert M. Schwartz, *Servant Leaders of the People of God*

by offering prayers and sacrifice. The Letter to the Hebrews follows this path when it describes Jesus as the High Priest who offered one sacrifice forever for his people. All Christians agree that, when we come to the deepest meaning of the word, Christ is our *only* priest. We have no other intermediary with the Father.

The term "priest" appeared only gradually in the Church

Scholars note that the earliest Church never used the sacred title of "priest" for its ministers, perhaps to avoid confusion with the Levitical priests among the Jews. In the New Testament, only the Jewish priests, Jesus (in Hebrews), and all the baptized (in I Peter and Revelations) are called "priest." There was no historical trace of anything called the Melchizedek Priesthood.

From the beginning, there were those in the Church who acted in the name of Christ. In the Gospel of St. John, Jesus breathed on his disciples and said, "As the Father sent me, so I also send you." In the different Christian communities, different names were used to designate those who ministered: *Apostle, the Twelve, Episkopos, Presbyteros, Deacon, Shepherd, Prophet, Teacher, Evangelist, Preacher, Father, Servant, Overseer,, Leitourgos, Neoteros*. Osborne tells us: "There does not seem to be any standard pattern or universal preference for one title over the other, even at the end of the New Testament period."

To repeat, *from the very beginning, ministers acting in the name of Christ were active within the Church, even though they were not called priests*. We can reasonably argue that the presence of ministers was part of the Church's divine foundation. All ministry was seen as a call and commission from the Lord. Not even the community could appoint someone to ministry, although it could acknowledge that someone had been called by God.

The ministry of authority

Only gradually did the Church develop the ministerial structure we see today. Around the year 111, Ignatius of Antioch noted that three offices were in place which would be familiar to a modern Catholic: bishop, presbyter (or elder), and deacon. During that same period, the ritual of ordination appeared. Catholics see this development of leadership as a Spirit-guided process.

Christians who lived at that time accepted the authority of the bishop, presbyter, and deacon, along with the ministries of the prophet and teacher. A perceptive Christian who lived a century or more later day might also have noted the beginnings of a new trend. More and more, the bishops–and sometimes the presbyters–were finally called "priests." This term was used first to describe the leaders of the church communities, emphasizing the role they played in the celebration of the Eucharist.

By 1000, "priest" had replaced the term presbyter completely. The priesthood focused more and more on the Eucharist. The priest's sacred power to consecrate the bread and the wine made him different from all other members of the Church. By 1100, the Eucharist, the sacrament of reconciliation, the performance of marriages, and the anointing of the sick were all reserved to the priest, ordained to those tasks.

The Catholic Priesthood after the Vatican Council

A ministry rooted in the mission of Jesus

The bishops of the Vatican Council moved away from a focus on a priesthood narrowly centered on the Eucharist to a priesthood based on the *entire mission* or ministry of the Risen Jesus, who is Head of his Body, the Church. In order to understand priesthood, we have to begin with the ministry of Jesus, which was threefold: prophet, priest, and king. 1) *Jesus the teacher or prophet*: By his words and by his very life, he instructed his followers about the coming of the Kingdom. 2) *Jesus the priest:* We have seen that only Hebrews call Jesus the "High Priest" who offered the sacrifice of his own body and blood for his people. The Gospels and St. Paul portray Jesus in a very priestly way. He was the sanctifier who brought holiness to his people. 3) *Jesus the pastor or shepherd:* Jesus is the good shepherd who led his followers to Jerusalem. As the Word made human flesh, Jesus came to minister to us by proclaiming the Kingdom and by offering his life on the cross.

A two-fold priesthood within the Church

Vatican II teaches us that, as a baptized people, the entire Church shares in Christ's priesthood

Risen and glorified, Jesus Christ is the Head of his living body, the Church. The *entire* Church has received the mission and ministry of Jesus. If the mission and ministry of Jesus is described in the threefold manner described above, so is the ministry of the Church. Through their Baptism, *all Christian people* share in the "priestly, prophetic and kingly office of Christ." [143]

The Council speaks of "the common priesthood of the whole church." By the power of the Spirit, Christ the Priest continues to be present in the wounded, grace-filled humanity of his Church. The Church is his sacrament, a sign and instrument of God's healing, saving compassion.

The baptized members of the Church are Christ's voice, Christ's hands and Christ's heart in a troubled world. The baptized act as priests above all when they join in the Eucharistic sacrifice by their prayer, thanksgiving, and the

---

[143]*Lumen Gentium*, n. 31

reception of the sacraments. They are priests when they teach, when they carry Communion to the sick, when they encourage and minister to each other. The Council emphasizes two special areas where the common priesthood can exercise Christ's teaching or prophetic role. The first is in marriage and family life, where spouses witness to each other and to their children. The second is in the world, where lay people prophecy as much by deed as by word.

> *The faithful must...acknowledge the inner nature and the value of the whole of creation and its orientation to the praise of God. They help one another...to achieve greater holiness of life, so that the world may be filled with the spirit of Christ and may the more effectively attain its destiny in justice, in love, and in peace.*[144]

After centuries of emphasizing the ordained priests who offer Mass and forgiveness to the community, Catholics have only begun to understand the priestly role that comes to them through Baptism. Instead, they leave holiness and ministry to priests and religious within the Church, and often adopt the manner and attitude of the world instead, contributing to the human tragedy. I will bless the day when most lay Catholics are anxious to organize together in order to learn how to do Christ's work as priests to their families, to their parish, and to their community.

The ministerial priesthood

When most Catholics think of priests, they think of the ordained members of the ministerial priesthood, who are called by God above all to stand before their people every

---

[144] Ibid. n. 36

day to preach and celebrate the Eucharist. They are the ones who celebrate the Sacrament of Reconciliation. They are the ones who bring anointing to the seriously ill. In the words of Pope John Paul, they stand in the place of Jesus Christ, Servant-leader of his priestly people. It is their task to serve the baptized and aid them in their priestly service. They are the living sacraments of the living presence of Christ, Servant of his Body the Church. Through them and in them, Christ the servant continues to act as teacher, priest, and leader of the whole people of God. Catholics call these men "Father."

I am one of those men others call "Father," The fact that they see me in this way drives me to my knees because I know I am a sinner often burdened by my weaknesses. I see myself as a *servant* of the Catholic community called by the Holy Spirit to priestly ministry in Christ's name. Catholics recognize that the risen, glorified Christ acts *in* his priest, using him as an instrument. But in spite of myself, I become the voice of Christ announcing redemption won on the cross, the voice of Christ offering his eternal sacrifice, the voice of Christ the Shepherd healing and nurturing his sheep.

The bishop has the fullness of the priesthood

The bishops of the Vatican Council, acting as the official teachers (ordinary magisterium) of the Church, taught that the episcopacy is the fullness of the priesthood. The bishops have received the mission and ministry which Christ gave to his apostles, and because they have received that mission, they are considered successors to the apostles.

Called to be a sacrament of Christ, the servant-leader of his Church, the bishop is the servant leader of a "particular church," more commonly known as a diocese. He has an organic relationship with those who share the common priesthood of the Church. He forms a collegial structure with his ministerial priests; together they become what is called a "presbyterium." He does not and cannot act alone.

This is the official talk. Any bishop must look at the job description the Council gave him, and tremble. He knows that he is just another sinner with a more daunting task than the sinful priests who are united with him to do Christ's work. I have served under seven bishops. Each led the diocese in his own way. The bishop when I was a seminarian was a tyrant who kept priests trembling in their beds. Our Diocese has seen several bishops who gathered with their Presbyteral Council for a total of several days a year. Our current bishop gathers with his Presbyteral Council for a total of six hours a year. Two bishops rescued the diocese from bankruptcy. My previous bishop was quite liberal; my current bishop is very conservative. There are bishops who delegate authority, and other bihops are CEOs who keep authority close to their vest. My current bishop is doing good work as he understands it, part of the Church on its journey in my part of the world. But like anybody else, he is limited in his vision, energy, and personality. He can use my prayers.

A priest in his parish

Over the years, I have learned what it means to be a servant leader to the people of God in my parish. I am a weak and sinful man, but I am very conscious of the anointing I have received. As the Council taught, I am, first of all, a preacher and teacher of the Word. This proclamation of the Word reaches its most profound moment when I lead the parish in the celebration of the Eucharist at Mass. I always think of Christ the priest, dying for us on the cross. When I proclaim the Eucharistic Prayer which tells again the story of our salvation in Christ, the people present join me within that moment in God's time, and our hearts are one with the suffering heart of Christ. I have the same experience when I celebrate any sacrament. I become the voice of Christ, the servant leader of his people, and he uses my hands to baptize, anoint, forgive, and bless in marriage. When I celebrate the Mass, I also remind myself that I am the voice of the people, raised in prayer, praise, and thanksgiving.

I have to confess that, when it comes to executive ability, my leadership skills leave a lot to be desired. With the help of strong members of the parish, I have been able to serve my parish as its shepherd, a sign of Christ the shepherd in their midst. Long after I have left a parish, people thank me for my shepherd's role, and tell me that they felt the presence of Christ in the work I tried to do in their midst.

Catholic Growth Points

Do I understand that, through my baptism, I share in the priesthood of Christ? As spouses, are you priest to each other and priests to your children, ministering, healing, bringing love? Your bishop can be a distant shepherd, but when he comes to your parish, he is there in Christ's name. Do you welcome him if your paths cross? Your pastor struggles with his own weaknesses as he tries to serve you. Do you offer him your respect and support? Do you pray for your priests? Would you support a child if he considered becoming a priest?

21

For Mormons, a Restored Apostolic Authority

For Catholics, the Magisterium

Both Catholics and Mormons base their authority on the apostles. The LDS claim that apostolic authority that was lost in apostasy. They teach that, on an undetermined date and in an unknown place, with no other witnesses present, Peter, James, and John came down from heaven and ordained Joseph Smith and Oliver Cowdery to the Melchizedek Priesthood, thus restoring apostolic authority. In contrast, Catholics talk about apostolic succession. There was no empty time when no apostolic authority existed in the Church. It is rooted in the bishops, who can claim an unbroken line back to the apostles.

Authority in the Mormon Church

An outline of the basic LDS teaching

In his *A New Witness for the Articles of Faith*, Apostle Bruce R. McConkie demands that the Catholic Church and other churches prove their authority:

> *Where, if anywhere, are the modern legal administrators who have power to represent the Lord on earth? If there are legal administrators now on earth, how and in what way were they called of God? Where, if anywhere, are the apostles and prophets today?*

Mormons believe in a series of "dispensations." Beginning with Adam, each dispensation was led by a prophet holding "every power, right, prerogative, priesthood, and key."[145] The same gospel was "proclaimed by Adam, Enoch, Noah, Abraham, Moses, and all of the ancient prophets and patriarchs."[146] Despite the power and credentials granted to its leaders, each dispensation ended in apostasy and the prophetic authority was lost.

In the fullness of time, Jesus appeared. One of his first acts was to restore the official authority structure called the Melchizedek Priesthood. Like Catholics, Mormons are fond of Matthew 16:13-16. There on Mt. Tabor, Peter confessed that Jesus was the Christ, and Jesus responded, "Blessed art thou, Simon Bar Jona: For upon this rock I will build my church." Mormons teach that the "rock" is the Melchizedek Priesthood, the power of the keys, and ongoing revelation.

---

[145] Ibid., p. 320-21

[146] Ibid., p. 137

In his *New Witness for the Articles of Faith*, Bruce McConkie tells us,

> *Jesus then created the authority structure of his church. First, he named and ordained the other apostles, who formed "the quorum of the Twelve," which would be an ongoing institution guiding the church. Most important were Peter, James, and John, who were appointed to "the first presidency" on the Mount of Transfiguration. After the apostles came the "seventies," who were seventies had been called, ordained, and endowed with all the "keys, gifts, powers and blessings essential for the growth of the Church."* [147]

He goes on. "Branches were then established and other officers were ordained by the apostles to officiate in their respective localities." [170] Organization was from the top downward, "first the apostles and prophets, then the various authorities as growth in the by prophecy and revelation:

> *Holding these keys, Peter would have power to preside over and regulate all the affairs of that church which is the kingdom of God on earth...power to do all that was necessary to assure men of an inheritance of eternal life in the kingdom of heaven.* [148]
> *This is the gospel and the Church as established by Jesus Christ: the Church was called the Church of Jesus Christ; the officers herein enumerated were essential; the officers were divinely called and endowed with authority; they were ordained by the*

---

[147] . Ibid. P. 149 [170] . Ibid.

[148] Ibid., p. 320

imposition of hands by those previously so ordained of God...and revelation was to continue.[149]

When Smith speaks of the gospel, he is talking about godhood and eternal progression. McConkie imagines Jesus and the apostles establishing church branches all over Israel. The New Testament shows no glimpse of any of this. For Mormons, this is proof positive that wicked priests have removed the true gospel from the Scriptures.

Authority in the modern LDS Church

Mormons believe that, after long centuries of apostasy, the divine pattern is alive again on earth. First, their Church is custodian of modern scriptures which restore much of the lost gospel of Christ. Second, the church is guided by a living president/ prophet and is led at all levels by authorities who have been called through prophecy and ordained by someone possessing the power and authority of the Melichizedek Priesthood. Third, the Mormon leaders rule their church by "divine authority through direct revelation."[150] Fourth, the temple has been restored, with its "essential ordinances and practices." [151]

Authority granted at an unknown time in an unknown place

In the quote that began this chapter, Bruce McConkie snarls at those who claim apostolic authority in the Catholic Church. He asks, *How in what way were they called of God?*

---

[149] . Ibid. P. 152

[150] . David O. McKay, *Gospel Ideals* (Salt Lake City: *Improvement Era*, 1953) p. 533

[151] . *Encyclopedia of Mormonism*, vol 1, under "Catholicism and Mormonism."

Our Catholic Survival Kit examined one of those blurry stories so familiar in any discussion of Joseph Smith. During the year 1829, at some unknown time in some unknown place, the apostles Peter, James, and John appeared to Joseph Smith and Oliver Cowdery and ordained them to this apostolic rank. Nobody else witnessed this, of course. Mormon sources say that Smith began to ordain men to this priesthood in 1831. The Melchizedek Priesthood appears for the first time in Section 27 of the *Doctrine and Covenants*. The Survival Kit noted the maneuver that puts the whole thing in doubt. Without explaining that words had been added and paragraphs removed,the Melchizedek Priesthood and the Power of the Keys were inserted into earlier revelations appearing in chapter 28 of the *Book of Commandments*. In the modern world, this could be grounds for a charge of fraud. The Mormon claim to apostolic authority stands on this shaky foundation.

The Melchizedek Priesthood with its apostolic authority has the structure of a pyramid.

At the top, the First Presidency and the quorum of the Twelve

The supreme power in the Mormon Church belongs to the *Quorum of the First Presidency*, which is made up of the president of the church and two counselors. They have "the ultimate power of appointment, presidency, interpretation of doctrine, and all other matters pertaining to the Church. Thus, all other quorums, councils, and organizations of the Church operate under the authority of this quorum."[152]

---

[152] . *Encyclopedia of Mormonism*, Vol. 2, under "First Presidency."

Next are the *Quorum of the Twelve Apostles,* which possesses a missionary role. The Quorum holds "the keys to open up the authority of (God's) kingdom upon the four corners of the earth." (DC 124:128) They are "special witnesses of the name of Christ...and they (are) equal in authority and power" to the First Presidency. (DC 107:23-24) The Twelve can perform any and all functions in the church, but only under the direction of the First Presidency.

The awesome role of the president of the church

> The *Encyclopedia of Mormonism* tells us:
>
> *The President of the Church is the prophet, seer, and revelator who is authorized to direct the affairs of the Church throughout the earth. He speaks and acts under divine guidance from Jesus Christ, who is the head of his church...The Doctrine and Covenants specifies that the President's duty is "to be like unto Moses" (D&C 107:91-92; 28:2), relaying the will of God to his people and teaching them the gospel.[153]*

Mormons expect their prophet to receive revelations about doctrines, organizational matters, proper moral conduct and disciplinary actions. He can speak with authority about the correct meaning of scripture, the spiritual concerns of the faithful, and the problems besetting the world. His words are considered scripture.

The keeper of the keys

It is hard for non-Mormons to fully understand the authority of the president of the Mormon Church. The

---

[153] . Op. Cit. Vol 3, from LDS Collectors Library '97

Encyclopedia of Mormonism tells us that the keys to all the fundamental principles, government, and doctrines of the Gospel were given by revelation to Joseph Smith and the "designated prophets" (ie, presidents) of the church.

We continue down the pyramid. There are ten leadership roles in the church. The first three belong to individual men and their counselors, the other seven are occupied by men scattered across the church. There are five offices within the church, which include Apostles, Seventies, Patriarchs, High Priests, and elders. All exercise their role by "the power of the keys," a power given by ordination at the hands of a person who presides and holds keys at a higher level. But nobody can exercise his priestly powers unless he has been delegated by the president of the church.

> *The president of the church, who is the senior apostle, holds all the keys presently on earth and presides over all the...work of the church. He delegates authority by giving the keys of specific offices to others.*[154]

As a living "prophet, seer, and revelator," the LDS president has the authority to change or add to scripture

God's living "prophet, seer, and revelator" holds power *even over the Word of God*. The *Encyclopedia of Mormonism* tells us: "His official statements in his time may take precedence over revelations in scripture pertinent to other times or over statements by previous presidents of the Church."[155] In other words, the president of the Church can overrule St. John or St. Paul, or any other author in the Bible. The

---

[154] . *Encyclopedia of Mormonism*, Vol. 2, under "Keys to the Priesthood."
[155] . Op. Cit. Vol 3, under the article "President of the Church" [180] . Ibid.

Encyclopedia hastens to assure its readers that the LDS president and revelations from other dispensations "rarely are in conflict."[180] But it is clear that they can be in conflict, and when that conflict occurs, the prophetic authority of the current president prevails.

Some examples

In his *New Translation* of the Bible, Joseph Smith did not hesitate to add to, change, or delete hundreds of passages in the Old and New Testaments. Here is an example. With no knowledge of Hebrew, any copies of the original, and operating strictly through the power of revelation, this semi-literate man made changes in the first chapter of the Book of Genesis. Joseph Smith turns the Creation story into a long monologue spoken by God himself:

> And it came to pass, that the Lord spoke to Moses, saying: *Behold, I reveal unto you concerning this heaven and this earth: write the words which I speak. I am the beginning and the End; the Almighty God. By mine Only Begotten I created these things. Yea, in the beginning I created the heavens, and the earth upon which thou standest. (Genesis 1:1-3 Inspired Version, my emphasis)*

Succeeding presidents dared change the teaching of Joseph Smith himself. For instance, no doctrine had a more dramatic impact on the lives of the Saints than the doctrine of plural marriage. When Smith received this revelation, it included a stern warning from Jesus himself:

> *For behold, I reveal unto you a new and everlasting covenant; and if ye abide not by that covenant, then are ye damned; for no one can reject this covenant and*

be permitted to enter into my glory. (D & C 132:4, my emphasis)

Utah had become a territory and wanted to become a state. LDS teaching on polygamy stood in the way. In 1890, President Wilford Woodruff issued his famous Manifesto, a revelation in which God withdrew his command to practice plural marriage. Gordon Hinkley, a modern prophet/president, pronounced polygamy a grave sin, something that could mean ejection from the church.

In appreciation

To show how Joseph Smith brought order to chaos, Mormons point out the sad plight of Christianity. As we now know by heart, there are more than forty-three thousand different Christian churches in America today, a babbling confusion of different Christian voices, mostly of the Evangelical variety.

The Latter-day Saints have avoided spiritual meltdown by their submission to a living prophet who alone has authority over the power of the keys. With the exception of the president, every Saint is under the prophetic authority of someone higher. This powerful structure preserves the unity of the church.

Authority in the Catholic Church

Put on your thinking cap! In the long section that follows, we will discuss the role of the prophets in the Bible, as seen from a non-literalist perspective. Next, we will ponder apostolic succession, the role of the Twelve, and the apostolic tradition. This will lead to a discussion of the meaning of an unfolding Church Tradition and the role played by the Magisterium. We will explore the authority of the papacy, including a discussion of papal infallibility. Finally, we will show why the Church rejects the concept of ongoing revelation.

Biblical scholars describe the actual role of prophets in the Old Testament

Joseph Smith claimed to be a prophet and all Mormon presidents are considered modern prophets. We need to go back and listen to scholars who have examined the role of the prophet in ancient Israel. *First*, with the exception of Elijah, they did not volunteer and they were not ordained. Their calling came as a gift from God.

Second, with one notable exception in Ezechiel, the prophets did not receive new revelations. Instead, they were the conscience of Israel, challenging the people to remember the Covenant at Sinai. In defense of that covenant, they were not afraid to denounce either king or people for idolatry, for mistreatment of the powerless, or for dishonest business practices. They threatened God's judgment in the face of disloyalty, and promised blessings if the Covenant was kept.

Third, they were aware that they voiced the word of God. Sometimes they talked about God, but more dramatic were the times when they spoke in the first person in God's name, beginning with, "Thus says the Lord!"

Fourth, they were great poets. Because their words were full of images and metaphor, they were not precise and their message was sometimes vague.

Prophets in the New Testament

The New Testament speaks frequently of Old Testament prophets. In the New Testament, "Prophecy" was either the gift given to an individual, or the prophetic word itself. John the Baptist was the most famous prophet in the New Testament, and there were other prophets who are listed among the leaders of the Church. There is no evidence of ordination. A prophet achieved his role as a gift from God. He did not possess an office that was part of the established church institution. Even though some would say that prophecy disappeared after the ancient Church, there have always been prophets within Catholicism who challenged believers and non-believers alike, such as Francis of Assisi, Catherine of Sienna, and the modern Dorothy Day, Oscar Romero, and Saint Pope John Paul II.

We conclude then, that neither the Old nor New Testaments support Latter-day Saint conclusions about the role of a prophet. They were not ordained. They did not occupy an office within Israel. They were not revelators of new truths. Their role was to demand fidelity to the Old and New Covenants and warn the people of the consequences of infidelity.

Apostolic authority

Catholics believe that the ancient apostolic authority continues on in the church through its bishops. In *Dei Verbum*, the Vatican Council tells us,

> *This holy synod...teaches and declares that Jesus Christ, the eternal pastor, established the holy church by sending the apostles as he himself had been sent by the Father. He willed that their successors, the bishops, should be the shepherds of his church until the end of the world.*[156]

---

[156] . *Lumen Gentium*, # 18

Historically, there were sometimes gaps in the papacy, or times of shameful power struggle. We saw this during the Dark Ages and during the years before the Reformation. But all over the Church throughout the long centuries there has always been an unbroken chain of bishops. The Church is referring to these bishops when she speaks of "apostolic succession."

The role of the Twelve, a brief history

We begin by clarifying the difference between the apostles and the Twelve. They were not identical terms. Biblical scholars argue that the word "apostle" was coined after the resurrection of Jesus. The following were called apostles in the New Testament, even though they were not members of the Twelve: James the "brother" of the Lord, Paul, Barnabas, Andronicus, and Junia. Junia was a woman.

The Twelve occupy a strong role in the Gospels. Mormons say that Jesus established the Twelve as a permanent governing body within the church. True enough, the Twelve were personally chosen by Jesus to be his constant companions. But the historical evidence shows that Jesus did not create an ongoing office within the Church called The Twelve, because they did not survive the first generation. Why? In part, it is because membership in the Twelve was based on certain requirements, which Peter described when it came time to replace the traitor Judas.

> It is necessary to choose one of the men who have been with us the whole time the Lord Jesus went in and out among us, beginning from John's baptism to the time when Jesus was taken up from us. One of these must become a witness with us of his resurrection." (Acts 2:21-22)

This job description limits the members of the Twelve to the first generation of disciples.

It is important to ask ourselves about the significance of the number "twelve" in the Bible.

We think of the Twelve Patriarchs in the Old Testament. These were the *twelve sons of Jacob in the Book of Genesis*, who became the foundation stones for the twelve tribes of Israel. To be one of the ancient patriarchs was not an ongoing office. Nobody was appointed to succeed Judah or Joseph or any of the others.

In the New Testament, Jesus speaks only once concerning the purpose of the Twelve: "Truly, I say to you, in the new world, when the Son of Man shall sit on his glorious throne, you who have followed me will also sit on twelve thrones, judging the twelve tribes of Israel." (Mk. 19:28) The *New Jerome Biblical Commentary* says: "The Twelve were understood as unique: they were the representatives of the renewed Israel who would be seated on the twelve thrones of judgment."(Mt 19:28; Lk 22:30)[157] McKenzie's *Dictionary of the Bible* adds that, even as the twelve patriarchs were the foundation stones of the old Israel, *"the apostles are the foundation stones of the New Israel of the Church."*[158]

The apostles were witnesses who gave us the "apostolic tradition"

All Christians agree that the apostles were chosen by God as the authorized witnesses to the life, death, and resurrection of Jesus. Their teaching set the rule of faith for

---

[157] . Op. Cit. 81:155

[158] . Op. Cit. p. 47, under "Apostle."

the ancient Christian community and lives on in the Church today.

The apostles witnessed to an encounter with *a living person*

As we saw in our chapter on revelation, the apostles handed on more than a list of religious truths and practices. Most of all, they announced a living person. St. John writes:

> That...which we have heard, which we have seen with our eyes, which we have looked at and our hands have touched, this we proclaim concerning the Word of Life. The life appeared; we have seen it and testify to it, so that you may have fellowship with us; and our fellowship is with the Father and with his Son Jesus Christ. (1 John 1:1-3)

And so the apostles were not witnesses simply to the teachings of Jesus. They were witnesses to the Word Made Flesh himself. They wanted us to hear what they heard, to touch what they touched...the living Jesus Christ who was always more than any doctrine or any gospel could ever express. Their testimony about the life, death, and resurrection of Jesus Christ formed the solid foundation of all subsequent Christian belief.

The apostles witnessed to *a Way*

The apostles witnessed to Christ not only through their preaching and writing, but also through a way of life, prayer, and worship which helped early Christians put on the mind and heart of Christ. This means that beliefs, rituals, and a rule of life are also part of the apostolic tradition.

Proclaiming Christ, the apostles needed to find *words* to express who he was and what he had done. Proclaiming his way of life, they needed to outline *rules* expressing his heart. Proclaiming his living presence, they needed to find *rituals* that would bring him alive again into the lives of his disciples when they remembered his death and resurrection.

The *Catechism* reminds Catholics that the heritage handed on from the apostles was entrusted, not to a single individual or group of individuals, or even to a pope exercising his office in Rome. The apostolic heritage was entrusted *to the whole Church*. As the Vatican Council explains it:

> *The apostles entrusted the Sacred deposit of the faith...*
> *to the whole of the Church. "By adhering to (this*
> *heritage) the entire holy people, united to its pastors,*
> *remains always faithful to the teaching of the apostles,*
> *to the brotherhood, to the breaking of the bread and the*
> *prayers.* (Dei Verbum, #10), quoted by the
> *Catechism,* #84

The faithful witness of the Spirit-filled Church includes the two elements contained in the apostolic tradition: 1) the proclamation of a living person, Jesus Christ, and 2) the beliefs, doctrines, rituals, and scriptures of the ancient Church, which bring us into contact with Jesus Christ. The Church accepts the apostolic tradition as the guide for all Christian belief. If something contradicts this original witness, or does not flow from it, it cannot be accepted as part of Christian faith.

The Magisterium of the Church

Historical roots

We saw that the New Testament was characterized by considerable diversity. But the early Church was also concerned about *unity*, which prevented diversity from crumbling into chaos. After the death of the apostles, the Church guarded the unity of her faith in her ancient creeds and through her liturgy. But above all, she guarded the unity of her faith through the ministry of her bishops in communion with the Bishop of Rome. We call their united authority the *Magisterium*.

Catholics believe that in every age, there are men who proclaim and guard the Gospel as the apostles did. Quoting the Vatican Council, the *Catechism* tells us,

> *In order that the full and living Gospel might always be preserved in the Church, the apostles left bishops as their successors. They gave them 'their own position of teaching authority.*[159]

In this way, "the apostolic preaching, expressed in a special way in the inspired Books, was to be preserved in a continuous line of succession until the end of time."[160]

Leadership in the Church today

The mission of those ancient bishops continues today in the bishops of the modern Catholic Church. Catholics are on solid ground when they believe that this development

---

[159] . Ibid.

[160] . D.V. 7

was guided by the Holy Spirit and was part of God's design. Quoting the Vatican Council, the *Catechism* teaches us:

> *The bishops have by divine institution taken the place of the apostles as pastors of the Church, so that whoever listens to them is listening to Christ."*[161]

The local bishop, the College of Bishops, and the pope

In the words of the Vatican Council,

> *The individual bishops are the visible source and foundation of unity in their own particular churches."*[162]

Catholics believe that Peter and the other apostles were part of the very foundation of the Church. They formed a kind of "college" with Peter at their head. Today, Catholics teach that the body of bishops throughout the world form a "college," with the Pope at their head. United under the primacy of the pope, the college of bishops has "supreme and full authority over the universal Church." (*Lumen Gentium* 22) The college of bishops exercises this authority in its most solemn manner when it gathers together in an ecumenical council, such as Vatican II.

St. Peter, Shepherd of the flock: The role of the pope

According to the Gospel of St. Luke, Jesus gave Peter a special task.

> *"Simon, Simon, Satan has asked to sift you all as wheat. But I have prayed for you, Simon, that your faith may not fail. And*

---

[161] . *Lumen Gentium*, 20 #2
[162] . Ibid, 22

when you have turned back, strengthen your brothers." (Luke 22: 31-32)

In this way, Jesus commanded Peter to be a stronghold of faith for his "brothers" and for the whole community. In the Gospel of John, the risen Jesus made Peter shepherd of His flock. (John 21:15-17) In the Jewish world, it was the task of the shepherd to find pastures and watering-places for his flock. The shepherd defended his sheep against wolves and led them to safety each night. Catholics believe that, when Jesus the Good Shepherd commanded Peter to "feed my lambs...feed my sheep," he appointed Peter to watch over his flock in his name.

The successor of St. Peter

Peter and Paul both died as martyrs in Rome. We know from ancient Church Fathers like Ignatius of Antioch, Dionysius of Corinth, and Irenaeus of Lyons that the church in Rome was held in special esteem. Catholics believe that the successor to St. Peter is the Bishop of Rome. The Bishop of Rome was official witness to the apostolic tradition handed on in his church, and other churches acknowledged his authority, turning to him for answers to questions about doctrine and practice. The Bishop of Rome gradually continued the functions exercised by Peter among the apostles. He was the rock of the Church's unity, the guardian of its faith. In this way, Catholics can say that the papacy is willed by Christ. The *Catholic Catechism* sums up Catholic teaching about the pope, bishop of Rome, and Peter's successor in a brief paragraph:

> *(He) is the perpetual and visible source and foundation of the unity both of the bishops and of the*

whole company of the faithful. For the Roman Pontiff, by reason of his office as Vicar of Christ, and as pastor of the entire Church, has full, supreme, and universal power over the whole Church, a power which he can always exercise unhindered.[163]

But this does not mean that the Pope is a monarch with absolute power. He is bound by revelation contained in Scripture and by the defined teachings of Tradition. He cannot receive new revelations for the Church, and he has to speak and act as part of the college of bishops.

Infallibility

Under the leadership of the pope and bishops, the Church has framed the words of her creeds, celebrated her worship, and crafted her teaching. When we are talking about the infallibility *of the pope or an ecumenical council*, we are talking about a gift of the Spirit that applies only in very restricted conditions. Neither pope nor council can speak outside the meaning of the Scriptures and the context of its long Tradition. This gift preserves both the teaching Church and the believing Church from error regarding the truth revealed to us in Jesus Christ.

The *Catechism* explains the meaning of infallibility in careful terms. The Pope does not speak infallibility simply by himself. It is a gift exercised *within the Church*, a gift given by Christ in order to preserve "the purity of the faith handed on by the apostles." (#889) It is a "supernatural sense of faith" which enables the People of God, guided by the living Magisterium, to live an authentic faith. But the Church knows that this power has its limits. The *Catechism* quoted the Vatican Council:

---

[163] # 883

This Magisterium is not superior to the Word of God, but is its servant. It teaches only what has been handed on to it. At the divine command and with the help of the Holy Spirit, it listens to this devotedly, guards it with dedication, and expounds it faithfully.

Popes have chosen to speak infallibly only twice, about the immaculate conception and assumption of Mary. They were careful to ground their words in Scripture and Tradition, after consultation with their fellow bishops. Their proclamation followed a carefully worded formula that made their intention clear.

Final thoughts: A blessed Church...a sinful Church

The Vatican Council pointed out the difference between those who happen to be baptized Catholics, and those who are "fully incorporated" into the Church. Those who are fully incorporated live lives of deep faith that are filled with the Holy Spirit and the grace of God.

These are the Catholic saints. Some were popes, bishops, or priests, and many lived quiet lives in convents and monasteries. But the majority were saints of the hearth and home, busy earning a living, busy as parents, busy as ordinary sons and daughters of God. Only a few of these saints have been officially canonized by the Church. Most lived and continue to live lives recognized only by those who love them. In them the Church is made flesh, and in them, she will continue to proclaim the gospel and live in the truth.

No individual Catholic—not even a pope as a private person—has any guarantee that he will never fall from the true faith. That promise belongs only to the Church. Within her body there will always be the Spirit-filled faithful who trust in the grace of God. Because of them, the ancient apostolic witness will never be forgotten. One can see this through a study of Church history. Those who scorn the Church point to the so-called "black popes," but those who love the Church notice that great saints flourished alongside the blackest of the black popes. Again and again in the history of the Church, "dead ashes" have suddenly burst into flame with the fire of the Holy Spirit.

Catholics do not believe that her dialogue with God came to an end with the last book in the New Testament. The Church hands her life on to future generations, and this Spirit-guided process is a conversation with the living God. And so, under the leadership of our bishops in communion with our pope, we continue to live the words of Scripture and the teachings of Tradition. What was not clear in one generation becomes clear in another. The saints still live and the prophets still speak. The life of the Church is like the marching of the seasons of the year. Sometimes we burn with love, but at other times we shiver with the cold. The perfect God seems content with our imperfection. He leaves us in the struggle, to stumble in our weakness, to stand tall in the refreshing breeze of the Holy Spirit.

Catholic Growth Points

Let me return to my explanation of the word "conversion." It can happen on many different levels. In our present context, it means I change one church for another. We could call this religious conversion. But there are other kinds of conversion. All of them have a single common element: I am willing to be personally responsible and personally accountable for some element of my life.

In *religious conversion,* I take responsibility for my religious choice. This does not mean I join a different church, although it might. It does mean that I hold myself accountable for growing in my faith. I choose to be accountable to God, to my conscience, and maybe to someone I respect and love. But sincere religious conversion implies other forms of conversion. For instance:

— *Moral conversion.* I decide to live in a Christ-like way. I observe the way of grace, love, and virtue. I keep the moral rules and values implied by my religious conversion. I choose to use the sacrament of Penance as a source of moral responsibility.

— *Intellectual conversion.* I resolve to grow intellectually. This means reading books and magazine, taking classes, following good sites on the Internet, listening to solid voices. There can be a lot of self-deception here if I never get outside my comfort zone. We need to grow in breadth, not just in depth. If I consider myself a liberal, I need to listen respectfully to conservatives and their point of view. If I am conservative, I need to be challenged by liberal thinking. If I can't do this, I become part of the divisive problem afflicting our Church today.

— *Emotional conversion.* We are all wounded people. If we do not face up to our inner wounds, we can live distorted lives. This means a better understanding of our personal stories, self-awareness, and choice of friends who make our lives better and not worse.

— *Socio-economic conversion.* In a way, this is the most difficult form of conversion of them all. We live within a world, a culture, in a nation, and in a community. It involves an ability to look at our world and its institutions with an important question in mind: How does this help build the Kingdom of God? This is where Catholic social teaching comes in. When I bring Catholic social teaching into my sermons, I can count on the angry reaction. Here I would suggest a thoughtful study of the third section of the *Catholic Catechism,* called "Our Life in Christ."

PART SEVEN

Was there a Great Apostasy?

When Joseph Smith founded his church, he was a latecomer. By the time he arrived on the religious scene there was the Catholic Church, the Orthodox Churches, all the Protestant churches founded during the Reformation, and hundreds of Protestant Evangelical churches based on somebody's unique understanding of the Bible. But when Smith gathered his handful of followers in a ramshackle cabin and founded The Church of Christ, he boasted that his was the only true church on earth. All the other churches were lost tools of Satan, abandoned by God after a great apostasy that occurred sometime after the death of the last apostle.

The bald arrogance of such a claim takes my breath away. But it occurred to me that the question of a great apostasy is almost a side issue, a slight of hand that distracts us from the most basic of all questions I posed at the beginning of this book: Who is your God? Is God an exalted man of the human species with wives and countless children, who is literally our father? Or is God the mysterious reality existing outside the realm of being, who called the universe forth from nothing and holds it in his hand? An accusing finger pointed at the sins of the Catholic Church does not explain the meaning of God and the role God plays in our salvation. But our story is not finished if I do not address Mormon accusations about corrupted scriptures and a great apostasy.

22

Did the Bible Survive Its Journey

Through History Unscathed?

Mormons answer NO
—and claim that the present version of
the Bible is corrupt
Catholics answer YES
—and point to the results of a modern
science called Text Criticism

The Book of Mormon tells us that an "abominable
church" removed "plain and precious things" from
the Bible. And so the Bible may be useful, but it is also
flawed beyond redemption. For this reason, Latter-day
Saints argue that we need the truths supplied by new
scriptures and a living prophet.

For the LDS: A mutilated Bible

As we will see in the next chapter, Latter-day Saints say that, sometime after the death of the last Apostle, the Church fell into sin and darkness. The Scriptures fell prey to false prophets and wicked priests. Lost somewhere in the past were the perfect originals of a badly distorted Old Testament and New Testament. An LDS sponsored flyer that appeared in newspapers all over my corner of the Northwest summarized the Mormon position:

But as is well known, the Bible does not contain all the doctrines and truths taught by the prophets and apostles, nor have the teachings preserved in it come down to us in an absolutely perfect form....Mormons fortunately, however, are not forced to rely only on the testimony of prophets and apostles of the Old and New Testament times and lands. They have modern day revelation.

—From *Jesus is the Christ,* a 1995 newspaper insert

Whatever date they offer for the apostasy, Mormons say that the Church of Jesus was taken back to heaven, leaving behind a Bible so badly bent it cannot be used to jump start a restored church. The only hope is modern prophet and new revelation.

And so Mormons believe that the Bible once contained the Mormon Gospel. Once upon a time, the Bible told the story of eternal progression and a chance for the sons of Heavenly Father to fight their way to the level of godhood and join the cascading line of gods on their way to infinity. Weaving in and out of the story was a tale of gods without number, those family men with wives and billions upon billions of spirit children. For Mormons who believe in Smith as their prophet, the fact that there is no trace of this anywhere in the Bible today is sure and certain proof that it must have been there, once upon a time. Now, thanks to modern prophets and modern day revelation, we have a gospel restored.

New scriptures retrieve what was lost

As we know by now, Mormons believe that restoration began with the publication of the Book of Mormon. But other books would appear, which would also restore the lost gospel:

> *And after it (the Book of Mormon) had come forth unto them I beheld other books, which came forth by the power of the Lamb...And the angel spake unto me, saying: these last records...shall establish the truth of the first...and shall make known the plain and precious things which have been taken away from them. (1 Nephi 13:40)*

Mormons believe that those "other records" refer to two books by Joseph Smith which Mormons also consider scripture: the *Doctrine and Covenants* and the *Pearl of Great Price.* The plain and precious things restored to the world are most clearly expressed in two smaller books appearing in the *Pearl of Great Price,* called the *Book of Moses* and the *Book of Abraham.* As I explained before, the Mormons also consider the words of their modern prophet to have the authority of scripture.

SCHOLARS PONDER THE JEWISH SCRIPTURES

The Mormon explanation comes as close to reality as the caped heroes who fight crime and injustice on TV. I invite my reader to return to Chapter Three in this book, which asks the question: Are Mormons Christian? There, I describe an ancient religious movement called Gnosticism, with its claim of secret knowledge, lost books, and prophets proclaiming restored truths. Joseph Smith and the Mormon Church have dragged us once more into this ancient morass. I call them modern Gnostics.

In rebuttal, I turn to the Jewish, Protestant, and Catholic biblical experts who have searched out the origins of both the Old and New Testaments. This search has been sketched out in many books on modern Scripture studies. We will base our discussion in this chapter on two excellent sources: *The Jewish Study Bible,* published in 2004 by Oxford Press, and the *New Jerome Biblical Commentary,* published in 1990 by Prentiss Hall.

Let's begin with the Old Testament. The first thing I note is that it was written by Jews, for Jews. And so I will use *The Jewish Study Bible* as my source. The Jewish religion was born from the experience of people who could not read or write. When the writing began, the different books were united into three different groups. The Jews call their scriptures the TANAKH, an acronym that stands for the *Law,* the *Prophets,* and the *Writings.*

The **Law**, also known as the *Torah,* refers to the first five books of the Jewish Scriptures. Jewish scholars tell us that the Torah is a composite reflecting many traditions and sources. It explores several themes, including the story of the ancient forefathers like Abraham and Moses, and the early development of Israel as a people, its covenant with God, and the promise of the land. It is a narrative interspersed with instructions and collections of laws about proper living, proper worship, and the way God deals with the world.

Scholars speak of the *"Yahwist,"* because that was his preferred word for God. But they also speak of the *Elohist,* who used the word "Elohim", the *Priest,* and the *Deuteronomist.* These are not individuals. The names represent different schools that were part of the writing during different time periods along the way. These books were considered authentic scripture sometime around the destruction of Jerusalem by the Babylonians. Carried off into exile, the Jews took the Torah with them. It played a key role in their religious survival.

As time went on, the community added more books to the official "canon" or collection of books considered the authentic Word of God. These were the Nevi'm, or the **Prophets**. They include Joshua, Judges, Samuel, Kings, Isaiah, Jeremiah, Ezekiel and the Twelve Minor (because they were shorter) Prophets. The fact that histories like Joshua, Judges, Samuel, and Kings could also be numbered among the prophets means that we need to think harder about the meaning of the word "prophet."

The last books to be considered an authentic part of the Jewish Scriptures are the Kethuvim, or the **Writings**. This includes historical works, prayers, books of wisdom, and apocalyptic prophecy. Community discernment about these books was still going on during the time of Jesus.

I have asked my readers to slog through this discussion because it explains why I consider the Mormon charge that "plain and precious things" were erased by evil priests to be a cartoonish effort by Joseph Smith to explain away the total absence of gods and their wives, spirit-children, and eternal progression. Instead, the Jewish Scriptures are what they have always been, born from the rich story of a people chosen by God, called to Covenant, and challenged to become his holy nation.

THE SCIENCE OF TEXT CRITICISM

Catholics will argue that, through the new science of "Text Criticism," biblical scholars have been able to retrieve the ancient texts familiar to the first Christians. Text Criticism reveals that the Scriptures handed down to our generation are amazingly intact. There is no evidence that "plain and precious things" were removed from the Bible.

Text criticism is an incredibly exacting tool which has enabled Protestant and Catholic biblical experts to set out in search of the original texts of both the Old and New Testaments. This search has been sketched out in many books on modern Scripture studies. We will base our discussion on an excellent source called *New Jerome Biblical Commentary*.[164]

Pope Pius XII said in his *Divino afflante Spiritu*, that the first responsibility of biblical scholars is to make sure that the text handed down from ancient times is the best and most accurate possible. This is not easy. Ancient Hebrew was written without vowels, and somebody had to decide whether "Kng Dvd Lvd" meant "King David lived," or "King David Loved." The meaning came from the context.

Since all the ancient manuscripts were hand-copied, a scribe usually wrote while someone read from an older manuscript. But if he got tired or distracted, he might omit part of his text, or copy it twice, or copy it wrong. Handwriting could be sloppy, and sometimes scribes ran words together and made a new word with a different meaning. And so on...including the possibility that somebody deliberately changed or dropped part of the text.

The mission: come as close as you can to the original text of the Bible. At first, the task seems impossible. How do you recover an original copy that everyone admits has been lost in history? If the owners of that book had made only one

---

[164] . *New Jerome Biblical Commentary*, (Prentiss Hall, Englewood Cliffs, New Jersey, 1990) 68:6-188

copy, it would be impossible. *But what if the original had been copied many times? What if copies had been made from those copies of the original? What if other writers had quoted hundreds of thousands of words from that book? The lost book might not be so lost, after all.*

Enter the science of text criticism

When Smith was alive, scholars were translating the Old Testament from a Hebrew manuscript that dated from the year 900. AD. It was the oldest copy any Jewish synagogue possessed. The reason is simple. When the rabbis decided to replace old and worn-out copies of the TANAKH, they produced a new edition and destroyed all the old scrolls in every synagogue.

But then the new science of archeology began to uncover many more ancient manuscripts for both the Old and the New Testaments. After 1920, the discoveries multiplied. Some of the manuscripts were debris from the passing time, mere fragments shuffled together in a clump. But others were almost as legible as the day they were written. Through a stunning combination of technology and pure hard work, text critics have been able to assemble whole manuscripts out of scattered pieces. They have learned how to compare one manuscript with another, sorting out the best reading for each word and phrase appearing in the Bible. Patiently, doggedly, they have come very close to the original books of the Bible. Thanks to their work, we can appreciate the care with which the believing community preserved and copied the sacred books over the centuries, and we can be confident that we are reading accurate translations of the words the original authors meant for us to read.

A choice of manuscripts

It would twist history to think there was only one "official" version of Hebrew Scriptures during the time of Jesus. Researchers have discovered that a well-traveled Jew living during those days could pick between different versions. Scribes in Jewish religious centers located in Babylon, Palestine, and Egypt had been copying manuscripts for some time, and as a result, distinct "editions" of the Hebrew Scriptures were already in circulation. Some copies were longer with sections added on, while others were shorter with sections omitted.[165] At about the same time, a popular version of the Old Testament appeared in Greek. This translation, called the *Septuagint,* played a very important role in the history of the Church, because the Greek speaking writers of the New Testament used the Greek Septuagint when they quoted from the Old Testament.

Scholars conclude, therefore, that ancient Judaism possessed no "official" version of what we now call the Old Testament. There were different interpretations and different flavors even in Jesus' day. There is no historical evidence that Jesus or anyone else argued over the "correct" version of the Hebrew scriptures. So, it is up to the Mormons to find some ancient mention of a single official manuscript of the Bible without begging the question. Otherwise, the charge of changes made in some basic original Old Testament or New Testament is a heavy-handed self-serving imposition of modern issues onto an ancient world where such questions had never been asked.

---

[165] . Mormons who learn about the different "editions" will use that fact as proof of the corruption of the original biblical text. But the burden of proof is on them. In order to do this, they will have to study the work of text criticism, and will have to ponder seriously the conclusions of modern biblical scholarship.

An official text at last

Shortly after the destruction of Jerusalem and the Temple by the Romans in 67 AD, Jewish leaders were trying desperately to pick up the pieces of their shattered religion. If the Jewish faith was going to survive, it would be through the prayerful study of its scriptures. The Jewish rabbis finally decided to settle on one official text. And so they examined the several versions of the Old Testament that were available to them, searching for the best text they could find. For the Torah, they followed the Babylonian tradition, but in the other books, they followed the Palestinian type text. This was the beginning of Rabbinic Judaism as we understand it today. From then on, the Jews survived, not by their Temple and its sacrifices, but by building their lives around *Torah*. They were very conscientious about preserving their Hebrew Scriptures with the greatest possible accuracy, and scholars today admire their precision.

But were the rabbis faithful to the original books?

For a long time, this was an impossible question to answer. As we just said, it was the Jewish custom to destroy worn-out scrolls, and so the oldest scroll available at the time of Joseph Smith dated only to around the year 900 AD. But starting in 1948, scholars were suddenly able to take a thousand year leap back into the past, thanks to the discovery of the famous Dead Sea Scrolls, which gave us complete copies of most books in the Old Testament. Written two hundred years before the time of Christ, they reflected an even more distant tradition. Scholars could place these texts on a table and compare them to the text used today by modern Jews and Christians.

Other ancient manuscripts were also located, including translations made in other languages. Translations are valuable, because they give a glimpse of the manuscript from which they were made.[166] Following a painstaking process, scholars were able to use these manuscripts to establish an ever more accurate collection of the Hebrew Scriptures, which is used now to make modern translations.

Text criticism and the New Testament

Written on fragile materials, the original books of the New Testament have all been lost. When Joseph Smith was alive, the oldest manuscript available to the scholars of that day dated from the 300's or 400's. But since 1890, ninety papyrus manuscripts of New Testament books have been discovered, dating from the second to the eighth Centuries. Ancient translations—such as a Syriac version of the New Testament—have also been found. Scholars use these translations to determine the accuracy of more recent manuscripts. In addition, the ancient Fathers of the Church quoted so many passages from the New Testament that an expert could virtually reconstruct a New Testament from that source alone! The quotations used by the ancient Fathers were compared with the New Testament manuscripts.

From these sources, and with their accustomed painstaking precision, the text critics have been able to reconstruct the New Testament as it was probably read during the earliest years of the ancient Church. There is no evidence of glaring gaps, of apostate priests deliberately slicing out words and verses that did not meet their evil

---

[166] The *King James Version*, for instance, gives a very accurate rendition of many Hebrew words and expressions. These "Hebraisms" give the *King James* its unique sound and rhythm.

vision. The real Gospel of Jesus, handed on from the witness of the apostles, is what any person can read for himself in any modern translation of the New Testament today. The "missing" parts of the Bible will always be missing, because they were never there.

In conclusion

The science of Text Criticism has been able to recover most of the originals and there is no evidence that "plain and precious things" have disappeared from the pages of Scripture. An argument from silence is no argument at all. It is simply based on an old fallacy called begging the question. It is up to those who make such accusations to find the concrete evidence that will back up their charge.

Catholic Growth Point

I hope you have a Bible in your house. As I pointed out in the chapter on the Mormon missionaries, a favorite tactic is to catch you without one. Check the front of your Bible and see what translation it is. Some still have the old Douai-Rheims. This translation is not a good choice because — even though it was a good effort and earlier than the King James version so popular with Protestants — it lacks modern scholarship. Most Catholics have a copy of the *New American Bible*, translated by Catholic scholars.
Catholic and Protestant scholars have achieved, sometimes apart and sometimes together, good modern translations that are acceptable for Catholics. If you get a modern Protestant translation, make sure it contains "the Apocrypha," a derogative term for the books written in Greek that have always been part of a Catholic Bible, but were left out of the Old Testament by Jewish scholars after the destruction of Jerusalem. Martin Luther and the King

James rejected the ancient Christian numbering, choosing to ignore the ancient Christian list of books included in the Old Testament, and follow the Jewish numbering, instead.

23

Did the True Church Survive its

Journey Through History?

Mormons answer NO
—and accuse the ancient
Catholic Church of Apostasy Catholics
answer YES
—and speak of an unfolding Tradition
faithful to Christ

Preliminary thoughts

The world of great affairs did not even notice the life and
death of Jesus Christ. Historians tell us that Christianity
lived in obscurity for seven generations. We have a
sentence here, a paragraph there, a handful of Christian
writings, and the passing notice of Roman writers. But
in the larger world, things were a blank. For instance,
during the reign of Emperor Alexander Severus (222-
235), a respected scholar named Cassius Dio wrote many
volumes about the history of the world without once
mentioning the Christians.[167]

Respected scholars steeped in the history, culture,
and archeology of those distant times humbly admit

---

[167] Hubert Jedin and John Dolan, eds, *History of the Church,* Vol I: From the
Apostolic Community to Constantine" (New York, 1965), p 132, quoted in *A*
history of Christendom, Vol I, by Warren H. Carroll, Christendom Press, 1985

that the best history of the ancient Church contains gaps and a certain amount of speculation. Unfortunately, there are those who assume they know the whole story beforehand. Some are Catholic fundamentalists trying to defend a very simplistic understanding of Church History. Others are disbelievers trying to prove that the original church lost its bearings and went astray. Whatever their purpose, they pick and sort through the rock pile of history, leaving any stone behind that does not support their foregone conclusions about the life and times of the first centuries of Christianity. This is the only part of the book where we engage in a debate.

Mormons level the worst accusation one church can make about another. They say the Catholic Church fell into apostasy and never returned to the true path. Even though they try to be decent about it, they teach that ancient Catholics entangled themselves in immorality and false doctrine, abandoning the "one Christ... one gospel, one plan of salvation, one set of saving ordinances,(and) one group of legal administrators" who made up the "one true church."[168] This is either true or it is slander of the worst order, and Catholics have the right to an energetic reply.

The key question: how to remain faithful

For both the LDS and the Catholic churches, it is about the meaning of hope and how to remain faithful. A Mormon will ask how his church can arrive safely home in a world whose history is surely drawing to a close. A Catholic is confident that his ancient

---

[168] Ibid.

church will remain true to the Gospel, even when she is being carried headlong into the questions and challenges of the twenty-first century, with the end nowhere in sight.

THE GREAT APOSTASY

Jesus said to Peter: "Upon this rock I shall build my church and the gates of hell shall not prevail against it." (Mt 16:18). But Mormons say that Jesus made this promise in vain. The gates of hell did indeed prevail, and very quickly.

Once upon a time, Christ restored a church, but it perished

If you remember from our first chapters, Mormons teach that the gospel Jesus preached was a *restored* gospel that goes back into infinity. As far as the inhabitants of this earth are concerned, it was first proclaimed to *Adam* in the Garden of Eden.[169] Mormon President Joseph Fielding Smith Jr. once told the faithful:

> *Contrary to the generally accepted belief, the Gospel of Jesus Christ was first proclaimed to Adam....When the Savior came into the world, he did not present a new plan for the salvation of mankind, but he came to restore that which had been taken away because of apostasy and the hardness of heart of the people of former times.*[170]

---

[169] Joseph Smith told his people that the Garden of Eden was in a location now occupied by the city of Independence, Missouri.

[170] . Joseph Fielding Smith Jr., *The Way to Perfection*, p. 55-56, quoted in the LDS Collectors Library '97.

Fielding Smith is basing his words on the usual assumption. The Gospel of Jesus was actually the good news about mortal men who could raise themselves to the level of godhood, marry women who would be their eternal companions, and bear them billions of spirit children. As I have said a few times with a small bit of sarcasm, the fact that none of this appears anywhere in Scripture is sure proof that evil priests must have erased it from every page.

The *Book of Mormon* predicted a great apostasy

In the very first book of the *Book of Mormon*, the Lord warned the Prophet Nephi that the church founded by Christ would also dissolve in apostasy. It would be the fault of an abominable church.

> *Thou seest the formation of that great and abominable church,*[171] *which is most abominable above all other churches; for behold, they have taken away from the gospel of the Lamb many parts which are plain and most precious; and also many covenants of the Lord have they taken away. (1 Nephi 13:26)*

Naming the villain

What was the name of the abominable church? Modern Mormons seem reluctant to blame Catholics alone. My distant relative Doctor Hugh Nibley, still considered one of the great Mormon scholars, tells his readers, "You must not identify this (the apostasy) just with the Roman Catholic

---

[171] As we have seen, "church" was another term that meant nothing in the Jewish world of Jeremiah

Church. People do because that's a simplistic answer."[172] Bruce R. McConkie wrote in a carefully researched and very popular book called *Mormon Doctrine:*

> *The titles church of the devil and great and abominable church are used to identify all churches or organizations of whatever name or nature—whether political, philosophical;, educational, economic, social, fraternal, civic, or religious—which are designed to take men on a course that leads away from God and his laws.*[173]

Other Mormon scholars would probably concur, but they try to soften the verdict. The authors of the *Encyclopedia of Mormonism* go out of their way to point to the good accomplished by the other churches and seem reluctant to identify the abominable church with any church or organization existing today. But in the end, all agree that the "plainness of the gospel" has been violated and the Bible is in shreds.

When did the apostasy begin? For many authors, the time was 200. Apostle James Talmage wrote that the original church had vanished by the year 300. Other authors suggest a lingering downfall, with the year 600 the probable date. Nibley uses the analogy of a tunnel: "The church which comes out of the tunnel is *not* the church that went into it."[174](His emphasis) All the Saints agree that the church plummeted into a chaos so deep that God was forced to take

---

[172] . From class notes, "teachings of the Book of Mormon," by Hugh Nibley, Semester 1, p. 196. Quoted in the *Encyclopedia of Mormonism*

[173] . Op. Cit., p. 137, Quoted in the LDS Collectors Library '97

[174] . Hugh Nibley, *BYU Studies*, Vol 16, No. 1, p. 149

priestly authority and his one true church away to the safety of heaven. All that remained were the fallen Church of Rome and the fruitless churches created by the Protestant Reformation.

How Latter-day Saints prove there was a great apostasy

Proof from the Bible

So, where is the proof? *The Great Apostasy*, by James E. Talmage, is the classic volume on the subject and his arguments are endlessly repeated. LDS apologists mine the New Testament for proof–a rather strange tactic in view of their belief that the Bible is corrupt. But Mormons select, for instance, St. Paul's warning in Acts 20:29-30, where he said to the Church of Ephesus,

> *After my departing shall grievous wolves enter in among you, not sparing the flock. Also of your own selves shall men arise, speaking perverse things, to draw away disciples after them.*

Surely, these words predict that an apostasy was standing at the very door of the Ephesus Church. Mormons bolster this evidence with a collage of New Testament proof texts taken from St. Paul and the Pastoral Epistles. To Latter-day Saints, these texts offer reasonable evidence that dry rot was eating at the heart of the whole Church even while the New Testament was being written.

Greek thought corrupted the true gospel

Many LDS apologists reason that the next generation of Christians allowed the pristine gospel to be contaminated by pagan Greek philosophy. They point out, correctly, that ancient Apologists like Justin Martyr used Greek patterns of thought to speak to a Greek-speaking world. One author says that this led to the "importation" of unacceptable pagan ideas into Christian belief. This was because God was no longer with his church, as Nibley assumes when he writes: "In the absence of direct divine guidance it was only natural for there to have been some drift from the pure faith."[175] All this culminated in St. Augustine, whose doctrine, framed in Neo-Platonic thought patterns, "even now...forms the bulk of Catholic doctrine."[201]

Next came moral collapse. Mormons who follow Talmage charge that the church fell into total mortal disarray in the early 300's, after Constantine ended the bloody persecutions of the Christian religion within the Roman Empire. The emperor's favorable attitude toward the church meant sudden prestige and worldly influence for Church leaders. Dazzled bishops left the simple customs of the apostolic Church behind, choosing instead the trappings of royal authority.[176]What little was left of the true church of Christ blew away on the dank wind of compromise and immorality.

As history unfolded, so did apostasy. Talmage describes "disorder and confusion" in the list of popes, the presence of anti-popes, and note the gaps when no pope ruled the Church.[177]I pointed all this out when I discussed Tradition. Talmage also listed "unauthorized changes in the Order of Christ's Church." These include: the doctrine of the Trinity, changes in "priesthood officers," with "unauthorized leaders" such as pope, cardinal, archbishop, monsignor, etc... Other "unauthorized changes" would be papal

---

[175] Ibid. P. 50 [201] Ibid.

[176] Many Catholics would agree that there was too much compromise with Roman power. But did this cause apostasy in a Church guided by the Holy Spirit?

[177] . Joseph Fielding Smith, Jr. *Religious Truths Defined*, (Bookcraft, Inc. Salt Lake City, Utah, 1959), pp 172-173

infallibility, the complicated ceremony of the Mass, the Seven Sacraments, the Sign of the Cross, the intercession of martyrs and saints, bowing or genuflecting before statues and images, and the doctrines about Mary. Also mentioned are "Original sin, indulgences, relics, lying wonders, feasts, asceticism, monasticism, celibacy, transubstantiation, pardons and almsgiving."[178]

Granted an apostasy, how do Mormons prove that their church is the one true church?

At this point, the LDS are only half-finished with their argument. The question they still face is a formidable one: *Even if you grant that a universal apostasy destroyed the original church, how can the Saints prove that their church is the true church?* After all, they appeared only two hundred years ago, and other, older churches make the same accusation, and the same claim.

Protestants say, thanks to a good understanding of the Bible alone, they have reformed or restored the true church. But as I said before, the Mormons do not even grant the Protestants a place in this discussion. They are building their argument on sand, because the Bible they study is flawed, its plain and precious passages changed or erased by false and evil priests. The Bible is no longer a valid proof for an issue as serious as the existence of the one true church.

Only the Mormon Church can call itself the true restoration. Why? Because God raised up in this church a man who was prophet, seer, and revelator. Through him, lost books have been rediscovered, old covenants remembered, and new revelations received. For the first time in at least fifteen centuries, the world has sure access

---

[178] . Ibid. pp. 180-183

to the word of God in the continuing authority of the LDS Church.

Even though the LDS use rational arguments against Christianity, they consider their church above the same critique. Their faith does not depend on scriptural or historical or rational arguments, because they have a greater proof: the witness of *testimony*. We discussed testimony in our second section, and saw the decisive role it plays in Mormon life. The average Saint believes that God has given him a direct revelation proving that the Mormon Church is God's only true church. Thanks to testimony, no other evidence is really needed.

A CATHOLIC RESPONSE

Catholics do not have to accept the burden of proof

Since the Catholic Church can trace her roots back to the witness of the Apostles, she does not carry the burden of proof. The LDS face a two part burden. *First*, it is up to them to prove beyond a shadow of doubt that the church founded by Christ disappeared. This is no easy task because the charge of apostasy questions the power of the Holy Spirit and the ability of Jesus Christ to protect his Church from the gates of hell.

Second, they have to prove that the LDS Church is now the true Church of Christ. As I just said, Mormons do not bother with this question because they have received a testimony, a revelation assuring them that theirs is the true church, and they usually feel no obligation to look any further. In the three short sections that follow, I will demonstrate that the Mormons have failed to prove that they are the true church. Then I will turn to the larger question of the Great Apostasy.

1---There is no proof that "plain and precious things" were removed from the Bible

The Mormons realize how far they have departed from Christianity. There is no hint or trace in the scriptures about Heavenly Father, eternal progression, eternal wives, and spirit children. The reason is simple. "Plain and simple things" have been removed from the text, as it says in I Nephi. This is a self-serving, unproven accusation used by Smith to justify his creation of yet another church to clutter up the spiritual landscape. As I have noted again and again, using an argument without proof is called "begging the question," and it is a logical fallacy. A fallacy is called a fallacy because it cannot yield the truth. But as I demonstrated in the previous chapter, Biblical scholars have revealed how the Old and New Testaments developed from the very beginning. They have proven beyond a shadow of a doubt that the Old and New Testaments are what they have always been. When the Bible was written, there was no trace, hint, or glimpse of the Mormon gospel. And so Mormons with their strange doctrines have failed to prove that theirs is the true church.

2---The Mormons are Gnostics, not Christians

Gene Fadness, a deacon in my diocese, expresses it perfectly in the title of a little pamphlet he calls *My Conversion to Christianity from Mormonism.* As I noted in the third chapter of this book, when the missionaries knock at a door and offer a discussion about Jesus, their listener usually imagines that this is a conversation among Christians, and say yes to the discussion. But even though

Mormons have great love for the Jesus their church presents to them, they are not Christians.

I ask the reader to go back to my third chapter, where I describe an ancient religious movement called Gnosticism. The Gnostics were like the alien Borg in the television series *Star Trek*, who announced to their victims, "You will be assimilated." As the Gnostics moved across the ancient world, they absorbed one religion after another into their system. As their unfortunate host tried to defend itself, the Gnostics appealed to the discovery of lost books, new revelations, and secret knowledge.

The Mormons follow this pattern

What do the Mormons offer the world? They are a modern form of Gnosticism. They appeal to a lost book on gold plates that can never be examined by ordinary eyes, with Jesus speaking through the mouth of his prophet, featuring ongoing revelation, new books of scripture, secret knowledge, the lost rituals of ancient temple of Solomon restored, the old order of celestial marriage once again on the earth, and on and on. When the scholars of the Congregation of Faith finally pondered Mormon teaching and discovered an infinite universe populated by gods of the human species, with heavenly wives and uncountable numbers of children called to be gods in their own right, they must have gasped. One of them might have exclaimed, "this is so far from Christianity that we cannot even call it a heresy!" We remember this when we ponder the Mormon claim that they are a Christian church.

3---It boils down to the credibility of a single

man

Mormonism rests on the word of Joseph Smith, Jr.. He was the one who had the visions. He was the one who found and translated the golden plates. As God's self-proclaimed prophet, seer, and revelator, he would stand before his people and the words of Jesus himself would resound in a New England twang from the mouth of a poorly educated man. Secretaries took frantic notes. But nobody saw Jesus standing above Smith on the brink of heaven. They had to take it on faith. They had to base their religious world on that peaceful feeling in their hearts. Mormons face disbelievers with a defiant question. Was Joseph Smith a con-man, a mad-man, or a saint? My response is found in Section Two of this book. I invite you to read chapters eight and nine again.

4---The great apostasy

The accusation that there was a great apostasy rests on the existence of something like an official religious handbook revealed to Adam, restored by Jesus, and lost again in a great apostasy. Let's imagine that there was such a "handbook." One of its elements would have been about doctrine, including a careful explanation of the meaning of the Cross. Another element would have been about essential church structure, including the Quorum of the Twelve.

1) If there was a "handbook" which contained an explanation of the true

**meaning of the Cross according to the
Great Plan, then Peter, James, and Paul
had failed to read that chapter**

After Jesus ascended into heaven, a great crisis quickly rocked the infant Church. We find this in the Letter to the Galatians and in the Acts of the Apostles. Paul and Barnabas belonged to the same Christian community in the great city of Antioch. Their community was a mixture of Jews and Gentiles. It did not demand that its male converts be circumcised, and was not strict about observing the dietary codes prescribed by the Mosaic Law. Peter came to live in that community and seemed very comfortable with what was going on.

Then James, one of the Twelve and the leader of the Church in Jerusalem, sent men to observe church life in Paul's Christian community. The visitors were scandalized by what they found. St. Paul tells us in his letter to the Galatians that Peter hastily returned to a strict observance of the Mosaic Law. Outraged, Paul was forced to "oppose him to his face," because Peter and the representatives of James "were not acting in line with the truth of the gospel." (Gal. 2:11-14) We are saved by the Cross, and not by the works of the Law.

If the Mormons are correct and Jesus handed over a detailed "handbook," this makes a puzzling story. Assuming that Jesus had carefully explained the great Plan for godhood and his atoning death on the cross in fulfillment of the Plan, it would seem that James, the head of the Church in Jerusalem, and Peter, the Keeper of the Keys, had already fallen into apostasy. In his rebuttal, Paul does not mention the Plan. As far as Paul was concerned, the reason was obvious. Evil priests had carefully removed that detail.

2) Jesus gathered the Twelve around him. But did the "handbook" say that the Twelve was meant to be an ongoing office in the Church?

The New Testament has plenty to say about the Twelve. We have lists of their names. LDS art portrays Jesus ordaining an ecstatic and solemn group of apostles into this quorum, with Peter on his knees to receive the Power of the Keys. Mormons say that the Quorum of the Twelve is an *ongoing* authority structure, and the true church cannot exist without it. But if the Quorum of the Twelve was meant to play that role, the apostles again had a very short attention span. The Church did not survive the *first* generation, because Peter and his brothers failed to maintain the Quorum of the Twelve.

What??

This Mormon interpretation of the scene has to pass through the strainer of the Acts of the Apostles. If the Mormon claim is true, then Peter, James, John *allowed the crucial Quorum of the Twelve to disappear in their own lifetime.* The Acts tell us that Herod murdered James, one of the Twelve and the leader of the Jerusalem Church. Mormons argue that James the Brother of the Lord was chosen as his replacement. But the Acts of the Apostles, the epistles, and the ancient Fathers of the Church have nothing to say about a matter so important. Admitting that they have no real proof, the Mormons take refuge as usual behind the argument from silence and blame the lack of evidence on those evil priests who destroyed the evidence from Scripture and the writings of the earliest Church Fathers. Once again, they beg the question.

But supposing the Mormons got it right? What if, according to that now vanished handbook, Peter and the

Quorum of the Twelve *were* members of a crucial ongoing office that marks the true church? Then the Church did not fall into apostasy after the deaths of the apostles. By not choosing men to replace the Twelve as they died, Peter and the other apostles were the architects of a catastrophe that engulfed the Christ's Church in the *first* generation. Smith claimed that Peter, along with James and John, ordained him to the Melchizedek Priesthood. But if the three had died apostate, why was that ordination valid?

Catholics argue that the Church did not begin with an instruction manual containing the great Plan and all the details about doctrine, worship, and morality. As we have just seen, the best proof is found in the New Testament itself. There is no trace of Heavenly Father and godhood. There is no trace of a carefully organized body of rules, worship practices, and doctrines. What we find instead is a step by step, Spirit-led journey toward a deeper understanding of the Gospel and how it was to be led, lived, and celebrated. In Chapter Fifteen, I discussed Tradition, which shows how the Church unfolded, guided by the Holy Spirit. You might read this chapter, and the chapter on authority (Chapter 20) again.

3) A story that must have confounded the angels

When I observe the modern LDS Presidency and the Quorum of the Twelve during one of their televised conferences, I see good and prayerful men who support and advise each other. I also see the devout body of LDS faithful asked to listen to the Holy Ghost and "sustain" their priesthood holders in some teaching or the election of a new church authority. In the midst of this atmosphere, it is hard for me to imagine the leaders of the church infecting each other with apostasy. It is hard for me to imagine their famously conservative membership sustaining such a spiritual calamity without a fight.

And so, *why the repeated fall into apostasy, especially after the restoration by Jesus Christ himself*? God founded each dispensation on living prophets and revelators who were empowered to speak in the name of Jesus himself. The president's two counselors, the Quorum of the Twelve, and the Seventies knew all the divinely revealed principles and sustained their prophet. They all shared in the god-like power and authority of the Melchizedek Priesthood and were guided by the light of Christ and the friendship of the Holy Ghost. They could perform the saving ordinances. They had the power of their Patriarchal Blessing and their temple endowment. They could depend on the gift of ongoing revelation.

Bumbling prophets and an ineffective priesthood

If the prophet and his counselors and all the members of church government were *chosen by prophecy*, how could the Holy Ghost have so completely misled the church about the leaders who would guide their people over the cliff? If each living prophet was in direct contact with the Godhead, why didn't the Holy Ghost warn him when he was going astray? If the living prophet and his counselors were losing the way, why didn't the Holy Ghost warn the Twelve? If the Melchizedek Priesthood truly has the awesome power to act in God's name and with God's own power, why did it fail six times to guard the gospel? Was Satan that much more powerful than the living Prophet and the Priesthood? When Joseph Smith finally arrived, the score was Satan 6, God 0.

6) Divine malfeasance

Parachuting into burning oil

I have never heard a Latter-day Saint discuss the agony that must have gripped the heavens during those ages of apostasy. Heavenly Father had invited his sons and daughters to come to earth and accept their time of probation in order return to his mansion, enter the Celestial Kingdom, and eventually qualify for godhood. They gave a great shout of joy when they heard this news and hurried toward their destiny.

And then, from their vantage point in pre-existence, they watched in horror as each dispensation quickly lost its way. This sight must have been especially difficult for those who were next in line, about to make their leap to earth. They knew that they were doomed to be born into the darkness of apostasy. In an enormous unending tide, they kept their side of the bargain and left the security of their Heavenly Father's mansion for their chance to gain a body, prove themselves, and achieve godhood. But their memories were blank and their minds were darkened. Without a living prophet and the power of the priesthood, those beloved sons and daughters of Heavenly Father—at first in their millions and then in their billions—arrived spiritually naked in the midst of the malignant power of Satan without a missionary in sight.

Mormons say that part of their fate was decided by their good or bad behavior in pre-existence. Did they fight by Michael's side, or did they sit on the fence? Did they fall into other sins? Mormons believe that their life as spirit-children helped determine the families they were born into, their race, physical and mental strength and defects, and religious status in this new life. But it was reward or punishment for behavior they no longer recalled. They had come to play the game of godhood, but it was blind man's bluff and was rigged before they were born.

Did Heavenly Father do the math?

Why, after the apostasy of the church Jesus Christ himself founded, did Heavenly Father let as many as *seventy-five generations* pass without the voice of a prophet, the consolation of the priesthood, or the companionship of the Holy Ghost? If a real father knew that he was sending his children into deadly peril, wouldn't he do everything possible to protect and instruct them? Why did Heavenly Father wait *one thousand six-hundred years or more* before beginning his seventh and last dispensation? Didn't he do the math and understand that demographics and the approaching end to history would make it impossible for most of his children, now living as gentiles, to meet a missionary and begin the essential steps toward godhood?

In the face of long, long odds during these latter-days, almost all of Heavenly Father's children will die without knowing his name

Remember, Mormons they call themselves the *Latter-day* Saints. . If the people who keep track of human demographics are correct, the vast majority of Heavenly Father's children who have ever lived on earth are alive NOW. The Mormons teach that, as soon as Christ returns in glory, the world will be destroyed by fire. Angel Moroni might blow his trumpet announcing the end of the world before I take my next breath.

The future is grim. The LDS Church has only *sixteen* million members. How is this relative handful going to reach the *eight thousand million* and more sons and

daughters of Heavenly Father who are here *in our lifetime.*
Seventy thousand zealous missionaries carry the gospel to
stranded souls who have no memory of their purpose on
earth. Since the missionaries travel in pairs, the ratio is one
set of missionaries to two hundred sixty thousand gentiles
and–according to that recent report by CNN--the average
missionary makes 4.7 converts in a year.

How to solve the dilemma? With the seconds ticking
toward zero, good Mormons are doing genealogical
research to find names. The people on this list are then
baptized by proxy in a temple. When that is done, deceased
missionaries from Spirit Paradise will visit Spirit Prison, call
the baptized by name, and offer them salvation. Maybe that
is why Mormons are building so many temples today.

It is a heroic effort. But factor in the unknowable,
uncountable number of gentile people who have lived and
died in Europe, Asia, Africa, and the Americas since the
Great Apostasy and now. The angels must shake their
heads as Mormons in their few millions try to find salvation
for brothers and sisters in their billions upon billions upon
billion.

Three levels of heaven

Mormons soften this stark tale of spiritual castaways by
assuring us that a merciful Father will send his children to
one of three levels of heaven: the telestial, the terrestrial,
and the celestial. Even the lowest heaven will not be that
bad. But we cannot forget that for Mormons, the only real
salvation is exaltation and godhood. As one apostle put it:
"Salvation in its true and full meaning is synonymous with

exaltation,. and consists in gaining an inheritance in the highest of the three heavens within the celestial kingdom."[179]

The fate of most of Heavenly Father's children

If all this is true, then Satan succeeds far, far more than he fails, because the vast majority of spirit children who come down to earth for their one chance at godhood will never return to the mansion of their Father. In the cold words of Bruce McConkie, *"They will, therefore, be damned; their eternal progression will be cut short; they will not fill the full measure of their creation."*[206]

Is there a rumbling in the eternities?

According to Mormon teaching, gods beyond naming fill the infinite expanse of the universe, but the only god who concerns us is Heavenly Father. Mormons say he is literally our father and we are only accountable to him.

But I find myself wondering, to whom is Heavenly Father accountable? To his Heavenly Father? Do Heavenly Grandfathers have a concern or two about the fate of those brave spirit children who left heaven for the chance to become gods or married to a god, and their journey is in vain?

What about all those unnamed eternal companions who are the mothers of those billions upon billions of spirit sons and daughters? As I pointed out, most of the people who have ever lived on earth are living at this moment in a world rocketing toward its conclusion. What do all those mothers say when they realize that most of their

---

[179]*Mormon Doctrine*, p. 670, under "Salvation." [206] Ibid., p 669

children don't have a hope or a prayer for exaltation? Do they simply shrug and put it down to bad luck, or do they have strong words for a divine husband who didn't convene the final dispensation until the very last minute, with time running out?

And what about those gods who could be considered peers to Heavenly Father? Do his brothers, uncles, and cousins who have also become gods wonder why so many children of Elohim live beyond the reach of the LDS church and its missionaries, even though it is not their fault?

The gods and heavenly spouses who look on can surely see that the missionary effort and all the heroic research of legions of genealogists is like someone trying to empty Lake Erie with a spoon. Could there be such a thing as divine malfeasance? Is there a rumbling in the eternities because Heavenly Father has only a short time to do what he should have been doing for at least one thousand five hundred years?

5) Texts taken out of context

When we examine the New Testament texts used by Mormons to prove an apostasy, we discover that they are words plucked out of time and out of place. They do not describe the generally positive tone of the books and letters from which they were taken, nor do they take into consideration the time-frame within which they were written. One can see apostasy only if he focuses on carefully selected negative passages while ignoring the rest of the New Testament.

The proof texts used by Mormon apologists dance in thin air, disconnected from their surrounding historical and church framework. Focusing on the negative, they bypass the countless words of confident hope that fill the pages of the New Testament. Talmage and his imitators buy into the literalist assumption that the New Testament was written by eye-witnesses during the lifespan of the twelve apostles. They are unaware of the conclusions of modern biblical scholarship: The New Testament was written during the course of at least three generations–from St. Paul, who wrote in the '50's, to Second Peter, which was probably written around the year 120. Most of the New Testament was written after the apostles were already dead.

A closer look at some of the proof texts used by Mormons to prove a great apostasy.

That quote from St. Paul

Mormons quote St. Paul's warning to the elders of the Ephesian church, *"After I leave, savage wolves will come in among you and will not spare the flock."* (Acts 20:20) Surely here is proof that apostasy was about to break loose! But Paul spoke this warning sometime around the year *fifty*, while the words we just read were written in the Acts of the Apostles sometime around the year *ninety*.[180]

Much had changed during the forty year span separating St. Paul from the writing of the Acts of the Apostles. Jerusalem had been completely destroyed by the Romans and the Jerusalem church had disappeared forever as a nerve center for Christian faith. Antioch and Rome were now the dominant churches. Scripture scholars say that the Letter to the Ephesians was written during that time. Anyone who has meditated on the soaring poetry at

---

[180] Modern biblical scholars say that the Gospel of St. Luke was written around 85 A.D.. Acts, which continues the narrative was probably written around the year 90. See the New Jerome Biblical Commentary or similar books for more information.

the beginning of the letter, or pondered its moral demands, knows the Ephesian community was alive in Christ.

There is another witness: The Book of Revelations also dates from around the year ninety, and the author said this to the Church at Ephesus:

> *I know your deeds, your hard work and your perseverance. I know that you cannot tolerate wicked men, that you have tested those who claim to be apostles but are not, and have found them false. You have persevered and have endured hardship for my name, and have not grown weary.*
>
> (Rev. 2:2-3)

Ephesians and Revelations describe a church that took St. Paul's warning to heart and resisted the temptation to fall away from Christ. The Book of Revelations survives because people heeded its warning.

We can study the other proof-texts offered by Mormons to make their case, with the same results. The passages are quoted with no respect for the real time-frame, with no appreciation of the loving Christian communities who wrote and preserved the New Testament. What we really find is a faithful church intent on following the teaching of the apostles.

6) The role of Greek philosophy

When the first Christian missionaries left Israel behind to proclaim the Good News in another language and another culture, they found themselves in a pagan world teeming with gods. When they announced the gospel, the citizens of that world said, "you are talking about a god. But which god do you have in mind? Zeus? Hermes? Dionysius?"

The Christian missionaries had to find the words and concepts that would proclaim the God of the Old and New Testaments to citizens of a Greek world. Missionaries from an Asian cultural universe would have to find the words to announce its message to people whose understanding of reality was very different.

When Paul wrote to the Romans, he appealed to them in a familiar way:

> *For what can be known about God is plain to them (the non-Jewish peoples), because God has shown it to them. Ever since the creation of the world his invisible nature, namely, his eternal power and deity, has been clearly perceived in the things that have been made. (Romans 19-20)*

Paul is using an argument straight out of the Greek philosophers, especially the Stoics. His words are a mixture of faith and reason. Paul was not alone. In their effort to explain Jesus to a Greek world, Christian missionaries found an unexpected ally in the Greek philosopher Plato, who gave them intellectual tools which helped the rational Greeks understand the Christian message.

A heresy based on Plato that resembles basic Mormon teaching

During the fourth century, some Christians did let Greek philosophy distort their vision of Christ. For instance, a priest named Arius confused the *Logos* of St. John's Gospel with the *Logos* of Plato. Plato taught that a world of perfect Ideas formed the peak of reality. The material world was its dim reflection. The *Logos* was an intermediary who brought the world of Ideas and the material world together. By identifying the *Logos* of St. John with the *Logos* of Plato, Arius turned Jesus into a being less than God the Father. Interesting enough, Mormons teach that their Jesus is inferior to their Heavenly Father. Since they pray to Heavenly Father in his name, Jesus is an intermediary. And so Mormon teaching about Jesus resembles the heresy of Arianism, which was based on Greek philosophy.

A bishop named Athanasius realized that Arius had departed from traditional Catholic teaching. In 315, the Council of Nicea refuted the Arians by returning to Scripture, its liturgy, and its Tradition. The result was the doctrine of the Trinity, proclaiming our faith in one God, and in the divinity of Jesus Christ. The Church convened other great councils to clarify other questions about the relationship between Jesus, the Father, and the Holy Spirit.

Speaking Greek and Latin instead of the Hebrew and Aramaic of the Jews, they found the words we now translate as "Incarnation," and "Trinity." For Mormons, this is proof of apostasy, because such terms are not found anywhere in the New Testament. For Catholics, it is evidence that a faithful Church agonized long and hard to use words and concepts which could express the deepest doctrine of the Christian faith without snapping the thread leading to the apostolic witness.

7) What about a later apostasy?

Okay, but what about the history of the Church after that? We have the miserable story of the Papacy during the Dark Ages and the Renaissance, when powerful families schemed to seize the papacy, when popes were murdered by their rivals, when popes had "nieces and nephews" in their royal palaces, and when greedy popes lived in luxury. We have the bloody Crusades and the Inquisition. It is important for Catholics to learn about all of this, and weep.

Talmage describes "disorder and confusion" in the list of popes, the presence of anti-popes, and points to gaps when no pope ruled the Church.[181] His imitators list "unauthorized changes in the Order of Christ's Church." As we have already seen, these include: the doctrine of the Trinity, changes in "priesthood officers," with "unauthorized leaders" such as pope, cardinal, archbishop, monsignor, etc... Other "unauthorized changes" would be papal infallibility, the complicated ceremony of the Mass, the Seven Sacraments, the Sign of the Cross, the intercession of martyrs and saints, bowing or genuflecting before statues and images, and the doctrines about Mary. Also mentioned are "Original sin, indulgences, relics, lying wonders, feasts, asceticism, monasticism, celibacy, transubstantiation, pardons and almsgiving."[182]

This list is built on that mythical box containing all the essentials of Christian religion, a box that was supposed to be preserved intact with no deletions or additions. Since there is no proof that such a box ever existed, to argue from the basis of that belief begs the question. Talmage's list has done a good job mixing up Tradition with tradition. It is a hodge-podge of realities essential to the Church and its mission, and realities that can change and have changed.

Talmadge and his followers are speaking within the limited world of the Mormon imagination. Their observations have no application within the rich sacramental realities of a Catholic universe. Religious beliefs are expressed in observable, concrete ways. And so

---

[181] . Joseph Fielding Smith, Jr. *Religious Truths Defined*, (Bookcraft, Inc. Salt Lake City, Utah, 1959), pp 172-173

[182] . Ibid. pp. 180-183

Mormons wear garments while Catholics make the Sign of the Cross, Mormons go to the temple for endowments and Catholics meet Christ in the Mass, Mormons base their claim to apostolic authority on Joseph's Smith's supposed ordination by Peter, James, and John, while Catholics base apostolic authority on an unbroken chain of bishops. If I wanted to be tedious, I would go through Mormon accusations point by point and show that the essential Catholic realities mentioned there are well-grounded in Scripture. I did this, for instance, in my discussion about the Mass.

I have already mentioned the complicated story of the papacy, a list of saints and sinners. But the essential leader of the Church is not a pope. It is the Holy Spirit. And even in the worst of times, the Church had its bumper crop of saints, proof that God, in a sulk, has not picked up his church and packed it off to heaven.

History surrounds us and changes us and to demand otherwise is to hope for a moral impossibility. Let me roughly repeat my thumbnail sketch of the history that unfolded after the death of the last apostle. When the Jews revolted against Rome, and the Roman Army completely destroyed Jerusalem, the Church had to move into a world dominated by the Greek culture. The Roman Empire was the single, overpowering reality, but then it split into two parts. Over-run by barbarians, the western half collapsed and entered into the world some call the Dark Ages. The Moslems appeared and conquered most of the East, all of North Africa, and all of Spain. Vikings ravaged northern Europe and even captured Sicily and southern Italy. European nations began to emerge, but were plagued by constant warfare. Great plagues destroyed one third of the population. Moslems finally conquered Constantinople, and the world of Eastern Christianity was gone. Columbus discovered America. Galileo changed our understanding of man's place in the universe. The Reformation fragmented the Catholic world. Wars and disease killed half the population in some parts of Europe. The Enlightenment, with its trust in reason alone, replaced the world of faith. The American Revolution proved that tyrants were not forever. The French Revolution turned Europe inside out. There were the great, destructive wars of Napoleon. Nationalism became a dangerous, driving force. Two world wars followed, with millions dead. There was the rise of communism, and then the atom bomb. Predatory capitalism emerged, with its emphasis on materialistic consumption.

Restoration churches imagine that, during two thousand years of tumult, the Church was expected to march through all of this, unchanged and unscathed. But that is not the way history works. Bruised, battered, and glorious, the Catholic Church is history's longest surviving institution. It's story is one of the greatest stories ever told.

8) The Mormon Church has experienced its own changes

Less than two hundred years old, the LDS Church has already made its own alterations to its original self-definition. In the beginning, Smith's church was supposed to be a restored version of the simple, primitive Church of the New Testament. But soon, the church soon had an Aaronic and then a Melchizedek priesthood, a temple, and a more and more intricate authority structure. The church Smith founded in New York State did not resemble the complicated church he governed in Nauvoo, just before his death.

Smith's theology also continued to evolve. I have noted the unexplained deletions and additions he made in the *Doctrine and Covenants* to justify changes he had made in his theology. And then there was polygamy. The *Book of Mormon* condemned the practice. But in Nauvoo, Jesus proclaimed through his faithful prophet Joseph that polygamy was necessary for salvation.

The 20,000 faithful converts who joined Smith in Nauvoo voted as a single block. He boldly involved what was supposed to have been a simple church in state and national politics. It was a wild move that cost him his life. After Smith's death, the changes continued. Guided by an early revelation, Smith had attempted to make his church into a community where the rich handed over their possessions, and everything was shared in common. Today, the Mormon Church is a bastion of capitalism, with huge investments in America's wealthiest corporations. The words of Hugh Nibley can be applied to the Mormon Church: the church that entered the tunnel was not the church that emerged.

Some of the changes have been forced by outsiders. In the 1880's, Utah hoped to become a state and join the union, but polygamy stood in the way. In 1890, President Wilford Woodruff ended the practice. Today, any Mormon practicing polygamy is excommunicated. In the *Book of Mormon*, people with dark skins were cursed. After Smith died, blacks were excluded from the Melchizedek Priesthood and could not enter the temple. In the 1960's, Mormons endured withering criticism for this practice. Suddenly, in 1972, there was another revelation, and now Blacks are fully included in Mormon life. In 1997, President Gordon Hinkley was interviewed by PBS, Time Magazine, and the San Francisco Chronicle. Journalists asked him about the Mormon belief that men could become gods. Hinkley gave cagey, almost Protestant-like answers that seemed to imply that Mormons were turning Joseph Smith's very explicit teaching into some kind of vague idea. And, as I have noted from my own experience, the Mormons who boasted they were not Christians sixty-five years ago now defiantly claim that they are.

9) On the long journey of history

The New Testament begins the story of a Church that has followed the Holy Spirit across the mountains, valleys, and deserts of history. During that long journey, she has spread from east to west, from north to south, and has traveled down through the centuries. The Gospel has been proclaimed in Aramaic, Farsi, Greek, Latin, Hindi, Chinese, Japanese, Vietnamese, Spanish, French, Portuguese, and in several Slavic and Germanic tongues, including English. Each of those languages represents a different culture with a different history and a different view of reality. The Church had to cross those boundaries, proclaim the Good News, and keep true to the Bible and Tradition.

For two thousand years, the Church has journeyed through a world often turned upside down. If I were to use an analogy, I would compare it to life inside a washing machine, with the dial set on spin. The restored churches say she fell into apostasy. They assume she was supposed to live through all this, and somehow emerge that simple Church Jesus founded in Galilee. This claim is ironic. These same churches often began as an effort to re-create the simple house churches of the Gospels. Now we find enormous buildings seating thousands of people presided over by preacher-stars who are sometimes millionaires. One group of cynics keeps track of the watches and shoes those preachers wear, which are often worth thousands of dollars. There is even a prosperity gospel which teaches that

God wants to make his faithful followers rich. Many of these churches have recently sold themselves to a controversial political figure, and seem to seek a union between church and state. All of this is done, of course, in the name of Jesus.

A Church exploring the Seven Seas of history

When Catholics look back two thousand years, they see *change in the midst of continuity*. The Church did not begin with an owner's manual. The deep questions contained within Scripture and Catholic Tradition were not answered until they were asked. Take, for instance, the question about the divinity of Jesus and his relationship to his Father. The Council of Nicaea returned to the Church's deepest roots, and answered the question. Then came the question about the Son's relationship with the Father and the Holy Spirit. A discussion about Grace came next, followed by a clarification of the living presence of Jesus within the Mass and the Blessed Sacrament. Before answering these questions, the Church always pondered the sources, which are found in scripture, liturgy, and Tradition. As I already noted, modern theologians call this the *Great Tradition*, a Spirit-guided river of growth flowing within the Church to this very day.[183]

Good times and hard times

The Catholic Church was born into, and outlived, the Roman Empire. With century following century, there was growth and holiness, but there was also weariness and the

---

[183] Any contextually based introduction to the New Testament will give the information I have summarized here. My remarks are based mostly on *the Beginnings of the Church*, by Frederick J. Cwiekowski.

temptation of a sinful mirage on the horizon. The Church admits she has failed to listen to the Spirit. Sometimes she allowed herself to see the world through the distorted lens of the culture that surrounded her, and fell into its sins.. She has had her blind or corrupt leaders in league with some of history's great sinners.

Any good Catholic reading Church history discovers these things, and weeps. But even in the worst of times, she has had her saints and prophets. We learn about spiritual triumphs and unexpected renewal. The arrogant Pope Julius is an embarrassing memory. His contemporaries Theresa of Avila and John of the Cross live on as guides for Christians seeking holiness. And so we rejoice at the stories of great faith and great love in the face of conflict and temptation. These are the rhythms of a living reality struggling through the pain and glory of its changing seasons.

Maybe that is why the ancient Christians loved to compare their Church to a ship. We first find this image on the walls of the catacombs in Rome, above the tombs of ancient martyrs. Safe in a snug harbor, the good ship called Church is not fulfilling her purpose. She has to set sail and risk the storms, the unseen rocks in the confusion of fog or darkness, and the weary complaints of her crew. Her bottom is heavy with barnacles and the debris of seven seas. But, with Jesus aboard, she will not shatter on the rocks. Catholics instinctively understand that their Church is an ancient, sturdy craft on a long journey. To some eyes, she isn't pretty. But, sails lifted by the wind of the Spirit and with her eyes on Christ who holds the helm, she confidently heads for distant horizons.

THE END

About the Author

The story begins when Fr. Bill was baptized with the rest of his family at the age of six. He was an altar boy when he was eight, and decided to become a priest when he was only nine or ten. He attended Catholic grade schools and then a Catholic high school. When he was sixteen, he joined his brother Tom at Mt. Angel Seminary, in Oregon. He was ordained a priest in 1964.

Along with service as a missionary in Cali, Colombia, Fr. Bill has served as a priest all over Idaho. He has been a campus minister twice. He retired at 72 and was soon back to work at St. Paul's Parish, Nampa, Idaho. He takes care of two missions in that parish.

Books on Mormon issues, by the author:

Joseph Smith, the Prophet King (2 volumes). Found on Amazon. This is the only novel ever written about Joseph Smith. After years of research into the life of one of the most interesting persons American has ever produced, I have tried to tell a respectful story that does not have a critical agenda. I invite the reader to make up his mind: Was Joseph Smith a liar, a mad-man, or a saint?

Mormon Missionaries Knocking at my door I wrote this short book to help Catholics understand who the missionaries are, and how they make converts. It then gives Catholics a lesson in spiritual karate, so they can deal with the missionaries in a more effective way.

A tale of Two Cities — Two Churches on the March into the Future I had two goals when I wrote this book. First, it helps you compare the Mormon Catholic churches in a number of different ways. Second, my description of the Catholic Church is a heart-felt meditation about a church I know and love. I

You can find these books on Amazon as a paperback or as an e-book. I hope you will include a review if you buy a book.

Glossary of LDS Terms

Aaronic Priesthood—The lower of the two levels of the LDS priesthood. Aaronic priesthood offices are deacon (received at age 12), teacher, priest, and bishop. The bishop administers his ward and sees to its temporal needs. The deacons, teachers, and priests are usually teenagers eighteen and under who perform minor roles in their ward, under the direction of the bishop.

Angels—Mormons see two kinds of angels. They are spirit children who have not yet received a body of flesh and bone, and they are creatures of body, flesh, and bone who are awaiting the resurrection. They can have a role as a messenger from God.

Apostasy—To abandon or willfully change teachings, principles, or practices of the LDS Church, or to rebel against the authority of the church. The GREAT APOSTASY was a general departure from the ordinances and doctrines of the church founded by Jesus. Mormons say this began after the death of the last apostle and continues to this day.

Atonement—At the great meeting with his spirit-children in heaven, Heavenly Father explained that the Plan of salvation involved the necessity of a fall, which would bring about mortality and the danger that the spirit-children would come down to earth only to be trapped in sin and death. But if someone volunteered to die on a cross in bloody atonement, sin and death would be defeated. Jehovah, Heavenly Father's first-born son volunteered. When the time came, he would enter a human body and die his sacrificial death.

Auxiliaries—organizations in the church which assist the Melchizedek Priesthood in carrying out its mission of instruction and spiritual care. The most important is the Relief Society, which involves all Mormon women. It has a governing structure parallel to the priesthood structure.

Baptism—an "ordinance" necessary for salvation. Valid only if it involves complete immersion in water done by someone who has the authority of the priesthood. Eight years is minimum age.

Baptism for the dead—a worthy Mormon can be baptized in one of the many Mormon Temples, serving as proxy for a non-Mormon who died without baptism. Usually, but not always, limited to people who are family members. This is the reason Mormons are so interested in genealogy.

Bishop—holder of both Aaronic and Melchizedek priesthood. Operates in Aaronic priesthood capacity. Ordained to the level of high priest, he directs all the church activity in a ward.

Bishop's Court—a judicial hearing presided over by the bishop and his counselors. Usually deals with issues of church law, but can also help solve a conflict between Mormons.

Calling—appointment to all Mormon church offices comes by revelation given to the pertinent church official. At the highest level, it is given by the general authorities, but at the lowest level, a bishop, guided by revelation, can give a calling to his people as he assigns one of the 250 tasks that make a ward run. Most Mormons will not refuse a call.

Celestial Kingdom—Mormons believe in three levels of heaven. The celestial kingdom is the highest level, which involves exaltation. Those who achieve that level are on their way to eternal life as a god, or as a heavenly queen, eternal companion to that god.

Common consent, law of—the congregation has the right to reject or accept its leaders. Their names are read for a sustaining vote, and opposition or acceptance is demonstrated by "raising the arm to the square." Even the president of the church is "sustained" at the semi-annual conference in Salt Lake City.

Conference—usually refers to the semi-annual meeting of the entire church in Salt Lake City, but also held at the ward, stake, or regional level.

Cultural hall—a standard feature for most Mormon chapels. It is an area for sports, dances, dinners, plays, etc.

Deseret—according to Joseph Smith, the word means "honey bee," and is a synonym for famous Mormon cooperation and hard work. The name chosen by the first Mormons to designate what became Utah and the surrounding area.

Disfellowship—to temporarily remove the privileges of membership except the privilege to attend all but priesthood and sacrament meetings.

Dispensation—Mormons believe that the true gospel has been given to humankind several different times but that each time it was lost through apostasy. I count seven dispensations.

Dispensation of the fullness of times—began in 1820 when Joseph Smith had his first vision. It will continue until the coming of Christ.

Dispensation of the Meridian of Time—the proclamation of the gospel that occurred during Christ's life on earth until it was lost in the great apostasy.

Elder—the basic office of the Melchizedek Priesthood. A holder of this priesthood continues to be called elder even if he has other offices. Mormon missionaries wear a tag identifying them as elders, even though they are as young as nineteen.

Elohim—the Mormon name for the Heavenly Father. In the Bible, it is a generic plural name for God used by Israel and the other Semitic peoples of the area.

Endowment—In Mormonism, it is a ceremony occurring in the temple which allows Mormons to become gods and eternal companions, kings and queens, priests and priestesses in eternity.

Exaltation—to reach the highest level of glory in the celestial kingdom after fulfilling all the requirements, including marriage in the temple.

On who achieves exaltation is on his/her way to godhood/eternal queenship.

Excommunication—a formal procedure in bishop's court, it involves having one's name removed from church records and loss of all privileges, including whatever one could have received in eternity. If one repents, he must be rebaptized.

Family Home Evening—a command coming by revelation from the president to spend one night in the week (usually Monday) with the whole family. The father, usually following a planned program, organizes the evening whose purpose is to promote the gospel in the family.

Fast Sunday—On the first Sunday of each month, Mormons abstain from food and drink. The money thus saved is a fast offering given to the poor. A the worship service, a member can give his testimony for the inspiration of other members.

Fireside—a social gathering, usually of youth groups, but also of other age or interest groups, to learn and be inspired.

First Presidency—the president of the Mormon church and his two counselors.

First Principles of the Gospel—basic requirements for membership in church. Includes 1) Faith in the Lord Jesus Christ, 2) Repentance, 3) Baptism by immersion for the forgiveness of sins, 4) Laying on of hands for the gift of the Holy Ghost.

Free Agency—A man is free to obey the Lord or not, but he must bear the consequences of his choice. A very important concept among Mormons.

Garments—Sacred clothing resembling underwear to be worn next to the skin 24/7 as a sign of covenants made during the endowment ceremony in an LDS temple.

Genealogy—Research to uncover names of non-Mormon ancestors so that they can receive (by proxy) baptism and other temple ordinances.

General Authorities—The First Presidency (president of church plus two counselors), Quorum of the Twelve, First Quorum of the Seventy, and the Presiding Bishopric. Men holding these offices have authority all over the world.

Godhead—Heavenly Father, Jesus Christ, and the Holy Ghost. They are three separate exalted beings who share one mind and one purpose. Jesus Christ is inferior to

Heavenly Father, and the Holy Ghost is inferior to Jesus Christ. He does not possess an exalted body.

Gospel—the great Plan of Salvation revealed by Heavenly Father to Adam and passed down through a series of dispensations to our day.

High Council—a group of twelve men called to assist the stake president administer the spiritual and temporal affairs of the stake.

High Priest—an office within the Melchizedek Priesthood that involves administration and spiritual leadership. The bishop is always a high priest.

Holy Ghost—the third member of the godhead. Has the omniscient powers of God, but is a human being without "tabernacle," or exalted body.

Holy Ghost, gift of—given only to Mormons after baptism, received through the power of laying on of the hands by a member of the Melchizekek Priesthood. The Holy Ghost becomes a sort of companion, offering light and wisdom.

Holy Spirit—not to be confused with the Holy Ghost, who is a member of the Godhead, the Holy Spirit is a kind of impersonal force that fills the universe, which can touch us and lead us to God.

Immortality—the gift of Jesus' resurrection. The spirit and the body of each individual are joined together and live forever.

Jehovah—the name of Heavenly Father's first-born in pre-mortal life, volunteered to die on cross, helped organize world, became god of Old Testament, entered body created by union between Heavenly Father and Mary, became Jesus Christ.

Keys, power of—The keys of the priesthood refer to the right to exercise power in the name of Jesus Christ or to preside over a priesthood function, quorum, or organizational division of the Church. Keys are necessary to maintain order and to see that the functions of the Church are performed in the proper time, place, and manner. They are given by the laying on of hands in an ordination or setting apart by a person who presides and who holds the appropriate keys at a higher level.

Kingdom of Heaven—The LDS church. Today it is an ecclesiastical kingdom, but during the Millennium, it will be a political kingdom ruled by Christ through the leadership of the church.

Melchizedek Priesthood—the power and authority of God. It is conferred upon worthy male members of the Church. Those who hold priesthood keys direct the administration of the ordinances of the gospel, the preaching of the gospel, and the government of the kingdom of God on the earth.

Mormon—a great prophet/general who was responsible for collecting, editing, and abridging the ancient records that were translated by Joseph Smith in the Book of Mormon.

Moroni—Son of Mormon and last guardian of the records of his father. He appeared to Joseph Smith and showed him where the records were buried in the Hill Cumorah.

Mutual—a nickname for the weeknight youth activity program involving members of the Aaronic Priesthood and the Young Women's Group.

Ordinance—a law, statute, or commandment of God. Often it is a ritual of the priesthood which brings blessing: includes baptism, laying on of hands, sacrament of bread and water, baptism for the dead, etc....

Patriarch—1) a man married in the temple who has a family. 2) an office of the Melchizedek priesthood who has the power to give blessings.

Patriarchal Blessing—a special blessing from a patriarch which gives a person comfort, direction for his life, and often establishes his lineage in the House of Israel. (My mother, for instance, was told she was of the tribe of Manasseh.

Polygamy—a revelation given to Joseph Smith commanding that plural marriage by practiced among priesthood members. Such marriages were for time and eternity.

President of the Church—the senior among the twelve Apostles. In him resides the keys, powers, and authority necessary to direct the church. He is prophet, seer, and revelator for the whole church.

Priest—the highest office of the Aaronic priesthood.

Primary—organization for children under the ages of twelve.

Prophet—one who speaks for God at the position of his responsibility. For the whole church, this is the president. However, a bishop can be a prophet to his ward, a man to his family. The spirit will give them the revelation they need for the spheres of their responsibilities.

Quorum—the bearers of various levels of the two priesthoods are joined into groups; e.g., twelve deacons, ninety-six elders, etc..

Recommend—a statement of worthiness to enter the temple to receive blessings and ordinances. Involves and interview with the bishop and stake president, in which one's moral life, commitment to church, tithing, and fast offerings are discussed. A person denied a recommend is publicly on the outs with the church. My brother was briefly denied a recommend when his financial situation made it impossible for him to pay tithing.

Relief Society—an organization for women in the church. Set up in every ward and run with an authority structure parallel to the priesthood and under the direction of the priesthood. Tries to involve all women in a ward in projects for their own social, spiritual, and cultural welfare. Also concerned with the poor.

Revelation—communication from god to man bringing instruction about religious truth but also about other practical matters. President of church has power of continuing revelation.

Sacrament—an "ordinance" observed every Sunday in the blessing and distribution of bread and water.

Sacrament Meeting—The main Mormon worship service on Sundays. Involves business and doctrinal talks and the sharing of bread and water.

Saint—the Mormons' term for themselves.

Sealing—to bind on earth and have the ordinance bound in heaven. In general, refers to the ceremony in the temple which binds a man to his wife for all eternity and binds parents to children.

Seminary—weekly classes for high school students held either before school or in a released time arrangement. Can refer to the building where classes are held, located near high school.

Seventy—an office of the Melchizedek Priesthood whose duty is to preach the gospel to non-members.

Soul—unique to Mormonism. The immortal pre-existent spirit is joined to a mortal body and becomes a *living soul.*

After death, the spirit lives in a place prepared for it while the body returns to the earth. Later, when the immortal spirit is rejoined to the resurrected body, the become together an *immortal soul.*

Spirit—unique for Mormons: Each person is born in "spirit" form in the world of pre-existence. Also refers to an impersonal force filling the universe.

Standard Works—the scriptures of the Mormon church: the Book of Mormon, the Doctrine and Covenants, and the Pearl of Great Price.

Stake—the next largest administrative unit after a ward. Made up of several wards under a stake president.

Teacher—the second office of the Aaronic priesthood. Also a man or woman called by the bishop to serve as a teacher in any of the organizations of the ward.

Telestial Glory—the lowest of the three degrees of heaven. A place for those who follow Satan rather than God in this life.

Testimony—a revelation from God about truth of Mormon church and teaching. Mormons are encouraged to publicly give their testimony on the first Sunday of the month.

Tithes—ten percent of one's gross income. A law of God and a key part of the advancement toward godhood.

Tithing Settlement—every Mormon is expected to attend a yearly meeting with the bishop to confirm the accuracy of the member's tithing record and to establish steps toward making up the difference if any exists.

Urim and Thummin—in the Bible, a pair of dice used by the high priest to discern God's will. Among Mormons, a pair of stone "spectacles" that enabled him to translate the Book of Mormon.

Ward—a geographical boundary including 300-1000 members of the church, and led by a bishop.

Welfare Program—the Mormon self-help program administered by the bishop.

Word of Wisdom—a name given to instructions in Doctrine and Covenants #89 which forbids tobacco, alcohol, an "hot drinks" interpreted as coffee and tea.

Zion—the scriptural name for Jerusalem but used by Mormons to refer to Utah, especially the area near Salt Lake City.

Index of Sources

Allred, Gordon, *God the Father* (Deseret Book, Salt Lake City) 1979

Andrus, Hyrum, *God, Man, and the Universe* (Bookcraft, Salt Lake City) 1968

Augustine, St. *De Trinitate, Sermon 56*

Brown, Raymond E, *The Churches the Apostles Left Behind* (Paulist Press, New York) 1984

Carrol, Warren H, *A History of Christendom, Vol I* (Christendom Press) 1985

Congregation for the Doctrine of the Faith, *Dominus Jesus, August 6, 2000*

Cox, James B, *How to Qualify for the Celestial Kingdom Today* (Ensign Publishing, Riverton, Utah) 1984

Cwiekowski, Frederick J, *Beginning of the Church* (Paulist Press, New York) 1988

Dulles, Avery, SJ, *The Priestly Office*, (On Amazon) 1997

Dreyer, Elizabeth, *Manifestations of Grace* (Glazier, Wilmington, Delaware)1990

Gregory of Naziasin, *Oratio*

Harris, Henry, *Affidavit, in Kirtland, 1:33*

Helwig, Monika K, *Understanding Catholicism* (Paulist Press, New York) 1981

Hill, Donna, *Joseph Smith, the First Mormon,* (WWW. Abe books) 1977

Johnson, Elizabeth, *She Who Is* (Crossroads Publishing Company, New York) 1992

Kasper, Walter, *The God of Jesus Christ* (Crossroads, New York) 1984

Kimball, Spencer W, *The Miracle of forgiveness,* (Bookcraft, Salt Lake City) 1969

Laurel Manuel 2 (LDS Publication, Salt Lake)

Ludlow, William, ed. *Encyclopedia of Mormonism* (EOM, BYU. Edu) 1992

Madsen, Truman G, *Christ and the Inner Life* (Bookcraft, Salt Lake City) 1978

Martos, Joseph, *Doors to the Sacred,* Kindle Edition, 1991

McConkie, Bruce, *A New Witness to the Articles of Faith* (Deseret Books, Salt Lake City) 1985

McConkie, Bruce, *Mormon Doctrine*, multiple printings starting
1956, now found on Amazon

McKay, David O, *Gospel Ideals* (Improvement Era) 1953

Millett, R. L., *Magnifying Priesthood Power* (Horizon, Provo, Utah) 1974

Morlin, Bill, *Idaho Statesman Review,* April 10, 2000

Mormon Miscellaneous, October, 1995, pp 11-16

New Interpreter's Dictionary of the Bible (Abington Press) 2006-9

O'Connel, Timothy E, *Principles for a Catholic Morality* (Seabury Press, Minneapolis) 1978

O'Donnell, John J, *The Mystery of the Triune God* (Paulist Press, Malwah, New York) 1989

Nibley, Hugh, *Collected Works* (Vol 9, Ch. 4); BYU Studies, Vol 116, No. 1

Osborne, Kenan OFM, *Priesthood* (WPF, Stock Publisher, reissue) 2003; *Orders and Ministry* (Paulist Press) 2003

Padovano, Anthony, *Eden and Easter* (Paulist Press, New York) 1974

Priests, Part B (LDS Publication, Salt Lake

Petersen, Mark E, *One Lord — One Faith* (Deseret book, Salt Lake City) 1963

Robinson, Stephen E, *Are Mormons Christian* (Bookcraft, Salt Lake City) 1984

Romney, Marion C, "How to Improve my Communication with the Lord," *Improvement Era, April, 1966*

Schwartz, Robert M, *Servant Leaders of the People of God* (Paulist Press, New York) 1989

Sixteen Basic Documents of the Vatican Council (Costello Publishing
Co., Newport, New York) 1992
Lumen Gentium
Dei Verbum
Sacrosanctum Concilium

Gaudium et Spes
Presbyterorum Ordinis
Unitatis Redintegratio
Dignitatis Humanae

Smith, Joseph Jr., *The King Follett Discourse* (Eborn Books) 1994
*Teachings of the Prophet Joseph Smith**
Journal of Discourses
History of the Church VI

Smith, Joseph Fielding Jr., *The Ways of Perfection* (LDS Collector's Library) 1997; *Religious Truths Defined* (Bookcraft, Salt Lake City) 1959

Talmage, James E, *Jesus the Christ* (distributed by Simon and Schuster) 1915

The Great Apostasy (Deseret book, Salt Lake City) 1909

The New Dictionary of Theology (Liturgical Press, Collegeville, Minn)
                                        A TALE OF TWO CITIES

The New Jerome Biblical Commentary (Liturgical Press)

Tiffany's Monthly, June, 1859

Welcome to the Kingdom

Webster's Encyclopedic Unabridged Dictionary, 1998 Edition

Made in United States
Troutdale, OR
11/25/2024

25264726R00226